Approaching College
with Purpose

Amy Lee, Ph.D.
H.T. Morse Distinguished Professor
Director of First Year Writing
University of Minnesota

Margaret Delehanty Kelly, M.A.
Director of Undergraduate Studies
Department of Family Social Science
University of Minnesota

Catherine Lee
Student
Occidental College

Maggie Bergeron, M.A.
Lecturer, Department of Theatre Arts
and Dance
University of Minnesota

Publisher
The Goodheart-Willcox Company, Inc.
Tinley Park, IL
www.g-w.com

Preface

Welcome to *Approaching College with Purpose*! This book is focused on the importance of students beginning their educational journey with intention, developing good habits, creating a strong mindset, and acquiring strategies to ensure a successful transition to college.

The idea behind this book is straightforward: To go beyond "what it takes" for college success and to delve deeper into the "how" of becoming a successful college student. *Approaching College with Purpose* is not just about acquiring specific and discrete skills—it is about translating those skills across contexts at increasingly complex levels. Students have an easier ability than most to absorb singular tips, tactics, and steps. What remains more challenging, and is often unsupported, is how students engage those ideas to make them their own.

Approaching College with Purpose focuses on these key areas:

- *Communication:* Strong emphasis on effective communication—especially writing.
- *Critical thinking:* Consistent application of reflective activities to encourage students to apply concepts to their unique situations and use their experiences to think critically.
- *Collaboration:* Awareness of each student's unique perspectives, values, and preferences in terms of the role each student plays in strengthening their personal, academic, and professional communities.

Information is provided in a concise, approachable, and modern tone that respects students.

Drilling in a bit more, the book seeks to:

- *Acknowledge and respect students' unique perspectives: Approaching College with Purpose* acknowledges that all students bring valuable, relevant, and diverse experience and wisdom to their first-year experience. This text strives to support the integration of these skills and leverage each student's own individual strengths and traits for a successful first-year transition.
- *Focus on students owning their experience:* Students are overwhelmed and distracted by the amount and variety of information available. This text is designed to give students tasks to try, offer them simple suggestions on how to approach problems, and suggest strategies to help them develop their own methods, as well as their own best practices, for approaching and managing college assignments.

- *Put the emphasis on communication: Approaching College with Purpose* offers a critical look at the writing and communication process. It asks students to think critically about "good writing" and their own ability to communicate effectively.
- *Provide just-in-time skill building resources:* The text provides a set of toolboxes to enhance critical skills related to time management and effective writing. These Toolboxes offer focused exercises and digestible bites of information that can be used as "just in time" resources on their own or be integrated into other chapters.

Approaching College with Purpose has 10 chapters, which are broken into three Parts: The Transition to College, Collaborating and Communicating, and Beyond College. Every two chapters is considered a set. The first chapter in the set provides current research about the topic, explains its relevance to student success, and guides students to assess their current mindset and habits in relation to the topic. The second chapter in the set focuses on practical application of the knowledge and awareness the students cultivated, giving them multiple opportunities to apply that awareness in the context of real situations. After Parts I and II, students will find Toolboxes with essential skills like time management and planning their writing.

A variety of features are included in each chapter to support the book's approach. Details on those features can be found in the *Guided Tour.*

About the Authors

Amy Lee is inspired by Gloria Anzaldúa's call to "do work that matters," and by Dr. Angela Davis's words, "I am no longer accepting the things I cannot change. I am changing the things I cannot accept." Amy is a Morse Distinguished Professor at the University of Minnesota and serves as Director of the First Year Writing Program and Director of Faculty Engagement for the College of Art's Career Readiness initiative. Her publications include eight books and numerous articles focused on undergraduate teaching, learning, and the first-year experience. Her specialization is pedagogy and faculty development that centers on equity and access. Amy has taught first-year writing and basic writing, community engaged learning, U.S. literature, multicultural literature, and various graduate seminars. She is a recipient of the University of Massachusetts-Amherst Distinguished Teaching Award and the University of Minnesota's Morse Alumni Award for Outstanding Contributions to Undergraduate Education.

Margaret Delehanty Kelly is the Director of Undergraduate Studies for the Department of Family Social Science at the University of Minnesota. Margaret has an M.A. in English as a Second Language and has spent the last 17 years teaching at the University, 11 of those teaching courses in the First Year Experience program in the College of Education and Human Development. She is currently the Training and Development Coordinator for the instructors of the First Year Experience course. She loves working with first-year students on challenging and critical issues.

Catherine Lee is an undergraduate student at Occidental College majoring in History and minoring in Cognitive Science and East Asian Studies. She hopes to attend graduate school in the future. Some of her most formative experiences have come from studying abroad in China and South Korea, experiencing nature during her childhood in Minnesota, and traveling with her family. She is passionate about education, history, and food.

Maggie Bergeron is a Lecturer in the Dance Program at the University of Minnesota, where she teaches courses on Dance Pedagogy, Dance Production, and Career Readiness. She has spent the past two decades working as a professional dancer, choreographer, curator, and teacher. As a first-generation college graduate, she is committed to helping students navigate their own college experiences with plenty of tools and resources they can then take with them the rest of their lives. Maggie graduated from Interlochen Arts Academy, holds a B.F.A. in Dance and an M.A. in Teaching, and is a licensed K-12 Dance Instructor.

Reviewers

Goodheart-Willcox Publisher would like to thank the following individuals for their honest and valuable input in the development of *Approaching College with Purpose*.

Barbara Audet, M.A.
Adjunct Professor of Student Development
Austin Community College
Austin, TX

Belinda Bartholomew, Ed.D.
Professor
Northampton Community College
Tannersville, PA

Julie Batten
Assistant Professor
Salem State University
Salem, MA

Linda Bolton, M.Ed.
Adjunct Faculty
Lone Star College Systems-University Park
Houston, TX

Meghan Cassidy, M.Ed.

Shandra Claiborne, Ed.D., M.Ed., B.S.
Director of First Year Initiatives
Virginia State University
Petersburg, VA

Charlotte Clark-Rowe, HSA
CEO/President of Medical Oasis Corporation
Professor
Florida State College
Jacksonville, FL

Nicole Collins, M.S., LPC
Mesa Community College
Counseling Faculty
Mesa, AZ

Ryan Echevarria, M.A.
Professional Academic Advisor
College of Lake County
Grayslake, IL

Dr. Jocelyn Evans
Professor and Associate Dean
College of Arts, Social Sciences, and Humanities
University of West Florida
Pensacola, FL

Kristen Goldberg
Director, Office of Learning Resources
Saint Joseph's University
Philadelphia, PA

Chad Hammett
Senior Lecturer
Texas State University
San Marcos, TX

Monique Hayes, M.Ed.
Assistant Professor/Counselor
Community College of Philadelphia
Philadelphia, PA

R. Edwin Hutchinson, Ph.D., LCSW
Adjunct Professor of Psychology, Independent
  Private Practice
Motlow State Community College
McMinnville, TN

April Klingonsmith, M.S.
Instructor
College of the Redwoods
Eureka, CA

Dr. Karen Laing
Professor, School of Arts & Letters
College of Southern Nevada
North Las Vegas, NV

Laura Manresa, M.S. Ed.
College Lecturer
Ocean County College
Toms River, NJ

Christine Metzo, Ph.D.
Director of First Year and Transfer Experience
St. Cloud State University
St. Cloud, MN

Marian J. Moore, Ph.D.
Professor of Sociology
Owens Community College
Toledo, OH

Dr. Cynthia Mosqueda, M.A., Ph.D.
Faculty Coordinator/Professor, First Year/
    First-Generation Student Programming
El Camino College
Torrance, CA

Jonathan Newman, Ph.D.
Assistant Professor of English
Missouri State University
Springfield, MO

Amanda Nimetz
Assistant Professor / Academic Coordinator
    for Student-Athletes
Midwestern State University
Wichita Falls, TX

Merry Olson, M.Ed., GCDF
Career Services Coordinator/Instructor
College of Southern Idaho
Twin Falls, ID

Jenifer Paquette, Ph.D.
Instructor
Hillsborough Community College
Tampa, FL

Elizabeth Reynders, M.Ed.
Assistant Director of First-Year Initiatives
Loyola University Chicago
Chicago, IL

Amy Siler, M.Ed.
Counselor, Assistant Professor
Community College of Allegheny County
Pittsburgh, PA

Stephanie Dee Smith, M.B.A./B.A.
Instructor
Brenau University
Gainesville, GA

Alyssa Stephens
Academic Advisor & Instructor
University of Alabama
Tuscaloosa, AL

Rebecca R. Todd, M.P.H.
Professor, Anthropology
Hillsborough Community College
Tampa, FL

Nirmal H. Trivedi, Ph.D.
Associate Professor of English and
    Interdisciplinary Studies
Kennesaw State University
Kennesaw, GA

Cheryl Veronda
Chair and Professor of Business
Centenary University
Hackettstown, NJ

Courtney E. Webb, M.A.
Instructor, Student Success Department
Pima Community College
Tucson, AZ

Pang Yang, M.S.
Student Engagement and Curriculum
    Coordinator
University of Minnesota, Twin Cities
Minneapolis, MN

TOOLS FOR STUDENT AND INSTRUCTOR SUCCESS

Student Tools

Student Text

Approaching College with Purpose is available as both a print text and an online text.

Journal

Reflection is a vital component of learning. Students can develop a growth mindset and assess their strengths with the *In Your Own Words Journal*, included with every new copy of the text. Each chapter of the journal includes key activities from the main text to help students focus, reflect, and reassess as they learn new concepts and build new habits to shape their goals for the material at hand. The journal provides students with creative space to document and to engage with their first year experience and ultimately, to make that experience their own.

Instructor Tools

LMS Integration

Integrate Goodheart-Willcox content within your Learning Management System for a seamless user experience for both you and your students. LMS-ready content in Common Cartridge® format facilitates single sign-on integration and gives you control of student enrollment and data. With a Common Cartridge integration, you can access the LMS features and tools you are accustomed to using, as well as G-W course resources, in one convenient location—your LMS.

G-W Common Cartridge provides a complete learning package for you and your students. It contains digital resources, including the textbook content in an online textbook format, to help your students remain engaged and learn effectively.

When you incorporate G-W content into your courses via Common Cartridge, you have the flexibility to customize and structure the content to meet the educational needs of your students. You may also choose to add your own content to the course.

For instructors, the Common Cartridge includes the Online Instructor Resources. QTI® question banks are available within the Online Instructor Resources for import into your LMS. These prebuilt assessments help you measure student knowledge and track results in your LMS gradebook. Questions and tests can be customized to meet your assessment needs.

Online Instructor Resources (OIR)

Online Instructor Resources provide all the support needed to make preparation and classroom instruction easier than ever. Available in one accessible location, the OIR includes Instructor Resources, Instructor's Presentations for PowerPoint®, and Assessment Software with Question Banks. The OIR is available as a subscription and can be accessed at school, at home, or on the go.

Instructor Resources The Instructor's Resources include components such as: Lesson Plans with Chapter Frames and Dialogue Drivers, Sample Syllabi, In Your Own Words journaling activities, and Chapter Assignment Grading Rubrics.

Instructor's Presentations for PowerPoint® These fully customizable, illustrated slides help you teach and visually reinforce the key concepts from each chapter.

Assessment Software with Question Banks Administer and manage assessments to meet your classroom needs. The question banks that accompany this textbook include ample questions, such as multiple-choice and short-answer questions, to assess student knowledge of the content in each chapter. Using the assessment software simplifies the process of creating, managing, administering, and grading tests. You can have the software generate a test for you with randomly selected questions. You may also choose specific questions from the question banks and, if you wish, add your own questions to create customized tests to meet your classroom needs.

G-W Integrated Learning Solution

INSTRUCTIONAL CONTENT
- Knowledge and skills
- Curriculum-based
- Standards-aligned
- Pedagogically sound

REINFORCEMENT AND PRACTICE
- Labs
- Media-rich assets
- Projects
- Illustrations
- Self-assessment

STUDENT SUCCESS
Technically skilled
Knowledge-rich
Career ready

ASSESSMENT
- Learning objective-based
- Multiple levels of learning
- Analytics and reporting
- Formative and summative assessments

INSTRUCTOR TOOLS
- Instructional strategies
- Lesson plans
- PowerPoints
- Test banks
- Standards correlations
- Answer keys

The G-W Integrated Learning Solution offers easy-to-use resources that help students and instructors achieve success.

▶ **EXPERT AUTHORS**
▶ **TRUSTED REVIEWERS**
▶ **100 YEARS OF EXPERIENCE**

EMPLOYABILITY SKILLS · TECHNICAL SKILLS · ACADEMIC KNOWLEDGE · INDUSTRY RECOGNIZED STANDARDS

Guided Tour

Approaching College with Purpose contains the following features in each chapter to help students learn and retain the content:

In Your Own Words

These are prompts for journaling to support mindfulness, metacognition, and reflection. They are featured at the opening of every chapter to orient the reader and are sprinkled throughout the chapters to prompt mindfulness of existing habits, mindset, and prior knowledge.

Critical Moment

These sections offer illustrative case studies compiled from interviews with, and reflective journals written by, first-year students, as well as their instructors. Case studies illustrate the principles or strategies discussed in the section.

Think About It

These prompts help students develop reflection and metacognition as habituated practice.

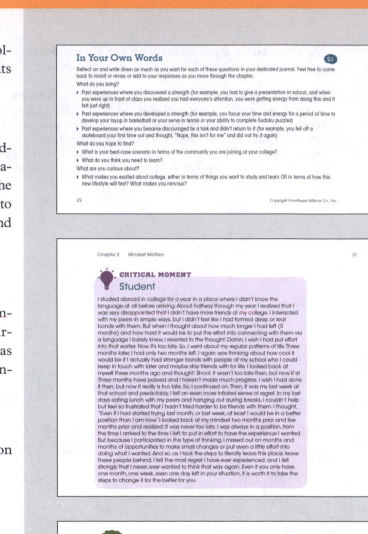

The power of Adichie's "single story" comes from "how impressionable and vulnerable we are in the face of a story." Once you have one view of something in mind, it is difficult to see the group of people or place described as anything but what has been described in that story. These visions are reinforced over time, often without actual exposure to the people one believes these things about. One component of the single story is that in our society, the groups who have less power have less access to the mediums that control the story (typically, the media and Hollywood). So their efforts to add more dimensions to the single story that's told about them are often ineffective.

TRY THIS _____ 2.4

The next time you are surprised by a person you are interacting with (either someone you perceive as similar or different from you in some way), ask yourself, "Why am I surprised?" "What had I been expecting?" "Where did that expectation come from?"

---

or let you continue your way of being. And so we invite you to think more about what this means. Now, we acknowledge that some of us need to hold on to protective layers in order to function or survive in a possibly inhospitable environment, depending on our identities. But we ask that you do your best to find places where you can pull back the reigns on "knowing things" to leave a little space for something new and different.

SIMPLE STRATEGIES

Look back at In Your Own Words 2.7, choose two or three items on your list, and commit to approaching these parts of your college life with vulnerability in mind.
- Brainstorm what you can do on a daily basis to practice bravery in these areas.
- Try writing a reminder of this commitment on a sticky note and put this somewhere where you'll see it every day.
- Consider discussing this idea with friends who can help you hold yourself accountable to this commitment.
- Reflect frequently on how this work is going, and be flexible to shifting your goals or reframing your approach as necessary, while being kind and understanding with yourself.

COMMUNICATION SITUATION

Seek out media coverage, or an Instagram post, or even a meme of a place that you know little about. Ask yourself:

- Who is telling this story and who is the audience?
- What choices is the speaker/writer making? What seems to be the reason for that choice?
- What reaction are they trying to evoke in me, the audience? Sadness? Fear? Pride? Laughter? Why?
- What is the goal of the communication?
- What's at stake in this communication?

Is this the complete story about this place? (The answer is always no, in all cases.) Now, do some research, even if it's just looking up the place on the internet and gathering more information (e.g., local news sources, school web pages).

- What details have you added to your understanding of this place?
- How do these details change or add to your original understanding of the news story, social media post, or meme?

Try This

These quick, low-stakes activities help students apply new concepts, explore new tools, and practice mindfulness.

Simple Strategies

These sections offer action-oriented tools to operationalize chapter concepts in students' day-to-day practice and mindset. They also provide easy-to-try strategies for internalizing and practicing what is discussed in the text.

Communication Situation

These scenarios prompt students to develop rhetorical awareness about interpersonal communication, drawing attention to the context (audience, purpose, medium), and fostering intentionality about communication choices.

Guided Tour

Takeaways

These chapter summaries help students to retain the chapter's contents and prime them for the "Keep. Quit. Start." section.

In Your Own Words: Keep. Quit. Start.

This is a more directive-oriented journaling activity that supports mindfulness and reflection by asking students three questions: After reading this chapter, what is a habit or approach you want to keep using? What is a habit, approach, or attitude you want to quit using? What is a new habit, approach, or attitude you will start doing?

Chapter Assignment

These end-of-chapter activities give students a chance to apply the concepts they have learned in the chapter.

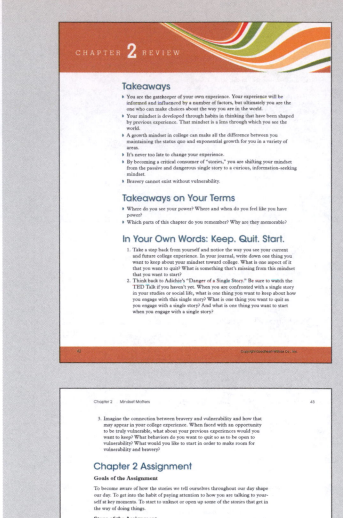

Figure 2.1 Thoughts from a Fixed Mindset

Focus on Illustrations

The illustrations in the book were developed by coauthors Maggie Bergeron and Catherine Lee, with input from the rest of the author team. The intent was to provide personal and colorful visuals to represent key concepts in the book and to model ways readers can interact with information in different modes.

Note: In order for students to be able to fully engage with the content and activities in this text, the authors made the purposeful decision not to include photos, especially images of students. This will allow students to envision themselves as they think about content, try out simple strategies, and reflect on concepts in their own words.

Brief Contents

Contents

Feature Contents

Think About It

Try This

Simple Strategies

Communication Situation

Takeaways

Takeaways on Your Terms

In Your Own Words: Keep. Quit. Start.

Chapter Assignments

Introduction

Welcome to college and *Approaching College with Purpose*! Chances are, you've heard a lot about what to expect from your first year of college, from friends and family, as well as from teachers and coaches, who wanted to share their experiences, offer advice, and tell you what college will be like. But now that you're here, we want to say: Your college experience is *your* college experience, and nothing about your experience will be fixed or predetermined. This textbook is written with that in mind, and we called this book *Approaching College with Purpose* because we want to encourage you to *own your experience*. Your experience, your goals, and your habits will all belong to you because you will shape them. This is an exciting and daunting idea, and we are honored and privileged to guide you through this.

Throughout this text, you will find multiple opportunities to reflect, journal, converse with classmates, and ask questions of yourself and others. This is intended to deepen your experience with the textbook and help you determine "the how" of your college experience. How are you going to engage with the people around you? How are you going to take advantage of the resources offered? How are you going to approach each new day and each new semester? How will you grow through these new experiences? How will you meet disappointments and learn from failure? Your answers to these questions will help you define your purpose in this college experience and reveal your expectations for how it will transform you.

As you engage with this book, both in and out of class, you will be asked time and time again to identify what you are bringing to any situation—your strengths, fears, preconceived notions, and goals. Identifying what you bring to the table allows you to build on the valuable assets you already have and discover what ideas or mindsets might be holding you back. Also, knowing yourself will help you approach each new situation with a strategy that is tailored to you as an individual, rather than based on the approaches of those around you, or ideas you have about how you should do things.

As you begin your college experience, it is important to be mindful, to take time to stop, reflect, and reassess. You will undoubtedly make mistakes, get lost, and fail sometimes. But the overarching goal of this text is to help you build awareness and habits that help you be resilient in the face of any and all setbacks. As long as you continue to practice reflection and work toward building positive habits that work for you, you will continue to grow, learn, and thrive. So, as you choose majors, build new friendships, discover new passions, and navigate setbacks, this book will support you in developing an intentional and purposeful approach to college, and life. This book's ultimate goal is to set you on the path toward owning your experiences, and approaching college and your life with purpose.

The authors wish to thank the literally thousands of students who inspired and contributed to our work on this book through our decades of teaching and research, as well as the colleagues and family members who directly influenced and supported this book.

Onward.

Amy Lee, Margaret Delehanty Kelly, Catherine Lee, and Maggie Bergeron

The Transition to College

Begin With Purpose: Own Your College Experience

> ❝ *Being a professional is doing the things you love to do, on the days you don't feel like doing them.* —Dr. J. Julius Irving
>
> *I believe, finally, that education must be conceived as a continuing reconstruction of experience; that the process and goal of education are one and the same thing.* —John Dewey ❞

In Your Own Words

1.1

You will begin every chapter in this book with a reflective journaling activity called "In Your Own Words." You will find these sprinkled throughout each chapter, with one always being the starting activity in a chapter, so as to get you focused and reflecting on concepts and habits, and put you in the relevant mindset for the material at hand. We suggest you dedicate a notebook solely to this purpose and make sure to keep all of your journal entries handy, whether it be in a notebook or a computer file. You will be prompted to refer to them from time to time to assess your growth in a particular subject matter and chart your development.

In your journal, spend some time reflecting on the title of this chapter. What does "Begin with Purpose" mean to you? The word purpose implies there is a reason, motivation, or intention for doing something. What is your reason or motivation for starting college? What is your intention? What is your role in taking charge of your experience in college?

Introduction to Begin with Purpose

This chapter, "Begin with Purpose: Own Your College Experience," focuses on the importance of beginning your educational journey with intention, developing good habits, creating a strong mindset, and acquiring strategies to support your transition to college and promote your learning and development. This chapter is subtitled "Own Your College Experience," because at the end of the day, nothing in this book matters unless you decide that it matters to you. No action will take place unless you decide to take it. *You are the gatekeeper to your own experience.* This is especially true now as you make your way into a new environment, with new knowledge, a new group of peers, new classmates, and new communities.

THINK ABOUT IT

Think about a typical day in your life. Where and when do you make decisions that are yours to make? (For example, do you get to decide the timing of your meals or which assignment you tackle first?) Where and when do you do things on purpose? When do you have limited decision-making capacity? (For example, are you eating in a cafeteria where there is a set menu and you only get to choose from the available choices?) And when do you have no choice at all?

The key message to be gained from this book is that being purposeful about how you begin is key to your college experience. Being purposeful specifically means that you stay open to your growth and change, are honest about habits and practices that haven't served you well in the past and you want to leave behind, and you are intentional about the new habits and attitudes you adopt.

In "Begin with Purpose," our goal is to prompt you to recognize, consider, and decide how to use the power that lies in your control to shape your experience of college, and to pave your own path for the future that lies beyond. Think about what is benefiting you (and also your family and community), and what is holding you back. It isn't easy, but it is within your power (and only yours) to work toward shifting your mindset. Later on, we will dig deeper into the idea of unlearning as a means of moving toward the mindset you want.

Obviously, none of us have control over every aspect of our lives. Your past experiences, beliefs about yourself, treatment from others, and a multitude of other factors influence your experiences and your opportunities. In many situations, it is not so clear-cut who has control or whether control is what really matters. That said, control and self-determination are not binary. In other words, it isn't an either-or situation: You either have control or you don't—either you have *all* the power or *none* of it. It is more likely that in most roles and relationships, you will be able to self-determine and exercise agency in some areas quite fully. In other areas, you may find a more complex situation, where the agency and authority are negotiated.

THINK ABOUT IT

What was a situation in your life where you felt you had a lot of power/agency/control? What was one in which you felt you didn't have any power? How did your approach to, or experience in, these situations differ?

The truth is, we all have power we might not even recognize. Each of us makes hundreds of micro-decisions every day that define who we are, impact how we feel, and determine the kind of experiences we have. In "Begin with Purpose," we invite you to reflect on the power you have and to develop awareness about how your habits of mind or action support or diminish a sense of empowerment. We will also guide you to set an intentional course about the kind of experience you will have in college and how you will use this book.

For every new college student, the First Year experience raises many questions with regard to navigating the first hours, days, and weeks of the semester, and also brings into focus the bigger picture of how these experiences will affect the rest of your undergraduate experience. This book centers on both the immediate transition and its connection to the big picture by providing you with the knowledge and information, tools and strategies, and activities of reflection and introspection to help you navigate both.

Transition is at the core of the college experience. You are navigating new and exciting grounds, taking in a lot of information, building new relationships, and exploring new ideas. You're seeing and experiencing many things for the first time, while also learning about yourself in a completely different environment. This leads to countless choices about how you should react in these situations and how to put your best foot forward. After all, you are presenting yourself to new people in new spaces, while still developing your own identity. Like many fellow students, you've left behind the security of a group of people who've known you since you were little, the people who "get you" on some basic level. You are now building an idea of who you are, side by side with others who are building their own ideas about themselves, and about you.

No matter whether you have moved away from home and are at college full time, or you are balancing jobs and family while pursuing a degree, you are doing something new and important—you are investing in your postsecondary education. This text, at its core, is focused on the transformation that occurs when you invest in higher education. Identifying yourself as a traditional student or a nontraditional student may impact how you navigate your day-to-day experiences, but it doesn't change your opportunity to shape how you approach college. It could be that everyone in the course of your day is now new to you, or perhaps the only new faces are those you see in classes, or maybe the faces in class are familiar from your own community—whatever the situation, this is a new avenue for you, one that offers you exciting potential for growth and change. The ideas in this text are ones that can apply to everyone, regardless of where they are in their education, family life, and responsibilities.

We wrote this introduction during the COVID-19 pandemic of 2020, a historic moment of disruption, change, and uncertainty for so many of us. In terms of college, for instructors and students alike, life as we knew it was rapidly turning upside down, without much time to plan or prepare for it. Most of us were required to shift to emergency remote teaching and learning. This was different than intentionally designed and planned online teaching and learning, and it had a profound impact on instructors and students, and their families. You will find particular strategies for remote and online learning in the "Tools for Managing Assignments, Workload, and Projects" toolbox. While your primary role at college is as a student, this book is focused on you as a holistic person, with skills, experiences, and insights that are valuable and will help you shape your college experience. A key component of well-being, in college and beyond, is being able to adapt during times of change. We have written this book with that idea of resiliency and adaptation front and center in our minds.

College as Transformation, Not Transaction

SECTION **1.2**

THINK ABOUT IT

What are your responsibilities while in college? What expectations do you have for yourself? What do you believe are the responsibilities of your instructors? Your friends?

One notion that should be dispelled is that college is a place where you come to make a tradeoff. You pay the school, and in exchange they give you some knowledge, hand you a diploma, and you walk away with this newfound information. This is a simple and non-encompassing version of the experience, but it's a common and limiting view. Ideally, through experience, you will come to see college as a laboratory where you go to experiment, learn, grow, and practice new skills to take into the real world.

To approach college as a transformative experience requires you to be mindful. Mindfulness versus mindlessness acknowledges the importance of being intentional, being explicit in setting goals, and adapting your behaviors and choices to support those goals. Mindlessness, psychologist Ellen Langer describes, is characterized by "...entrapment in old categories; by automatic behavior that precludes attending to new signals.... Being mindless, colloquially speaking, is like being on automatic pilot" (Langer, 1997, p. 4). Being mindful, on the other hand, resists a fixed way of seeing things, and means being open to new perspectives and adapting to change, which is inevitable. Approaching college as a transformative experience means anticipating that how you see yourself and others, and how you make sense of the world, will change.

Most people enter college with a lot of beliefs about themselves: Things like "I love animals" or "I'm not a math person" or "I can cook well." These are thoughts that have been constructed over time based upon what people say to us about ourselves, how we interpret our performance, how we think society sees us, and a multitude of complex experiences. Over time, we start to believe them, use them to guide our choices and therefore reinforce them with our actions, and thus they become even more believable and real to us. They are important because, without these ideas, we would have no idea what makes us who we are. They can be dangerous too, however, because we give them the power to influence our actions and choices, which can limit us. So, as you embark on your college journey, your challenge is to take stock of these thoughts.

In Your Own Words   **1.2**

1. In your journal, whether it's a paper notebook or an online document, write down a numbered list, 1 through 10.

2. Write down 10 phrases that describe the things that you do/don't do, like/don't like, are good at/are bad at. These should be things that you believe make you, you.

3. After you complete your list of 10, choose two of them that you could challenge the validity of. Ask yourself, "Is this really true?" Choose the ones that hold you back or shape your decisions, like "I don't like…" or "I'm not good at…"

4. In a few sentences at the bottom of your list, explain *why* you hold this belief about yourself. What's the origin story for this belief? Do this for both of the beliefs you identified in #3.

5. Finally, answer the question, could what you do/don't do, like/don't like, are good at/are bad at be more complicated than you originally thought? You can answer it simply yes or no.

Perhaps you haven't tried these things in the right context, or these ideas were formed a long time ago and you have changed. Being open to this change is very important to your ability to get the most out of your time in college.

Many students enter college believing they shouldn't "need" or utilize the many resources and services available to support them through college. Colleges invest in financial and human resources to ensure that students have services and support, including for mental health, career services, the writing center, and student support groups, as well as technology support desks and librarians. However, many students see these as only for people who "need" them, and this gets conflated often with an idea that "good" students *shouldn't need* these resources. But *all students benefit from, and should utilize*, these resources.

You hold the power to seeking and accepting support and help from others. As we have and will continue to stress in this book, one of the most important things you can do in college is actively seek out support in any way you can. Recognizing that you cannot do it alone cannot be emphasized enough. Using the support available to you can take many different forms, such as:

- Googling your TA's office hours and putting them in your calendar
- Signing up for a workshop to improve your ability to use Excel or Google Sheets
- Going to the writing center for help with an essay
- Sending an email to someone whom you want to query regarding an internship
- Raising your hand in class to ask a question you need answered
- Going to your school's counseling center to speak with a counselor
- Going to the library to see a tutor to help you edit video
- Attending a session or making an appointment with your school's career development office

These proactive decisions will help you maximize the benefits of the resources available (which you are paying for, by the way), thereby increasing your ability to learn and thrive, both there and beyond. Other ways you can help yourself succeed might be in opening up to a friend who asks how you are, or meeting with a professor who expresses interest in mentoring you, or listening to the advice of a therapist. While these don't include initiatives to seek help, they are just as important. Learning to accept and use this help as an asset will further allow you to take advantage of college and life beyond college. You need to work these muscles to get good at figuring out where you can get the help and support you need. The resources are there (as you can see from the preceding bullet list), but it's up to you to seek them out, or find someone who can help you.

🔑 **SIMPLE STRATEGIES**

Grab a piece of paper or a sticky note. Search on your institution's website for one of the following: your instructor's or TA's office hours, the campus writing hours, your school's student counseling office, your school's career development office, or your school's library. On the piece of paper or sticky note, write down the following regarding each resource:

- What (What service is offered?)
- Where (Do you need to go somewhere, or is there a virtual space you can access?)
- When (What are the hours?)
- How (Do you need to sign up for a slot, or can you drop in?)

Keep this piece of paper stuck to your wall, computer, or folder.

SECTION 1.3

Failure as a Trampoline

💭 **THINK ABOUT IT**

What is failure to you, in an academic context? What is one memorable time when you have failed? How did it feel? How did you know you had failed?

What aspect of failure causes fear for you? Why? What aspect of failure motivates you? Why?

Failure is not a pleasant concept for most, but by the end of this chapter, you will be prepared for it. Most students will fail in some form during college. It's a part of life, and learning to embrace failure and learn from it is an important lesson. Society stigmatizes failing, making it difficult to see the ways in which it can enrich one's life, provide lessons, and contribute to future success. (**See Figure 1.1.**)

Raphael Rose is a clinical psychologist who practices out of California. Much of his public work involves stress management and resilience. In one of his TED Talks, he argues that failure is a very key part of the process of success (Rose, 2018). In fact, he argues that it is a requirement for the process. He explains that we have choices to take action. For example, you can choose to take a challenging math class at school instead of another that you know would be easier for you. Rose essentially posits this as a win-win situation (although you may not see it that way). If you succeed in this math class, you have overcome a challenge, which has meant growth and learning on your part. You're more ready to face another challenge when it comes, and you might be more likely to take on new challenges.

Figure 1.1 Conversations with Yourself

On the opposite side, let's say you fail that math class. He argues that while on the surface this is a failure, underneath it's an opportunity to learn. Yes, it's painful to fail in anything, but from this experience you have an opportunity to decide how to proceed. You can reflect on what you did wrong, what you did right, and what you would change if you could do it again. Bouncing back from this setback is the equivalent of you looking at yourself in the mirror and saying "Hey, I still believe in you," which is powerful. The opportunity to grow from this enriches your life. And yes, if you just failed a test or a class, the last thing you probably want to hear is "Hey, it's just an opportunity to grow!" because failure stings. But the sting will subside, and then you can take that moment to look at your failure as a way forward.

Conversations with Yourself: If you find yourself unwilling to try something because you are afraid of failure, consider the prompts in Figure 1.1.

You will not escape college unscathed. You will fail at small things, big things, and things in between. And in these times, you should be able to call upon this knowledge of the function failure can play in your life to—after you allow yourself to wallow a bit—pick yourself up and move on to a new challenge, with the additional knowledge you've gained from this one. Rose says you need to "learn from your mistakes, not just avoid making them" (Rose, 2018). It's unrealistic to enter college expecting to walk a long tightrope of balanced success and make it the whole way without some falls. When you do fail, seeing the value in continuing on to your next opportunity, with a belief in your ability to face it and do better, or differently, this time contributes to your next success.

Figure 1.1 points to a few of the different questions we might ask ourselves when facing a situation that feels risky. How does this "self-talk" impact us and the decision we eventually make? In each chapter throughout this text, we will ask you to pause and consider some form of communication, usually between more than one person. However, for this first "Communication Situation," we want you to think through how we talk to ourselves, and how we sometimes talk ourselves out of trying something because we fear failure.

COMMUNICATION SITUATION

Choose one of the questions from Figure 1.1 Conversations with Yourself.

Think of a situation when you could imagine asking yourself this question. Really think about it: What's going on that could result in failure, or in success? If you ask yourself one of these questions, do you also consider what will happen if you succeed? How do these conversations make you feel? Once you've thought through the story of why you are asking yourself this question, think through the following:

- What is the benefit of thinking through potential outcomes of a choice you make? What is the risk?
- In your experience, does thinking through failure prevent or minimize failure?
- Does thinking through possible failure prevent you from actually trying something?
- Does thinking it through help you understand and prepare for different possibilities?
- How might the speaker reframe the question in a way that would remove the fear of failure?

Failure looks different to different people. One person considers an A- a failure, and another considers a C a failure. Failure is built and named in accordance with personal values, experiences, and identity. What may feel like a failure to you may look like a success to your peers. Or what feels like a success to you may be seen as a failure by your instructors.

Failure has different ramifications for different people, based on identity and past experiences. Your safety net for failure is different from others. You may not be able to fail an exam because you will lose your scholarship. Or maybe you feel you cannot fail your family by not being able to keep up a part-time job and continue to ace your studies. Part of understanding the nuance of failure is naming the "what if I do fail" things, because these could happen. They may indeed feel like the end of the world, too. Understanding and using failure as a trampoline does not mean you do not feel these things. It's about how you are after the crisis passes. How can you reflect on that and use it to move forward?

THINK ABOUT IT

How have you learned to react to failure? Do you tend to see it as an inevitable part of learning or developing? Or does it feel like a sign that you can't or shouldn't keep trying, or that you just don't have what it takes? Who has influenced your understanding of and response to failure?

Angela Lee Duckworth, a professor at the University of Pennsylvania, is also a psychologist. Much of her research and her writing centers on a term she calls "grit." You might read this and think *Oh no, this is one of those "you can do it if you just try"* type of things. In her TED Talk, Duckworth describes it this way, "Grit is passion and perseverance for very long-term goals. Grit is having stamina. Grit is sticking with your future, day in, day out, not just for the week, not just for the month, but for years, and working really hard to make that future a reality. Grit is living life like it's a marathon, not a sprint." (Duckworth, 2013) (Note: Ted.com is a website where you can search for any of the TED Talks referenced throughout this book.) In her research, she looks at things such as which kids do best in the national spelling bee, and which students in military school are most likely to persevere and graduate. She also studies which students will graduate from high school. Basically, she has found that the people who get through challenging situations learn to thrive despite adversity and end up succeeding; all have this grit. We often think of factors such as talent and innate intelligence as the most important indicators for success, but Duckworth disproves this.

Grit says that you have to work hard, build stamina, care deeply, and keep it up in the long run. Now, this isn't to propose that the world is run by just hard workers. There are quite a number of factors at play besides just hard work and perseverance. It would be a mistake to pretend that race, class, gender, and other parts of our identities don't also affect our ability to succeed. Grit is not pretending that this doesn't exist. The concept of grit identifies the internal factors each of us can control: being disciplined; staying focused; remaining steady and persistent. These are internal states that we have the power to control and develop. Doing so will make you more likely to succeed, in a world filled with distraction, adversity, and competing demands on your time. Duckworth's website offers a free, short questionnaire which you can take to be placed on a "Grit Scale", which measures your level of grit. It can be found online by searching for "Angela Duckworth Grit Scale".

TRY THIS _____ 1.3

Become aware of the multiple small decisions you make in the course of a day and how they shape your day.

Steps of the Assignment

1. For one day, notice and then list, on a piece of paper or a notes app on your phone, all of your microdecisions. A microdecision is a small decision you make in the course of your day that, under normal circumstances, you might not think has any impact. Examples can be:

   Deciding what time to wake up
   Deciding to snooze or not to snooze
   Deciding to take a shower or not to take a shower
   Deciding to check social media before a shower
   Deciding to skip breakfast or to eat breakfast
   Deciding what you'll listen to on your way to the campus
   Deciding where to sit in a classroom
   (This is just a partial list of possibilities. Make your own list.)

2. At the end of your day, look through your list of decisions. Which had a positive impact on your day? (For instance, you ran into a friend at breakfast, or you were reminded it was your grandpa's birthday and you sent him a birthday text, and you skipped your shower.) Which had a negative impact on your day? (Because you snoozed, there was no time for breakfast and you were hungry in class. Then you ate a bag of pretzels and a can of soda from a vending machine and felt gross.) In the margins of your list, identify what was positive, negative, or neutral and jot down a few notes about why you felt that way.

3. Write a paragraph summarizing the insights you had about microdecisions because of doing this activity. Are there any decisions you would make differently next time? Are there decisions you can make now to automatize or remove a particular microdecision? (For example, always carry a banana and a bag of nuts with you in case you have to skip breakfast.) Be prepared to hand in this paragraph or share it in a small group with peers to discuss what you all learned from noticing and reflecting on daily decisions.

If you're sitting here thinking that you hate studying, or that if you were good at school, it would come more easily to you, you're not alone. Completing an assignment given to you that may or may not grab your interest or feel relevant, and completing it while many other people and responsibilities and interests make demands on your time and attention is no easy feat. It takes energy, discipline, and commitment. Successful students do not love every moment of studying or being in class. Learning is meant to be challenging, and sometimes it is frustrating. But the reward is found in caring enough about the product to work through stages when it isn't coming easily and you want to give up. Effective students persist.

CRITICAL MOMENT

Instructor

When I started to work on the first chapter of this book, I decided to start with the chapter on writing because it was what I know best. I thought it would require the least amount of research and that the words and ideas would just flow out of me naturally. I began teaching writing in 1990 as a young graduate student barely out of college myself. I have written and edited eight books and many articles and chapters. I have never *not* finished a writing project. Yet when I sat down to begin the chapter, I got a sort of sick feeling in my stomach and I kept jumping up to go attend to other things. From dogs to dishes to email. And when I did try to stay seated, I got fidgety, a little stressed, and agitated. By most measures, I am an experienced scholar and a successful writer. I do both of those for a living. And yet I still get a little nervous about it. It requires labor, stamina, and effort to produce. I can't force myself to sit down and churn out greatness. I have to force myself to stay still long enough to churn out something that isn't very good at first. But it's a start and it gives me something to work with moving forward rather than a blank page. Coming back to even terrible writing is much easier than coming back to an empty screen.

—*Instructor and coauthor of this book, Amy Lee*

TRY THIS   1.4

1. Identify an upcoming assignment you have that you don't feel like starting or that makes you feel nervous, overwhelmed, or even just bored.
2. Read through the assignment.
3. On a sheet of paper or online document, name the assignment and due date.
4. Set a timer for 10 minutes and spend that entire 10 minutes freewriting about something related to the assignment. For instance, the actual content of the assignment, a list of what you think you need to do to approach the assignment, or perhaps a list of what skills you think will be necessary to complete this assignment successfully.
5. Don't judge any of the words coming out. Even just putting words down on paper and putting the effort into thinking about the subject can help you greatly toward getting started. If you're on a roll after 10 minutes, keep going!

Serena Williams, Toni Morrison, LeBron James, and Bill Gates weren't just born that way, with those abilities and that level of skill, agility, and fluency just ready to be unleashed. Anyone who has played any sport—whether softball, basketball, kickball, or badminton—knows that in the beginning you mostly miss whatever ball it is you are trying to hit, kick, or catch. Becoming a powerful athlete or writer or inventor takes a lot of less than perfect athleticism, terrible drafts, lost games, failed experiments, and missed opportunities. All of these endeavors are head games: You have to be in the right frame of mind to endure, even when life is distracting you, and all sorts of things are getting in the way of your focus. To be successful means conditioning yourself to keep your head (literally) in the game. Even when it is hard. Even when you are playing badly. Even when you are losing. Even when the refs are unfair. And that's how athletes, inventors, writers, and students *become* successful.

It's a process of learning from your mistakes, getting advice from experts, and mostly just doing it often to gain muscle memory. The more you practice (whether as an athlete, an inventor, a writer, a performer, an electrician, or an accountant), the better your instincts will become and the more fluency you will gain.

> *"Amateurs sit and wait for inspiration, the rest of us just get up and go to work."* —**Stephen King** (King, 2016)

The good news is that you are in the driver's seat. There is no excuse that you weren't born with enough talent for school or that you just aren't smart enough. If you care enough to put time and effort into your studies, you will improve. This means seeking help, revising, and caring enough to make it the best it can be.

TRY THIS   1.5

The next time you have a major test, project, or an assignment, make an appointment either with the Writing Center on your campus or with your professor, even before you begin, and ideally, long before the assignment is due. And then go—even if you don't think you need it.

SECTION **1.4**

Learning Is a Process

In *How Learning Works: Seven Research-based Principles for Smart Teaching*, Susan Ambrose, Michael W. Bridges, Michele DiPietro, Marsha C. Lovett, Marie K. Norman, and Richard E. Mayer review research on cognitive and learning sciences to outline seven principles of how we learn. Ambrose, et al. write, "To become self-directed learners, students must learn to assess the demands of the task, evaluate their own knowledge and skills, plan their approach, monitor their progress, and adjust their strategies as needed." (Ambrose, Bridges, DiPietro, Lovett, Norman, & Mayer, 2010) At its core, *learning is a process* in their book. We don't learn just by accumulating facts and knowledge and content. We need to learn how to *use* and *test* and *transfer* knowledge and context in different situations and contexts in order to learn and not just to memorize.

This book is designed to be interactive. Our goal is to offer you a blend of information combined with opportunities to explore and experiment with a variety of skills and habits that support effective learning. As the research presented in *How Learning*

Works makes clear, there is not one single recipe for learning, but there *is* a universal, essential ingredient: metacognition. In simple terms, metacognition means that you develop an awareness of what you know, how you know it, and how it connects to other information. (**See Figure 1.2.**) It means the ability to step back, assess, and plan. Reflection and assessment are those moments of pause, not of action but of *thinking*, when you are able to see connections—connections across areas of your life. No matter what course you're in, or what decision you face, or what project you're tackling, reflection and assessment are skills and steps you can take at any phase of the process to increase your understanding about *how* to tackle it, increase your efficiency, and lay out an intentional path that will save you headaches, surprises, and hassles. Metacognition empowers you to take responsibility for your learning and knowledge, making it something that belongs to you.

THINK ABOUT IT

Metacognition is basically thinking about thinking. Take a moment to think about how you think. Imagine you have three assignments due next week: an essay, an article to read, and a presentation to prepare. Which one are you most excited to start? Which one will you be least excited about tackling? Why? Is this reasoning based in: Past experience? The amount of effort you think it will take? Interest in the topic? The application of a skill you think you have? How will your feelings about the task inform your approach? Will it make you knock it out first? Put it off till last? Take it bit by bit, doing a little each day? Or do you wait, and then do it at the last minute?

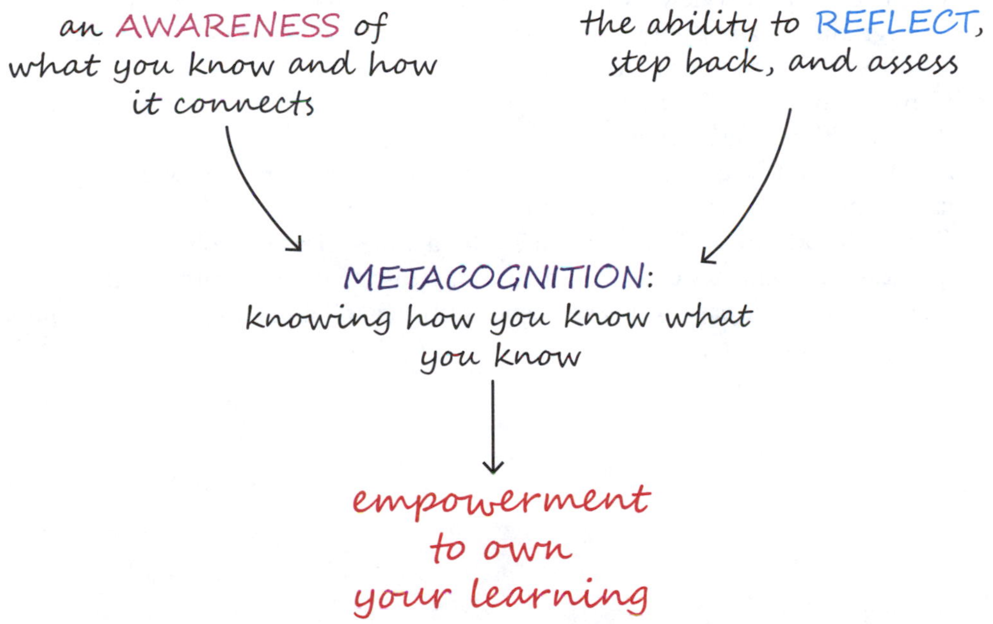

an AWARENESS of what you know and how it connects

the ability to REFLECT, step back, and assess

METACOGNITION: knowing how you know what you know

empowerment to own your learning

Figure 1.2 Metacognition

As you progress through this book, you can expect a variety of invitations to interact and experiment with tools that help you reflect on and assess your current habits and routines around learning, and that invite you to be mindful and intentional about the habits that you develop in college. In the Managing Assignments Toolbox, for example, we will come back to this same question and your approach. The goal is for you to become more self-aware and self-directed in your approach to your wellness, learning, and interactions with others.

The book has 10 chapters, which are broken into three Parts: The Transition to College, Collaborating and Communicating, and Beyond College. Every two chapters is considered a set. The first chapter in the set provides current research about the topic, explains its relevance to your success, and guides you to assess your current mindset and habits in relation to the topic. The second chapter in the set focuses on practical application of the knowledge and awareness you cultivated, giving you multiple opportunities to apply that awareness in the context of real situations. After Parts I and II, you will find Toolboxes with essential skills like time management and planning your writing. In each of the chapters, you will find the following features:

- **In Your Own Words**—These are prompts for journaling to support mindfulness, metacognition, and reflection. They are featured at the opening of every chapter to orient you, the reader, and are sprinkled throughout the chapters to prompt mindfulness of existing habits, mindset, and prior knowledge. We suggest you dedicate a notebook or online page solely to journaling, and save your journal entries because you will be asked to refer to them periodically to assess your growth and development.
- **Critical Moments**—These sections offer illustrative case studies compiled from interviews with, and reflective journals written by, first-year undergraduates and their instructors. Case studies illustrate the principles or strategies discussed in the section.
- **Think About It**—These low-stakes prompts help you develop reflection and metacognition as habituated practice.
- **Try This**—These quick, low-stakes activities help you apply new concepts, explore new tools, and practice mindfulness.
- **Simple Strategies**—These sections offer action-oriented tools to operationalize chapter concepts in your day-to-day practice and mindset. They also provide easy-to-try strategies for internalizing and practicing what is discussed in the text.

- **Communication Situation**—These scenarios prompt you to develop rhetorical awareness about interpersonal communication, drawing attention to the context (audience, purpose, medium), and fostering intentionality about communication choices.
- **Takeaways**—These chapter summaries of key points help you retain the chapter's contents and prime you for the "Keep. Quit. Start." section.
- **In Your Own Words: Keep. Quit. Start.**—This is a more directive-oriented journaling activity that supports mindfulness and reflection by asking you three questions: After reading this chapter, what is a habit or approach you want to keep using? What is a habit or approach or attitude you want to quit using? What is a new habit, approach, or attitude you will start doing?

The features in this book will take both time and attention. Your instructor might choose to assign these as individual or group projects, or classroom activities. You could also do them on your own. Not everyone reading them will be a person who loves his or her pen and journal and thrives in reflective practice. There are a variety of activities and prompts, some of which may resonate more with you than others.

Reflection is a skill, and even if it feels hokey at first, give yourself a chance with it. If it helps you, think of it in a different way, as perhaps you writing letters to a high school friend and telling a story. Or think of it as writing down what you might say for a future interview. Hopefully, you will pause throughout your reading of this book to take some time to reflect on your various selves—your past, present, and future self—and hopefully over time this will become a habit for you.

Depending on the context in which you are using this text (a face-to-face course, an online course, a non-course-related read), you may be asked to complete a feature and turn something in or be asked to share it with a peer. Completing something for an external audience can require a different type of attention to the product, because that external audience isn't in your head. This type of rhetorical awareness, as will be discussed elsewhere in this text, is part of how you translate the power of "you" to those around you.

Takeaways

▶ The first year of college is full of transitions. It brings with it an opportunity to harness your power in making these transitions purposeful.

▶ You bring preconceived understandings about yourself, that may or may not serve you, into your college experience.

▶ College is an opportunity for transformation.

▶ Everyone will fail in some way in college. Use this failure as an opportunity to learn about yourself.

▶ Your ability to reflect, self-assess, and be open to new ways of doing things will greatly increase your ability to learn more effectively.

Takeaways on Your Terms

▶ What in this chapter do you really believe without question? Why?

▶ What in this chapter feels like a stretch for you to believe? Why?

In Your Own Words: Keep. Quit. Start.

After reading this chapter, in your journal write down one thing you will keep doing as you transition to college. What is one thing you would like to quit so you can be more mindful and purposeful in college? What is one strategy you would like to start doing to engage with your college experience fully?

Chapter 1 Assignment

Goals of the Assignment

Spend time digging into the origins and story of a particular characteristic of yourself. Doing this may shine some light (for you) on whether it is part of a fixed mindset that comes from family lore ("After you were born, I had to stop serving anything with cheese on it because you simply refused to eat cheese!"), or if its origins are from the looking-glass self (the first time I got all As, my family took me out for ice cream and told me they were so proud of me).

Steps of the Assignment

1. Return to the In Your Own Words 1.2 section where you identified 10 things that describe you. Choose one of them and write a full (500-word) origin story. This is narrative, autobiographical writing. Tell your story in a way that people in your life can understand why you like/don't like, are good at/ are not good at a certain thing. Be creative. Have fun with it.

   The concept of this assignment comes from the prequels of superhero movies that reveal the hero's backstory and their personality traits. So, being dramatic in your storytelling is appropriate.

What You Need to Hand In

A 500-word narrative story explaining one characteristic that is part of what makes you, you.

Mindset Matters

> " *You have brains in your head. You have feet in your shoes. You can steer yourself any direction you choose. You're on your own. And you know what you know. And YOU are the one who'll decide where to go...* —Dr. Seuss
>
> *When I dare to be powerful – to use my strength in the service of my vision, then it becomes less and less important whether I am afraid.* —Audre Lorde
>
> *The most common way people give up their power is by thinking they don't have any.* —Alice Walker "

In Your Own Words

2.1

Reflect on and write down as much as you want for each of these questions in your dedicated journal. Feel free to come back to revisit or revise or add to your responses as you move through the chapter.

What do you bring?

▶ Past experiences where you discovered a strength (for example, you had to give a presentation in school, and when you were up in front of class you realized you had everyone's attention, you were getting energy from doing this and it felt just right)

▶ Past experiences where you developed a strength (for example, you focus your time and energy for a period of time to develop your layup in basketball or your serve in tennis or your ability to complete Sudoku puzzles)

▶ Past experiences where you became discouraged by a task and didn't return to it (for example, you fell off a skateboard your first time out and thought, "Nope, this isn't for me" and did not try it again)

What do you hope to find?

▶ What is your best-case scenario in terms of the community you are joining at your college?

▶ What do you think you need to learn?

What are you curious about?

▶ What makes you excited about college, either in terms of things you want to study and learn OR in terms of how this new lifestyle will feel? What makes you nervous?

What Is Mindset? Why Does It Matter?

In order to help you own your experience and recognize your power, this chapter focuses on both the power your mindset has over you and the power you hold to shape this mindset. This chapter will lead you through a few ways to think about your mindset, which are applicable to life in general, college, and the world beyond. Mindset is not an external motivator; rather, it helps you own the power that already lies within you and utilize that power to work intentionally toward your goals.

THINK ABOUT IT

Reflect on expectations you have for yourself and your experience at college. What are they? Where do they come from? How do they make you feel?

What is mindset? Put simply, mindset describes habits of our mind that are shaped by previous experience. Just as you have habits of action or ritual or routine, you also have habits of mind: mindsets. Mindset names habituated ways of thinking. Because it is habituated, we tend to be unaware of or less conscious about it—it becomes an automatic way of seeing something rather than a decision or intention. Sometimes, even when we have encounters or experiences that challenge our habituated beliefs or attitudes, we don't change them because they are so deeply ingrained in us. Instead, we think that the experience or encounter is an exception or a fluke. Or perhaps we just find it difficult to get out of a deeply habitual way of thinking. Mindsets can become self-perpetuating ways of ordering and anticipating our experiences and interactions. While that may save time, it is also problematic, because like many habits, (thumb sucking, eating junk food, binge watching), it might not be healthy, or productive. It's a habit because we engage in it automatically and without actively choosing it. Habits, or more specifically bad habits, get in the way of making a better choice. Habits of mind, our mindset, can get in the way of seeing old or new things in a new way. And just like it takes significant conscious effort to break a habit like nail-biting, it takes significant conscious effort to shift your mindset.

🔆 **CRITICAL MOMENT**

Instructor

My best friend believes that the world is against him. Not in a huge way but in a bunch of little ways. He stubs his toe or drops a knife and the look on his face communicates, "See, it happened to me again." Of course he doesn't pay attention to all of the times that he walks through a room without stubbing his toe and all of the meals where all the utensils stay on the table. This mindset or attitude has significant effects. (1) He's often paying more attention to the things that go wrong in the course of the day because he's always gathering evidence to support his theory that the world is against him. This makes him miss celebrating all of the things that are going right. (2) He sometimes has fear or anxiety about trying new things because of an expectation of being the unlucky one who doesn't succeed.

Your mindset is a purely internal thing, but its effects are found in all areas of your life. Although it only constitutes a pattern of thought in your brain, it shapes your actions, interactions, habits, and way of life. This is why it is so important to understand, deconstruct, and be critical of the origins and implications of your mindset. Working to do this won't just change the way you think; it also has the power to change the way you experience life.

One way to break down and understand this concept of mindset is to ask yourself what you're good at or what you could *become* good at. This is one way to understand your attitudes about different skills and activities.

Your mindset is fundamental to your college experience. You don't come to college with a blank slate and you can't pretend that now that you're here you get to decide everything about your life. There's no question that your previous experiences and entrenched beliefs have not disappeared. But if you can be aware of the mindset you're coming into college with, you can work to shape it, improve it, and use it to be successful.

SECTION **2.2**   # Facets of Mindset

Let's look at a few *facets of mindset*. We call them facets because mindset is a complex concept and scholars have taken many different approaches to understanding and explaining it. A facet is one side of a many-sided object. Imagine a gem and that each one of these frameworks is one side of the gem. The theories aren't in opposition to one another; they are simply multiple ways to understand the complex concept. We present these facets as interconnected and mutually

TRY THIS

Do you think you could "get better" at doing certain activities? If you were given a chance to improve your abilities in the following activities, could you? Would your mind and/or body actually be able to do these things and improve upon them with practice? For the purpose of this exercise, you can measure how you "get better" in whatever way you like.

Look at the following table. Open up your journal and either recreate the table or record your answers however you prefer. For each skill, decide whether or not you can get better at it, and if you would even want to. Make a note about it in your journal.

Skill	I can get better	I can't get better	Would I want to try?
Cooking			
Meditating			
Telling jokes			
Dancing			
Taking tests			
Organizing			
Basketball			
Drawing			
Singing			
Writing poetry			
Solving algebra equations			
Listening			
Other			
Other			

Table 2.1 Mindset Inventory

1. While looking at Table 2.1, ask yourself the following questions: Are there activities you are just good at? How did you learn you were good at them? Are there things you believe you simply aren't good at? These are the types of things where you might have said to yourself or someone else, "My head/my body/my finger simply doesn't work that way."
2. Look at Table 2.1 and write one sentence that states a belief you hold about your ability in an area and your capacity to change. You can use the following template for your sentence: I believe I (can) (cannot) get better at _____ (if) (because) I _____ _____.
3. Be prepared to share your sentence with classmates and explain why your belief is correct.

informative. By exploring and reflecting on these facets, you can better understand which apply to you best or illuminate your goals most effectively. Through determining which ones resonate the most for you, you have the opportunity to foster greater self-awareness around the way you approach college and life. Building on this awareness, you can cultivate a more intentional mindset that allows you to see college as a transformative experience.

Focusing on key theories advanced by contemporary thinkers in diverse fields (psychology, literature, social work) can contribute to your understanding and application of the concept of mindset. Many people have given TED Talks on these subjects that you can easily watch online. We've selected these particular facets because they have specific and significant relevance to your experience at college.

THINK ABOUT IT

Look back at your responses to Try This 2.2. Choose something you believe you cannot become better at doing. When did you first believe or decide you weren't and couldn't be good at this? Where did you get that messaging or input from? What is it about the item or yourself that makes you think you can't do it? How is it different from other things you have learned or gotten better at over time?

Facet #1: Fixed vs. Growth Mindsets

"And why seek out the tried and true, instead of experiences that will stretch you? The passion for stretching yourself and sticking to it, even (or especially) when it's not going well, is the hallmark of the growth mindset. This is the mindset that allows people to thrive during some of the most challenging times in their lives."
—Carol S. Dweck, Mindset: The New Psychology of Success (Dweck, 2008)

Professor Dweck's research on motivation suggests there is one very influential dimension of our mindset that shapes how we see the world, approach problems and challenges, assess our capabilities, and make choices. Dweck describes this dimension as a *growth* versus a *fixed* mindset. (See **Figures 2.1** and **2.2**.)

 A person inclined toward a fixed mindset tends to see their ability to learn as set, or *fixed*, at a certain level. They see challenges that they can't solve as being due to the limits of their intellect or abilities. A growth mindset, conversely, is oriented to chalk up failures to not investing enough effort or not being ready yet. This type of mindset makes a person more likely to be willing to take on a future challenge and thrive, seeing any failures as a reflection of their effort rather than a determination of their worth. For a simple example, picture how you would react to failing a test. With a fixed mindset, you would say, "Darn, I'm not smart enough to do well in that class." But with a growth mindset, you instead might say to yourself, "Okay, I need to work harder next time or try some new strategies."

Figure 2.1 Thoughts from a Fixed Mindset

Figure 2.2 Thoughts from a Growth Mindset

THINK ABOUT IT

Does this idea of growth and fixed mindsets resonate with you?

People develop these mindsets over time and in different contexts, based on messages received about themselves or what they are doing, but everyone has the capacity to change his or her mindset. For example, fixed mindset praise includes things like "You are so good at that," which tells the receiver, *"My level of proficiency in this is 'good.'"* In a growth mindset praise, you would say "You worked so hard for that," which tells the recipient, *I did the work needed to complete this well.* The implications couldn't be more different. The first student gains what they believe is a fact about their identity, while the second learns a lesson about hard work.

Dweck put this to the test in her research on elementary school students who were given a series of puzzles of varying difficulty. They gave one group of students fixed mindset praise ("You're so good at this!") and one group growth mindset praise ("You must have worked hard!") as they solved the puzzles. When given the choice between doing an easier puzzle and a more challenging one, the students given fixed praise chose the easier one, seeing this as an opportunity to be good at it. The growth mindset students overwhelmingly chose the more difficult ones, seeing it as an opportunity for growth.

This type of choice—leaning into and opting for challenge—has obvious implications for college and life in general. A person willing to choose *challenge* will take on riskier or more difficult projects and will grow more in the process, being less afraid of failing. Entering college with a growth mindset will prepare you to not only face challenges but seek them out and persevere through them.

THINK ABOUT IT

What is one area of your life where you are flexible and open to change or growth? What's one area where you are not?

At the end of the day, people with growth mindsets truly believe in their ability to grow, while those with fixed ones do not. Whether we cultivate a growth or fixed mindset deeply influences our view of the world and the opportunities available to us, as well as our place or role or power in it. Making the choice to cultivate a growth mindset, then, is one of the most powerful decisions you can make, and one that we encourage you to take action on.

🔑 SIMPLE STRATEGIES

When you're approaching an assignment, consider how your approach is affected by fixed beliefs you hold about yourself.

- Reflect on whether you believe you're "good" or "bad" at the type of assignment, whether it's public speaking, writing, art, or any other type of work.
- Take a moment to reframe your mindset and see this as an opportunity to shift your beliefs about yourself. How do you know you're "good" or "bad" at this, and how do you define this?
- What lessons about yourself have you learned from past experiences of doing this type of assignment (either failures or successes) could you apply to this experience?
- What are the things you can do, or the resources you can access, to support your completion of the assignment?

Who you think you are and what you think you are capable of doing is going to continually shift in college, and having a growth mindset allows it to shift in multiple ways. Becoming aware of your mindset now and understanding how a fixed mindset determines the end before you've even begun (you won't take a certain class if you believe you hate it/aren't good at it), will help you to be more open to a variety of possibilities.

A growth mindset in college can make the difference between maintaining the status quo and exponential growth in a variety of areas. A growth mindset means being open to new things, open to change, and open to ambiguity. This means letting go of assumptions, expectations, and rigidity, which may have governed your life in the past.

With the number of new opportunities and experiences you will no doubt be exposed to in college, it's natural to feel the ground you stand on shaking a little. For example, you might come in absolutely set on studying chemistry, only to find out you don't like how it operates at the college level, or maybe you discover that the economics course you're taking is calling to you.

Approaching opportunities with an open mind will help you to navigate these times where suddenly things you used to "know" are being questioned. For instance: What are you interested in? What motivates you? What is exciting to learn about? What are you good at? These are the types of questions you may have thought you knew the answer to in high school, but now, after a semester in college or even a year, your answer could be completely different. Not only is this normal, it's a wonderful aspect of personal discovery in the college experience.

CRITICAL MOMENT

Instructor

When students score less than 60% on the multiple-choice exams I give in class, I ask the students to meet with me individually so we can assess "what happened" and what is in their control to do differently. Often, when students first sit down with me, they will say, "I'm just really bad at taking tests."

While I believe that we do have different abilities at some level for taking tests AND that some tests are not really testing what has been learned in class (they're actually testing the student's ability to guess what the person writing the test was thinking at the moment they wrote it) AND that some tests are written in ways that give advantages to some students over others, I also believe that many students are stuck in a fixed mindset related to test taking. Because they believe they can't improve, they don't put in the effort. When they do poorly on an exam, they don't blame it on lack of effort or misplaced effort, they simply think they're not good at test taking.

When I work with these students one-on-one, we'll look for the easy fixes of how to get better on the tests. Do they understand the core theoretical framework we use in the class (and that appears in about 20% of the exam questions)? If they don't, we talk about it until they understand it and then we look at the questions that ask them to apply the framework. Next, have they done all of the reading for the class? What is their approach to reading? Do they annotate the text or take notes on it in some other way? Do they take notes during class? How did they prepare for the exam? Once we've talked through these things, then we go through the exam, question by question and they do a "talk-aloud" about *why* they chose what they chose. Almost always, once we've met and gone through this one time, their results on the next exam improve. And many will tell me, "I guess I'm getting better at taking tests."

"It's never too late to change your experience." This simple sentence is the best advice. It might not seem particularly life-changing, but when you start to convert this into action, it is. To elaborate, this refers to the feeling that many of us experience when there is a gap between the way we are experiencing something and the way we want it to be. Perhaps it is in a class, or on a team, or in a relationship, where you're dissatisfied with the results or quality of your experience and you know you could invest differently and change the outcome, but you just don't. Maybe you figure that it's not worth it to change. This comes from general laziness, which we all experience, where we think "It's not worth the effort to take steps to fix this." You'll only be in college for a certain amount of years. It could be three, four, five, or more, but it will certainly not be forever. With experiences that have time limits, it's easy to fall into this mindset because of the knowledge of a set end.

CRITICAL MOMENT
Student

I studied abroad in college for a year in a place where I didn't know the language at all before arriving. About halfway through my year, I realized that I was very disappointed that I didn't have more friends at my college. I interacted with my peers in simple ways, but I didn't feel like I had formed deep or real bonds with them. But when I thought about how much longer I had left (5 months) and how hard it would be to put the effort into connecting with them via a language I barely knew, I reverted to the thought: Damn, I wish I had put effort into that earlier. Now it's too late. So, I went about my regular patterns of life. Three months later, I had only two months left. I again was thinking about how cool it would be if I actually had stronger bonds with people at my school who I could keep in touch with later and maybe stay friends with for life. I looked back at myself three months ago and thought: Shoot. It wasn't too late then, but now it is! Three months have passed and I haven't made much progress. I wish I had done it then, but now it really is too late. So, I continued on. Then, it was my last week at that school and predictably, I felt an even more inflated sense of regret. In my last days eating lunch with my peers and hanging out during breaks, I couldn't help but feel so frustrated that I hadn't tried harder to be friends with them. I thought, "Even if I had started trying last month, or last week, at least I would be in a better position than I am now." I looked back at my mindset two months prior and five months prior and realized: It was never too late. I was always in a position, from the time I arrived to the time I left, to put in effort to have the experience I wanted. But because I participated in this type of thinking, I missed out on months and months of opportunities to make small changes or put even a little effort into doing what I wanted. And so, as I took the steps to literally leave this place, leave these people behind, I felt the most regret I have ever experienced, and I felt strongly that I never, ever wanted to think that way again. Even if you only have one month, one week, even one day left in your situation, it is worth it to take the steps to change it for the better for you.

What about this student's reflection and experience is familiar to you? What stands out to you?

This student's reflection is very applicable to the college experience overall. It's a short and intense experience full of opportunities where it is so important to remain engaged and continue to ensure that you're having the experience you want to be having. Whether this is socially, academically, emotionally, intellectually, or in any other category, it is so important that you are in touch with what you want and need. This, of course, circles back to the unique power you hold in your own life because this is about you taking steps to improve your own experience. It's about you caring enough to put in the effort to make a change in whatever situation you're in, whether it's a class, a relationship, or a family dynamic.

Facet #2: The Looking-Glass Self

It is important to discuss your self-concept, because the attitudes and expectations and beliefs you have about yourself—your worth, your capabilities, your limitations, your value—is critical to how you move through and interact with the world. From a young age, people attach labels to others and receive labels about themselves from others, such as "smart," "clumsy," "funny," "mean." These cues are verbal and nonverbal, direct and implied, personal and cultural. We receive them from family members, friends, strangers we encounter, the media, and our culture. Each message you receive explicitly and implicitly guides your view of yourself. You take it in and think, *"Oh, I guess I'm smart and therefore capable of doing well in school."* Or, *"Okay, I guess I'm clumsy and not good at anything athletic."* Internalizing these labels often leads you to actually carry out this identity. For instance, the first student might set high academic goals for herself and put most of her effort into school. The second student might avoid participating in sports in the belief that he won't be good at them. Taken together and over time, the messages we receive are heavily influential in how we view ourselves, or in forming what we call our *self-concept*. One's self-concept is heavily influenced and largely based on messages received from outside of ourselves, whether from people one is intimately connected with, or from broader societal and cultural messages.

Your self-concept is one of the most important facets of mindset. Self-concept refers to how you come to view yourself, and what you think about your abilities, worth, tastes, and talents. Your self-concept impacts your sense of self-worth, your belief in your potential, and these impact whether or not, and how, you pursue opportunities and interactions. How do we form a self-concept? Where do these intangible and important ideas come from and how do they pervade our brain?

To help you better understand this, it's useful to recognize a sociological concept called the *looking-glass self*, coined by Charles Horton Cooley. Cooley argues that our self-concept is created by seeing ourselves as we are constructed, created, or viewed by others. He puts it this way: "I am not what I think I am. I am what I think you think I am." (Cooley, 1902) Basically, we form our self-concept, in large part, based on how we believe others see us. This means that rather than form a sense of our self from our *own* experiences and our own interpretation of those experiences, we look to others, observe their reactions, and let our understanding of their response inform our sense of self. This, in turn, actually influences the type of experiences we have and how we interpret them. It becomes a bit of a self-fulfilling prophecy.

In Your Own Words

2.3

In this journal entry, you will need to think through the following questions, and then explain your answer by annotating an example.

1. Reread Cooley's words about the looking-glass self: "I am not what I think I am. I am what I think you think I am." Based on those words, how would Cooley explain the "like" button on Facebook, Instagram, and other social media platforms? How would Cooley explain the desire to have many "likes" and many "followers"?

2. Find an example in social media where you see Cooley's looking-glass self in action and make an argument about it. In looking for a good post to use, think about what types of posts and images get a lot of positive feedback. What gets ignored or scrolled by? How does this impact behavior? Where do you see posters to the site curating what is posted to maximize positive feedback?

3. Take a screenshot of a post. Put the image into an online document and, using the drawing tools, point to and explain what you are seeing and interpreting in this post.

If your identity is a construct based on your perception of your surroundings, does that mean you have very little to do with controlling your identity? On the contrary, recognizing the role perception plays in your construction of identity gives you agency to shape and change it. Hopefully, part of the college experience will be a chance for you to resee yourself. It's not easy, but it's slightly easier when you realize that what you know about yourself now is all constructed and, therefore, can be torn down and reconstructed, or revised, if you want.

THINK ABOUT IT

Cite a message you have received about your value or your worth that would have been different had the sender (the "you" in the "what I think **you** think I am") been different.

You aren't born with a sense of who you are and who you are meant to be. You create answers to these questions through your experiences and the messages you receive from family, peers, and society. And if you take it upon yourself, college is a time when you have the opportunity to challenge, reject, or build new beliefs and habits that become "you." As you work toward being an authentic version of yourself, you are working toward a personhood and voice that suits you. You won't be done in a year, and you won't be done in 10 years. However, as you hone your voice, it is imperative you utilize it and believe in its power. As expressed previously in Chapter 1 in Section 1.1, it is up to you as to whether any of this matters and affects your experience. The choice to use your voice is a powerful one.

THINK ABOUT IT

Cite a message you received about who "you" are or are supposed to be. Who or where did you receive it from? How did you respond? What was at stake?

"It took me quite a long time to develop a voice, and now that I have it, I am not going to be silent." —Madeleine Albright (Schnall, 2017)

Facet #3: The Danger of a Single Story

"The single story creates stereotypes, and the problem with stereotypes is not that they are untrue, but that they are incomplete. They make one story become the only story... I've always felt that it is impossible to engage properly with a place or a person without engaging with all of the stories of that place and that person. The consequence of the single story is this: It robs people of dignity. It makes our recognition of our equal humanity difficult. It emphasizes how we are different rather than how we are similar." —**Chimamanda Ngozi Adichie** (Adichie, 2009)

Chimamanda Ngozi Adichie is a prolific writer of fiction and nonfiction. She is also a social commentator and cultural critic, a feminist, and a powerful public speaker. She grew up in Nigeria and completed her postsecondary education in the United States. In her 2009 TED Talk, Adichie describes the powerful and pervasive practice of consuming and internalizing single stories about groups of people or entire cultures. She opens the talk with examples from her own childhood and how only having a limited view about a particular person meant that she could only see him and imagine his life in that narrow way until, eventually, she was exposed to more of his story.

She brings up the salient example of common American perceptions of Africa. Based on media coverage, representation in movies, and the way it is discussed in politics, Americans consume the single story of Africa as a struggling and desolate place in need of help rather than a continent with over 50 individual countries with vast political, economic, cultural and geographical diversity, and advanced technologies. Americans often tell a single story that fails to recognize there are enormous, bustling cities, entrepreneurs, people fighting for equality, educational institutions, and so many other hallmarks of a complex and modern society.

The power of Adichie's "single story" comes from "how impressionable and vulnerable we are in the face of a story." Once you have one view of something in mind, it is difficult to see the group of people or place described as anything but what has been described in that story. These visions are reinforced over time, often without actual exposure to the people one believes these things about. One component of the single story is that in our society, the groups who have less power have less access to the mediums that control the story (typically, the media and Hollywood). So their efforts to add more dimensions to the single story that's told about them are often ineffective.

TRY THIS _____ **2.4**

The next time you are surprised by a person you are interacting with (either someone you perceive as similar or different from you in some way), ask yourself, "Why am I surprised?" "What had I been expecting?" "Where did that expectation come from?"

The result of single stories is devastating, as Adichie describes: "It robs people of dignity. It makes our recognition of our equal humanity difficult. It emphasizes how we are different rather than how we are similar." In other words, retaining only a single story distances us from other people and dehumanizes them in our eyes. It doesn't matter whether it is intentional or done subconsciously, it happens to us all through the stories we consume every day.

The first step to improving this is being conscious that single stories permeate our consciousness and create a flat and inaccurate view of the world and people around us. The next step is to realize that we have the ability and responsibility to shift the way we understand the subject of the single story. Another step, which is much harder and less tangible, is to shift our mindsets accordingly. Everyone needs to take a critical view of the story—that is, the narrative in which we see the world. As Adichie argues, a single story—whether transmitted by social media or news agencies or family lore—limits and distorts truth and complexity.

COMMUNICATION SITUATION

Seek out media coverage, or an Instagram post, or even a meme of a place that you know little about. Ask yourself:

- Who is telling this story and who is the audience?
- What choices is the speaker/writer making? What seems to be the reason for that choice?
- What reaction are they trying to evoke in me, the audience? Sadness? Fear? Pride? Laughter? Why?
- What is the goal of the communication?
- What's at stake in this communication?

Is this the complete story about this place? (The answer is always no, in all cases.) Now, do some research, even if it's just looking up the place on the internet and gathering more information (e.g., local news sources, school web pages).

- What details have you added to your understanding of this place?
- How do these details change or add to your original understanding of the news story, social media post, or meme?

By doing this and becoming a critical consumer of "stories," you are shifting your mindset from the passive and dangerous "single story" to a curious, information-seeking mindset.

From now on, when you listen to someone's story, listen carefully to what they are saying, taking it in as one layer of a complex story but not the only layer. Acknowledge that there is likely more to what happened. You don't need to know every detail of the story, but you should consider the fact that it is only one story that has more than one perspective. As you process this information, you are activating your growth mindset. Keep it up!

Now, we will turn to the single story that you and others hold about you.

Your Single Story

THINK ABOUT IT

Think about one personal facet of your identity, such as your socioeconomic background, race, birthplace, sexual orientation, and so on. Now, brainstorm about a couple of stereotypes regarding the group you are categorized under. Where do you find these stereotypes reproduced or disseminated? How do they impact you, and why do they matter?

You may feel that others have a single story of you, due to where you come from, what you look like, or another part of your identity. You might meet people at college who are surprised about the things you know, your experiences, interests, mannerisms, or anything else about you because it contradicts the single stories they have heard about you.

Now think about the single stories you tell about yourself. At first glance, this might sound strange, because you know yourself well enough that you would think that your view of yourself is pretty nuanced. But single stories are those little phrases and beliefs, the refrain of the story that you might whisper to yourself as you see your reflection, or as you check your grades or your social media. You might not even hear them on a conscious level (I'm so bad at X. I hate Y. I guess I'm just Z.). Let's dig deeper and examine beliefs that we all hold about ourselves, which are based on reinforcement over time and that paint us in a light that doesn't fully encompass us as people or that may be just plain wrong.

THINK ABOUT IT

What's a script/label that was put on you by others when you were a child? This could be a memorable statement that was often said to you or about you (for example, "She's my athletic one" or "You're always so negative"). Or perhaps this might be a story that was often told about you to others. Or maybe this was an expectation that was communicated to you through other means—verbal, nonverbal, environmental cues, etc. Who produced the script or label? Who perpetuated it? How do you think it impacted your beliefs about yourself or your decisions?

Think about the discussion of the looking-glass self in the previous part of this chapter. If your identity truly is based on how you believe others see you, then how does the idea of a single story play into it? It means that the single stories you believe others have of you becomes your single stories of yourself—as in, *"Because I'm from a small town, people think I'm closed-minded, so I guess I'm not open to hearing new ideas."* It's so much more complicated than that, but it also is not. It's as simple as you believing these reductions of yourself, which are then reproduced in your actions and that reflect this belief. Thus, it's very important to be aware of what underlies your beliefs and actions as they relate to yourself.

Ultimately, everyone has single stories about other people and also about themselves. What we can't do is go back in time and reverse the beliefs we have settled into. What we *can* do is be critical of these beliefs, challenge them, and overturn them through conscious and intentional movements to facilitate a more open mind. We can also continue to reject single stories told by the media, our peers, or others in our lives. Resisting these simplifications of others and ourselves is a powerful step toward having a more complex worldview, which enriches our experiences.

The takeaway from the idea of a *single story* is that open-mindedness doesn't just mean you should be ready to try new sports in college or view drinking alcohol differently. Having an open mind extends to challenging the much deeper, more entrenched and more insidious types of beliefs inside us. No person or group of people deserves to be characterized by a simplification of their way of life, especially one which paints them as less human than others. Try to take some real steps toward chipping away at this mode of thinking and cultivating a mindset that resists this.

TRY THIS ────────────────────────────── 2.5

The next time you hear someone say something that sounds like a single story, challenge yourself and the speaker to be critical of it by taking on the perspective of one of the other people in the story.

Now that we've explained the concept of mindset and elaborated on a few facets of it, let's look at a more action-based (but still internal) battle. Mindset shapes your approach, but values of vulnerability and bravery will be expressed in your actions, which we will explain in the next part.

SECTION **2.3**

Exercising Vulnerability and Bravery

In Your Own Words   2.6

In your journal, name three images/scenarios that come to mind when you think about "bravery"? What about "vulnerability"? How are they different and similar?

When is the last time you personally felt vulnerable? Brave? Do you feel proud of either of these moments? Why/why not?

Vulnerability is a word with numerous connotations and misunderstandings in our culture. Brené Brown is a renowned researcher on vulnerability and shame. She is a research professor in social work, and her papers and public talks illuminate the tough, confusing, painful feelings people often have around the concepts of vulnerability and shame, and force us to reckon with them. Dr. Brown and her research team have interviewed literally thousands of people about their experiences in order to better understand how humans experience shame and vulnerability. For a moment, try to put away your preconceived ideas and engage your growth mindset with this definition: Professor Brené Brown defines vulnerability as "uncertainty, risk, and emotional exposure… Vulnerability is the core of all emotions and feelings." (Brown, 2010)

Ultimately, it's the experience of being open to possibilities and being willing to risk some degree of exposure. If you move into your college experience feeling you know everything and that campus life will be predictable, you will never get to a place of being vulnerable enough to truly feel and grow and change. If you begin college with a sense of being open, however, you have a greater chance to grow and change through your experiences, experiences that can only truly be felt when you meet them with a sense of vulnerability.

THINK ABOUT IT

Think back to past experiences, perhaps a retreat you went on, or something related to your first week at college, or something you remember as a "bonding" experience. What was the experience? Were there opportunities to try new things or challenge yourself in ways that felt risky (because of the people you were with or the actual task)? Did you feel vulnerable? How did you feel in the end—either about yourself or about your relationships with the other people in your group?

In Dr. Brown's 2010 TED Talk on vulnerability, one of the most impactful points she makes is about love and belonging. In her research, she found that one particular and critical barrier distinguishes people who possess a strong sense of love and belonging and those who struggle for it. The singular differentiating factor was that people who experienced a strong sense of love and belonging *believe* they are worthy of feeling love and belonging. These people are considered "wholehearted." It wasn't that the latter group didn't *want* love and belonging, but they lacked the belief that they were deserving of it, and because of that, they did not possess it.

THINK ABOUT IT

Think about a time when you had to make a decision between a choice that felt risky but the reward would be greater, and another choice that felt more comfortable or safer with less reward. What influenced your decision? What was your thought process? What can you learn about yourself from how you made the decision? Does this experience connect to your understanding of Brown's idea of vulnerability?

So, how does this connect to your college experience? Part of your college experience asks you to grow and change in a way that helps you become more and more yourself. This is really the power of you and the power of a transformational college experience. When you do poorly on an assignment and have to ask a professor for help, or when you enter into a new social situation, you have the opportunity to approach it in a vulnerable way that will support your growth and health. Thus, the more you can learn to step into your classes and your social life with an openness and a sense of vulnerability, the more you will be able to tell your story (as it unfolds) with your whole heart to a community that embraces you.

One of Brown's most significant findings is the connection between vulnerability and bravery. In society, we often see these two concepts as opposites. You can either be a courageous, strong, and dominant person, or a weak defenseless person who is open to harm. Yet what Brown discovered through her research is that bravery does not exist without vulnerability. The vulnerability, through the susceptibility to harm, is what makes actions we see as brave in the light we do. If there were no possibility of harm or failure, these actions would not require courage. Bravery can be discovered through vulnerability.

In Your Own Words   2.7

You have already demonstrated courage in getting yourself to college. Take a moment with your journal to write down and reflect on one step of your journey to applying, choosing, and enrolling in college that required you to be brave. What motivated your bravery in that moment? Was there someone who helped or inspired you to be brave? How were you vulnerable in this moment, and how did that make you feel? Now, make a list of things you're nervous about as you begin college. Be sure to consider personal, social, academic, community, and professional dimensions. And don't only focus on one dimension. Don't be shy—make a big list!

As you begin college, you may have more power to set your course and to form your mindset and habits than you have ever had before. You can hit "reset" and change a lot of things for yourself in the next few years, but all of it is up to you! For some of you, the idea that you get to define your own experience might be an obvious conclusion. Truly acknowledging and believing in your power is an example of a microdecision that will either allow you to grow into something new or let you continue your way of being. And so we invite you to think more about what this means. Now, we acknowledge that some of us need to hold on to protective layers in order to function or survive in a possibly inhospitable environment, depending on our identities. But we ask that you do your best to find places where you can pull back the reigns on "knowing things" to leave a little space for something new and different.

🔑 SIMPLE STRATEGIES

Look back at In Your Own Words 2.7, choose two or three items on your list, and commit to approaching these parts of your college life with vulnerability in mind.

- Brainstorm what you can do on a daily basis to practice bravery in these areas.
- Try writing a reminder of this commitment on a sticky note and put this somewhere where you'll see it every day.
- Consider discussing this idea with friends who can help you hold yourself accountable to this commitment.
- Reflect frequently on how this work is going, and be flexible to shifting your goals or reframing your approach as necessary, while being kind and understanding with yourself.

Hopefully, this chapter serves to help you slow down time just a bit so you can see the spaces for you to notice your surroundings, make mindful decisions, and invest time and energy in things that matter to you. If you come to really believe that you define your experience, you can make the most of your time and also make the most out of your experience in college.

Takeaways

- You are the gatekeeper of your own experience. Your experience will be informed and influenced by a number of factors, but ultimately you are the one who can make choices about the way you are in the world.
- Your mindset is developed through habits in thinking that have been shaped by previous experience. That mindset is a lens through which you see the world.
- A growth mindset in college can make all the difference between you maintaining the status quo and exponential growth for you in a variety of areas.
- It's never too late to change your experience.
- By becoming a critical consumer of "stories," you are shifting your mindset from the passive and dangerous single story to a curious, information-seeking mindset.
- Bravery cannot exist without vulnerability.

Takeaways on Your Terms

- Where do you see your power? Where and when do you feel like you have power?
- Which parts of this chapter do you remember? Why are they memorable?

In Your Own Words: Keep. Quit. Start.

1. Take a step back from yourself and notice the way you see your current and future college experience. In your journal, write down one thing you want to keep about your mindset toward college. What is one aspect of it that you want to quit? What is something that's missing from this mindset that you want to start?
2. Think back to Adichie's "Danger of a Single Story." Be sure to watch the TED Talk if you haven't yet. When you are confronted with a single story in your studies or social life, what is one thing you want to keep about how you engage with this single story? What is one thing you want to quit as you engage with a single story? And what is one thing you want to start when you engage with a single story?

3. Imagine the connection between bravery and vulnerability and how that may appear in your college experience. When faced with an opportunity to be truly vulnerable, what about your previous experiences would you want to keep? What behaviors do you want to quit so as to be open to vulnerability? What would you like to start in order to make room for vulnerability and bravery?

Chapter 2 Assignment

Goals of the Assignment

To become aware of how the stories we tell ourselves throughout our day shape our day. To get into the habit of paying attention to how you are talking to yourself at key moments. To start to unknot or open up some of the stories that get in the way of doing things.

Steps of the Assignment

1. Choose one of the facets (fixed vs. growth mindset; a single story; the looking-glass self; vulnerability) that resonates with you. Perhaps this is one that when you read the chapter you thought, "Yeah, I can see that."
2. Create some sort of string around your finger—something you will run into throughout the next three days that will prompt you to notice your current mindset. Some options that work for students are putting a sticky note on their laptop keyboard or a rubber band around their phone. This is your "attention device."
3. Throughout the next three days, when you notice your "attention device," ask yourself, "What is my mindset about this thing I'm currently doing?" or "Is there a single story that is relevant to this moment that I should challenge?" or "How does my idea of what I think others think about me impact me right now?" or "Is part of my feeling right now a resistance to being vulnerable?"
4. As you notice things, jot them down. Your journal is a great place to do this!
5. At the end of the three days, answer the question: "How did being aware of this facet of mindset impact my mindset?"

What You Need to Hand In

1. The original list of moments (aim for 20 across the three days), along with a sentence explaining what you were doing and what you found yourself thinking about it.
2. A two-paragraph writeup. Paragraph 1 should identify what you are telling yourself and how it impacts the moment. Paragraph 2 should answer the question: "How did being aware of this facet of my mindset impact my mindset?"

Engaging Diversity and Why It Matters

> " *The classroom environment is an especially important space for diversity to thrive, and can potentially affect all dimensions of campus climate. Research has demonstrated the positive impact that a classroom engaged with diversity has on student outcomes...* —Milem, Chang & Antonio*
>
> *Our ability to reach unity in diversity will be the beauty and the test of our civilization.* —Mahatma Gandhi "

In Your Own Words

3.1

Spend 10 minutes freewriting in your journal about this chapter's opening quotes. Which quote sparks a connection or resonates with you more? Why? Is it the ideas? The language? Gandhi describes diversity as both "the beauty and the test" of our humanity. What does he mean? What experiences or memories come to mind? Does entering this chapter's topic bring you excitement? Dread? Confusion?

Diversity is now a focus of many areas of our lives, from sports to media to law to education. It's likely you have some sense of what diversity is, but it's important to fully understand the concept of diversity and its implications for your educational experience, as well as your professional and personal development. College presents you with a significant opportunity to *engage diversity*, which is a concept we will explain more fully throughout this chapter. To make the most of this opportunity requires that you prepare for, and take full advantage of, the many opportunities you will have in college to cultivate the skills, knowledge, and mindset that are critical to engaging diversity effectively.

To engage is to become involved, to take part in, to participate. To engage something is to influence and be influenced; it is not to be passive or to simply observe. This chapter is not just about the recognition of diversity, but rather about the impact and importance of how to *engage* with it. The mere presence of diversity does not ensure that it will prove beneficial. People don't become interculturally effective or gain the benefits of diversity merely by being in a diverse environment. In this chapter, we will focus on some of the important concepts: Why does it matter whether we engage diversity? What does it entail? What skills and capacities does it require and help develop?

Why Does Engaging Diversity Matter?

College campuses bring together students from different backgrounds to create intellectual and social connections. . . . Research indicates that significant student growth occurs when (there are) structured opportunities for students from diverse backgrounds to learn and practice the skills and capacities needed (for) dialogue and interaction. . . .

Colleges must be ready to teach students how to listen actively to people who are different from themselves and hold competing ideological positions; to facilitate difficult conversations to ensure that students can think independently and creatively, expressing their opinions backed by evidence and reasoned judgment.

—**Report of the Commission on the Future of Undergraduate Education** (CUE, 2017)

In Your Own Words

3.2

In this journal exercise, it is important to get your ideas recorded/written down first, so you can review your responses while thinking through the questions. In other words, don't start analyzing before you have written down your answers. The first draft of your answers is just for you, but it should still contain complete answers to these questions. Your instructor might encourage you to share this journal entry with other students, so be prepared to discuss and analyze the results of the survey.

1. What are all the ways you would define "students from different backgrounds" compared to you?

2. Which of these might impact an interaction or conversation you might have with someone with a different background? Why?

3. What does a "difficult conversation" mean to you in the context of interacting with someone whom you perceive as different from you? What example comes to mind?

4. What kind of skills do you think are important for difficult conversations?

5. How confident are you that you have those skills?

We live in a historical moment where differences are often seen to divide us. You can seek out only those opinions and perspectives you already agree with. Thus, you can choose *not* to be challenged or exposed to alternative voices and ideas. However, the research is clear that being able to embrace, learn from, be changed by, and understand differences enriches us on every level, from our capacity to think and reason, to our capacity to communicate and collaborate. The CUE Report we cited previously argues that one of the most valuable aspects of your college experience is the opportunity to interact with, or engage with, diverse peers. Why is this so important? For one thing, there is abundant research in social science and higher education to suggest that those of us who learn to invite and engage with diversity will reap a number of benefits. Some of these benefits include:

- The ability to do more complex and critical thinking (Antonio, 2004; Gurin, Dey, Hurtado & Gurin 2002; Hu & Kuh, 2003; Milem, 2003)
- More expansive and sophisticated communication and interpersonal skills (Antonio, 2000)
- An increased capacity to cooperate and collaborate, and a greater openness to alternative views (Gottfredson, Panter, Daye, Allen, Wightman & Deo, 2008; Hurtado, 2001; Saenz, Ngai & Hurtado, 2007)
- A reduction in prejudice and an increased appreciation for racial and cultural diversity and identities (Allport, 1954; Bowman, 2010; Pettigrew & Tropp, 2008)

These are key skills that employers value in the workplace, as well as skills that are core outcomes of your college curriculum. Of course, these benefits don't simply happen, nor do they necessarily accumulate. It takes lots of practice, experience, coaching, and feedback. College presents a unique opportunity to pursue these outcomes because, whether your courses are in a classroom, online, or a hybrid of the two, each semester you are in a setting with many new people. As you take courses in different disciplines, you are also exploring different systems for assessing, creating, validating, and expressing knowledge and trying out different ways of knowing. You will also be collaborating and interacting with individuals who see the world differently than you do, and who have come to adopt different forms and styles of communication.

College offers a long-term laboratory in which you can explore and refine your way of approaching and interacting with differences in many forms as you develop an awareness that your way of thinking and communicating aren't universal or necessarily preferred, but rather represent one point on a continuum that has been shaped by your experiences, upbringing, identity, and interactions. Self-awareness, a willingness to listen, and an openness or humility when you encounter different perspectives, values, and communication styles are essential ingredients for this work.

CRITICAL MOMENT

Student

Learning within the walls of a classroom is necessary and extremely valuable. However, I feel that learning from peers and other individuals' experiences is also necessary and quite valuable as well. This is where *communication* comes into play, because it is nearly impossible to accomplish a goal or learn anything from anyone if you do not know how to communicate effectively. (In our class) not only are we learning quite a bit about a subject area, but we are also continuing to work on the necessary everyday *skill of working well with others*. And, finally, through working closely with a few other individuals, we are able to learn more about ourselves and about the lives of others', which may also end up teaching us valuable life lessons.

THINK ABOUT IT

If you could ask the student who wrote the preceding Critical Moment a question, what would it be and why? How have the perspectives of other classmates affected their experience? How have the perspectives of *your* classmates affected your experience in the classroom?

Defining Diversity

SECTION **3.2**

The term *diversity* in this usage refers to all the forms of human difference—social group and individual, visible or invisible—that define cultural identity as perceived, imposed, or self-defined (Lee, Poch, O'Brien & Solheim, 2017). (See **Figure 3.1**.) Diversity includes individual differences (personal history, life experience, educational background, learning preferences), as well as group or social differences (race, ethnicity, religion, language spoken, socioeconomic class, sexual orientation, country of origin) (Clayton-Pedersen, O'Neill & McTighe-Musil, 2009).

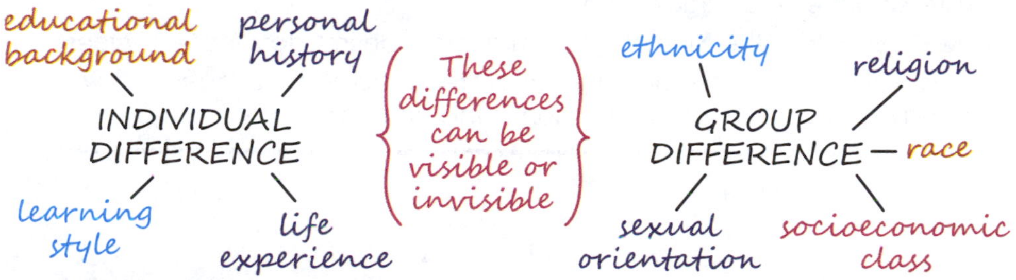

Figure 3.1 Diversity

Our way of seeing and interacting in the world is deeply influenced by our experiences and what we are exposed to, as well as by what we learn to see as "different," or choose not to see at all. The aspects of experience and background listed earlier in Section 3.1 and the facets of human difference identified in Section 3.2 shape what we value, how we see and approach one another, who we value, and even how we interact. For example, you might have grown up in a family or a culture that viewed interrupting someone as rude and disrespectful. In other families and cultures, however, jumping into a conversation is perceived as being actively engaged and participating. When someone who has learned from an early age not to interrupt finds him or herself in conversation with someone who has learned that interjections are okay, there may be dissonance and disconnects between them. One person may not feel heard; the other may feel judged if confronted about the interruptions.

Characteristics of our background and cultures aren't just passive descriptors that name where we come from—rather, our identity characteristics actively influence how we behave, what we value, and what we expect from others. As described in the chapter's first Critical Moment, they also influence how we interpret and assess interactions and information, and how we experience, and are viewed in, new or familiar situations.

COMMUNICATION SITUATION

Once we were assigned lab groups in my biology class, I emailed my lab group to tell them I prefer they/them pronouns. Everyone responded that they received my message. Once we started meeting weekly, I noticed that one person continually used he/him when referring to me. This person always spoke quickly and just rattled off the incorrect pronouns without pausing to correct them or apologize. Now it feels awkward to me to try and bring this up either in person or via email. I might ask someone else in my group to mention it to them.

—Student

- What choices were available to the speaker/writer in terms of framing and expressing their message?
- How do you think the form of the communication impacts these choices?
- This is a case where the message wasn't received. What suggestions would you have to support communication in this situation?

Acknowledging Difference

Some of the best writing related to difference comes from Audre Lorde in her essay, "Race, Class and Sex: Women Redefining Difference," from *Sister Outsider*. Lorde writes, "Certainly there are very real differences between us of race, age, and sex. But it is not those differences between us that are separating us. It is rather our refusal to recognize those differences, and to examine the distortions which result from our misnaming them and their effects upon human behavior and expectation" (Lorde, 1984, p. 115). In the essay, Lorde is taking on important issues related to inequality based on race, class, sex, gender, and sexual orientation in our American society. She gives us all some crucial things to think about as we prepare to engage diversity and understand ourselves better. We need to acknowledge difference, name it, and thereafter engage it.

Typically, we tend to be able to acknowledge, see, and understand many kinds of differences among the members of a group when we are a part of that group. Social scientists call this *in-group bias*. Because we are a part of the group—a religious organization, for example—we know there are all sorts of different types of people with different attitudes toward their faith within the organization. (See **Figure 3.2**.)

We tend to view groups we don't belong to as monolithic. We attribute sameness or generalized shared qualities to all members of the group. This can lead to the formation of *stereotypes* about a certain group of people.

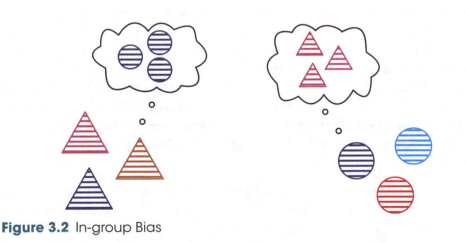

Figure 3.2 In-group Bias

THINK ABOUT IT

For this assignment, you will complete all four of the following parts, but only hand in or share #4. This is the conclusion you will come to by completing parts 1, 2, and 3.

1. Name three groups that you belong to. For example: soccer player; youngest child; multilingual speaker. What assumptions do you have about the people in these groups?
2. Name three groups that you do not belong to. What assumptions do you have about the people in these groups?
3. Looking at what you've written for questions 1 and 2, analyze the different qualities of your assumptions. Pay attention to whether the assumptions are broad or narrow, positive or negative, general or specific. How are the two sets of assumptions similar? Different? How does belonging to a group shape what you can assume about it?
4. (This answer is to be handed in or posted online on a discussion board. Length: 100 to 200 words.) How does membership in a group (your experience with it, your proximity/closeness to it) impact your assumptions about it? Give an example to support your statement.

Differences and similarities between us are complex and multilayered. Acknowledging this complexity and these multiple layers are the very beginning of this lifelong journey of engaging diversity. By engaging in this way, we will start to train our brain to see more than just our limited perspective and thus better view our various communities and recognize the strengths they possess and the complexities of the problems they face.

When we know someone well, we acknowledge how their values differ from ours, as well as recognize other differences, such as the way they deal with a setback, or their family situation, or the routine of their life. If you think about a group of good friends, you can list their differences. One friend might be really competitive and driven, while another might be someone you describe as really smart but who doesn't like school. Another friend could be really kind and supportive of you. If you spend time thinking about these friends, you can likely identify what in their life experiences gave them these differences. You can do this because you know them.

When we look at people we don't know—in a first-semester college class, for example—we tend to just categorize them in very flat and simple categories. Although most of us are not likely to admit it, our snap judgments about others often tend to be of the following type: "People who look like _____ are good (or bad) people," and "Students who have this kind of computer/jacket/hat are like _____." We use prejudgments and stereotypes to understand people who we don't know, and often this means seeing them as categorically the same or categorically different from us. When we see a person we've prejudged behave in a way that supports the stereotype, our idea is confirmed. When we see that person behave in a way that conflicts with our judgment, we tend not to notice it or we see it only as an exception. Social scientists call this *confirmation bias*.

SIMPLE STRATEGIES

Pay attention to thoughts or statements that are examples of a confirmation bias. You can sometimes catch these thoughts or statements because they begin with a big category of people, such as, "Students like that…" or "Women…" or "Men…" or "Athletes…" or "People from the Midwest…" When these come up, try to be reflective.

- Reflect on how you know this is an example of confirmation bias, and identify the underlying biases involved.
- Be mindful of how this bias affects your worldview or the worldview of people around you.
- Think about how you can challenge this bias and what breaking down this bias would look like for you.

CRITICAL MOMENT

Student

The more (small group editing and discussions) we do, the more comfortable we get with each other. One particular essay stands out to me because this individual revealed that they were gay… Growing up in a strong Christian family, things like that are not really talked about unless it is concerning what the Bible says and what we know as sin. However, that was not my reaction to this hardly shocking news, I was happy that my classmate felt comfortable with sharing that news with me and the story that came along with it… Now, going into a class where I am the only Christian or African American is not so much intimidating as empowering. I realize that I may be their only source of that particular group. This also gave me the opportunity to interact with other cultures or groups of people that I may have not communicated with without this class. I feel more equipped to confront the other challenges that will be presented here at the university.

THINK ABOUT IT

What parts of this student's story stand out to you? Do you feel you represent groups you belong to in a room? Do you have any memorable experiences interacting with other cultures or groups of people different from you? If so, what was that like? How did it make you feel?

College is an opportunity to train our minds to both observe and question. We want to always ask ourselves, "What do I see here? What might it mean? What else might it mean? And yet again, what might *others* think it means?" (Bennett, 2009, pp. 121–140). (See **Figure 3.3**.) Deep learning is interacting with new content or ideas in ways you can incorporate into how you see the world and the choices you make inside that world. As we noted in Section 3.1 of this chapter, there is abundant research to suggest that the ability to engage openly and meaningfully with multiple perspectives correlates to more complex and critical thinking (Antonio, 2004; Gurin, Dey, Hurtado & Gurin 2002; Hu & Kuh, 2003; Milem, 2003), more expansive and sophisticated communication and interpersonal skills (Antonio, 2000), and an increased capacity to cooperate and collaborate (Gottfredson, Panter, Daye, Allen, Wightman & Deo, 2008; Hurtado, 2001; Saenz, Ngai & Hurtado, 2007). Being able to consider multiple approaches to a problem and different perspectives on an issue are not only necessary to deeper learning but are critical to your growth as a person.

CRITICAL MOMENT

Student

We talked about our cultures related to how we identified ourselves regarding what we were talking about in John's class. We talked about our family history and where we were born and how it affects us. Like Gloria talked about how she was born in Mexico, that geography had to do a lot with her identity and of the people who lived in that area. For Najma, she mainly associated with her religion more than where she was from. She associates with Islam and it's part of her culture. For me, I identified with race not as much as place, more so than either of them. It was interesting to hear about their different cultures. It was a very deep discussion of our identities outside of class.

THINK ABOUT IT

In the preceding Critical Moment, the students involved talked about their backgrounds and openly shared information about their identities. What resonated with you most? What part of your identity would you like to share with the people around you? Do you feel comfortable doing so?

SECTION **3.4**   ## Engaging Diversity

As we established earlier, engagement is about more than observation. Engaging diversity is much more than just exposure to different perspectives. It is about interconnectedness and interdependence. It is about being able to communicate and form relationships with one another. Simply collecting a diverse group of

Figure 3.3 Multiple Perspectives

people together in one classroom, or one dorm, or on one campus does not guarantee growth or a change in mindset. Without some incentive or a structured and facilitated opportunity to connect with people whom we perceive to be different from us, many of us will tend to seek out or stick with what feels familiar to or like us, however we define that. There are many complex factors and abilities involved in engaging diversity. Similarly, without a reason to disrupt or detach from what we hold to be deeply true or familiar, we are unlikely to change our minds or develop new skills. Indeed, selecting to sit in communities of affinity (groups of people who are similar to us in some way) may be an affirmative choice in environments where our identities have been devalued, silenced, or marginalized (Tatum, 1997). On the other hand, we will need to develop the capacity to move among and between different groups, and to do so in ways that enable and facilitate inclusion, respect, and positive outcomes.

An example where we may self-select in ways that impede our capacity to engage diversity is in our news consumption from various media outlets, from feeds to podcasts to channels to programs. It is possible to consume "news" from a spectrum of sources, from conservative to liberal to radical, and from partisan to bipartisan or nonpartisan. However, it is also possible to get our news from sources whose purpose is not to inform or to investigate facts, events, or truth, but rather to espouse a narrow ideological position and to frame and interpret all facts and events through that lens. The problem is when consumers or purveyors of clearly partisan "news" aren't actively aware of, or interested in acknowledging, the "lens" of their news and its impact. Rather than engaging different opinions, interpretations, and points of view around a common set of facts, we get polarized narratives offering entrenched points of view rather than dialogue around collective interests and an array of positions and stakeholders.

🔑 SIMPLE STRATEGIES

Make a list of where you get your news. Include radio stations, newspapers, YouTube channels, TV stations, people, social media platforms, etc.

• How varied are the points of view? How do you know they're varied?

• Make a list of news sources you never engage with, maybe because you think you disagree with them, or you don't connect with them.

• Do some research into the news sources that you don't usually engage with, and think about how they're different or similar to the ones you do engage with. What do they bring that's different, and how do you feel about these differences?

• Identify one news source among a group of new possible choices that you could include in your viewing or listening that would broaden your diversity of perspectives in a way you feel is productive.

➡ TRY THIS   3.3

The following is an assignment from a public health course that uses small and large group discussion to prompt more complex problem analysis than would result from working alone. It also offers an opportunity to reflect on your perspective, and to adopt a different perspective. The activity is organized into three sections, each of which is indicated by a "STOP POINT."

Complete stop points 1 and 2 on your own by answering the prompts. You will refer back to your answers when you convene with your classmates to complete the third stop point.

Imagine you are in a public health course related to food and food security. The instructor is presenting information about programs that support families who are experiencing food insecurity. You listen to facts about the poverty line and who qualifies for EBT (electronic benefit transfer, often called "food stamps"). You hear some ideas about "food deserts" (urban areas that do not have access to affordable, nutritious, fresh food options) and learn that where a person lives can impact the food they have access to. The instructor also shares information on how food pantries work and the limits placed on clients in terms of the volume of fresh fruits and vegetables and the volume of meat they can take per week. Finally, the instructor asks you and your classmates to create a meal plan and food budget for a family of four (two adults and two children, ages 4 and 9) experiencing food insecurity, but who have access to government support (EBT) and a food bank.

STOP POINT 1: After taking a minute to think about what types of foods and meals you might put on the list for this family, map out one week of meals, including breakfast, lunch, and dinner. Plan for how often this family cooks at home and how frequently they go out to eat.

(continued)

TRY THIS ————————————————————————— 3.3

STOP POINT 2: How much of your list reflects your own food preferences and the type of food you ate while growing up? How much of your list reflects your beliefs about what a family experiencing food insecurity should eat? Label the different food choices with your assessment of why you put each on the list (e.g., inexpensive, very healthy, delicious, easy to make, etc.). Now, brainstorm a list of factors you might consider when making a meal plan like this. For example, are you driving or busing to the grocery store/food bank? How large is the family's refrigerator and freezer? See how many unique factors you can come up with.

STOP POINT 3: Share your work with your classmates and come up with a meal plan that represents the thinking and consensus of the full group. How many individual factors can you cull just from the diversity of the group? Different individuals will have different food preferences and food experiences. List the individual factors and the impact it has on your meal plan.

By completing the Try This 3.3, suddenly what started as a narrow list of factors and a simple solution (one person's sole view listed for Stop Point 1 and 2) shifts to a much more complex reality (the consensus that comes from working with a group for Stop Point 3). Because of the individual differences within your group—the diversity—you've worked with the course content at a deeper level, and you've engaged with the diversity in your group.

Factors raised when this question of food and food insecurity is posed to a large group of students, as opposed to an individual student, include the following: food allergies, foods forbidden by religion, the weight of food, the ability to buy larger (and cheaper) quantities when dependent on public transportation, the number of cooking pots owned by the family, the type of stove/oven owned by family, access to a microwave, the role of food in socializing (i.e., having food to offer a houseguest and the types of food expected), medical conditions that limit the ability to consume certain foods, the time available for food preparation, personal values related to organic versus conventionally grown food or food grown using sustainable farming practices, the perceived health qualities of different foods, the ethnicity of families and the types of dishes typical within that culture. And the list goes on and on. The complex diversity of the group is revealed through this discussion.

Interacting with others who think, feel, and behave differently from us requires that we develop practices and strategies that engage rather than oppose or isolate. These practices include how we react, approach, and behave in situations that are new or different—especially when encountering ideas and positions that don't align with our own. The following skills are not necessarily automatic or natural, but we can develop them over time and with intention, practice, and facilitation by instructors and peers (Lee, Poch, Shaw & Williams, 2012; Gudykunst, 1993, 1998; Deardorff, 2004, 2006).

List of Skills

- *The ability to tolerate ambiguity:* ability to function even in an environment of uncertainty; this means being able to produce and interact when there is uncertainty or conflicting directions or views.
- *Openness/humility:* the capacity to remain open to and influenced by new information, even if it contradicts ideas that may be deeply held or believed to be true.
- *Identifying multiple perspectives:* actively seeking different interpretations or ways of seeing an issue or idea, or approaching a problem from different directions.
- *Active listening:* taking in, processing, and focusing on what is being said.
- *Cognitive complexity:* ability to recognize and acknowledge differences, and to synthesize; ability to engage seemingly oppositional views or facts.

Engaging diversity is a process requiring practice, coaching, and mentoring to develop the skills and confidence needed for a globally interconnected world of work and life. Engaging diversity challenges individuals in different ways. To enter into it effectively and mindfully requires being aware of different realities, lived experiences, and perceptions. We will return to and continue building on the skills listed here in Chapters 4, 5, and 6.

The passages that follow are *Critical Moments* from first-year students reflecting on engaging diversity. As you read each passage, look back to the list of skills and attitudes cited in the previous passages, and consider which of them is relevant and important in each scenario. We will follow each passage with some reflection questions.

CRITICAL MOMENT

Student

...getting the opportunity to work with people I usually would not work with... the time in this class has opened my eyes to all different perspectives... I have had to learn to be more open to other opinions, and more willing to express my thoughts...I think having more than one opinion on something helps tons more when writing or explaining something later on... Being able to write out thoughts about a specific subject, and have someone else break it down and revise it, helps me to write better... I feel like three people's ideas are better than one person because we all see the issues differently.

THINK ABOUT IT

What about this student's story resonates with you? Refer to the "List of Skills" (that start on page 55 and continue on the top of this page) and identify a few skills this student gained from their experiences engaging with classmates. What can you take from this and apply to your experiences in the classroom?

CRITICAL MOMENT
Student

My class experience has also taught me that sometimes it's better to keep quiet when everyone else is. I can be intimidating, so when I am constantly voicing my opinion, not only does it get repetitive, but also I might be scaring someone else from voicing an opinion. The small groups have really helped me to work to do better with this. Rather than just voice whatever I'm thinking, I try to reflect more deeply.

THINK ABOUT IT

What about this student's story resonates with you? Refer to the "List of Skills" again and identify a few skills this student gained from their experiences engaging with classmates. What can you take from this and apply to your own experiences in the classroom?

CRITICAL MOMENT
Student

I am a very opinionated person, and when I feel like I'm right, I don't like to be challenged. This class has shown me that it's not about being right or wrong, but it's understanding that everybody looks through a different lens. My interpretation and my classmates' interpretation may not be the same, but that doesn't mean that one of us is wrong, it just means that due to different backgrounds and situations, we may not look at the problem the same way. We…can describe this as our schemata. I've also realized that's a good thing. If everyone were to think alike, we wouldn't be able to develop new ideas from the old ones. I've learned not to take disagreement personally and view it as a learning experience.

THINK ABOUT IT

What about this student's story resonates with you? Refer back to the "List of Skills" again and identify a few skills this student gained from their experiences engaging with classmates. What can you take from this and apply to your experiences in the classroom?

We imagine that you entered college assuming you would develop and acquire new knowledge. Learning the unique stories of others within the context of what you are learning in the classroom can produce a really powerful experience, one that is necessary for your future as a human being and as a member of our global community. Engaging with others allows you to open up understandings beyond your own way of knowing. As we have reiterated, the skills necessary to engage diversity, even one as seemingly straightforward as "really listening," are not simple. You don't develop them one at a time. And you don't cultivate them without a lot of practice. Any given situation will often put them all to the test at once. Growing in your capacity to engage diversity requires you to manage your uncertainty, sometimes take the riskier choice and open yourself up to being vulnerable, and practice humility.

We recognize this is a lot to think about and unpack for yourself, especially as you are probably just beginning to get your bearings in your college experience. We encourage you to come back to this chapter often to check in with the reading and the activities and to notice that elements of this chapter are woven throughout the book. This work of situating ourselves and others in the world is ongoing in our lives, and it's important to your education to circle back frequently to see if this information resonates differently.

Takeaways

- Diversity refers to all the forms of human difference, both visible and invisible.

- Engaging diversity is a process and it involves getting practice and experience, coaching and mentoring, so as to develop the skills and confidence needed to be prepared for life in the 21st century, a globally interconnected world of work and life.

- Increasing the capacity to engage diversity is about becoming more comfortable and confident, and being attuned to the interactions in dynamic and layered conversations or collaborations. It requires managing uncertainty and practicing humility.

- Seeing a group as having sameness or generalized shared qualities and projecting this onto all members of the group can lead to the formation of stereotypes.

- Differences and similarities between groups are complex and multilayered. Engaging diversity helps train our brain to see various communities anew: the strengths they possess and the complexities of the problems they face.

Takeaways on Your Terms

- How did this chapter challenge your understanding of the meaning of diversity?
- Where does diversity appear in your life and what does it mean to you?

In Your Own Words: Keep. Quit. Start.

Think about the way you have understood and approached diversity in the past, and what you have learned about it from this chapter. In your journal, write down what aspect of how you engage diversity you want to keep. Quit? Start?

Chapter 3 Assignment

Goals of the Assignment

Analyze a group interaction with a focus on how an individual's identity, and their individual perspective, impacts the interaction.

Steps of the Assignment

1. Find a YouTube video that is 2–3 minutes long. Recall movies and TV shows that you are familiar with and search for scenes that come to mind when thinking about group interactions where individual identities and perspectives are relevant.
2. Watch the scene with the goal of finding three to five moments where a character's identity, perspective, or experience impacts the words they use, their body language, their reaction, etc.
3. Dig a little deeper: This movie/TV scene is a product of mass media. Do you think this scene depicts complex identities accurately, or does it depend on generally believed stereotypes to get the laugh or the drama or the tears?

What You Need to Hand In

Upload the YouTube video to the online annotation tool called Videoant. Videoant (ant.umn.edu) is a free online annotation tool that anyone can access through a Google/Gmail or Facebook account. A tutorial is available on the web page (ant. umn.edu) as well. Using the tool, you will be able to annotate the video at the exact moments when you think an individual's identity is relevant to the group interaction. For each annotation you add to the video (three to five annotations total), explain what you think is going on and how an individual's actions or words are being impacted by identity, perspective, or experience (either theirs or that of others). Also include your analysis of whether or not you think this scene is playing into "single stories," the concept we examined in Chapter 2, or the simplistic and reductionist views of groups.

Share the Videoant link with your instructor.

CHAPTER 4

The Practice of Engaging Diversity

> *We have...been programmed to respond to the human differences between us with fear...and to handle that difference in one of three ways: ignore it, and if that is not possible, copy it if we think it is dominant, or destroy it if we think it is subordinate.* —Audre Lorde

In Your Own Words

4.1

For this journaling exercise, look carefully at Audre Lorde's words at the beginning of this chapter. Read the quote a few times to yourself—out loud is best. What stands out to you in this quote? Does it confirm something you know or feel? Does it challenge something you believe or have experienced? Where have you seen difference ignored? Copied? Destroyed? Lorde writes that we are programmed to respond to difference with fear. What do you think she recommends we replace that fear with?

Engaging diversity is a lifelong process. The more one does it, the more confident and competent one is likely to become. It begins with developing a diversity mindset, which is a process that requires skill and practice. This chapter offers a number of critical moments that illustrate the practice of engaging diversity and shows some of the outcomes. Hopefully, you will use these critical moments to identify and reflect on the necessary mindsets and focus on the specific strategies and skills that will support your development of engaging diversity. You don't need to wait to do this, because the opportunity to practice this is everywhere.

Take Every Opportunity to Practice Engaging Diversity

Engaging diversity is an approach to a class, or an experience, that includes interacting with classmates and seeking their perspectives. Not doing so is a missed opportunity. Every interaction is a learning opportunity, even if it doesn't seem memorable or appear to be a critical moment. One way to begin engaging diversity is to see each classmate in any given class as a human version of a course text, one of the resources available in the class. If you never hear that person's reactions, thoughts, and their interpretation of the course content, they're like a book sitting on the shelf, unread.

CRITICAL MOMENT
Student

"An interesting incident I had during the class is talking to a classmate from a country that is in tense relations with my country. I never imagined that I will have the chance to talk to somebody who I've always considered from an opponent nationality, but having the same class, reading the same books, and struggling with the same first-year experience made us talk. At the beginning of the semester, we were talking about class related themes, and that made us feel comfortable enough at some point to also have a discussion about the political topics that we disagree about."

What strikes you about the interactions between students in this moment? How would you feel being placed into the narrator's shoes? What do you take away from reading this critical moment?

Engaging with difference can provide exposure to new ways of thinking, some of which may go against your values or perceptions of right and wrong. What can be learned by paying attention to this feeling and experience? It's not about suppressing feelings or not engaging, but using this opportunity to both learn about yourself and go deeper. For example, as an instructor, Margaret (one of the authors of this book) leads an activity similar to the food insecurity exercise explained in Chapter 3. Some groups of students become very passionate during their discussions of the factors that can impact a family's meal plan and budget. Margaret has heard students fight for the right to buy microwavable pizza rolls. Other students reject pizza rolls as unnecessary, or a luxury. Other students reject them as unhealthy. Others argue for the ability to have a warm, easy-to-prepare snack after school. How can pizza rolls engage so much emotion? What are the values and beliefs that lie at the heart of this discussion?

🔑 **SIMPLE STRATEGIES** —————

The next time you are in a small group in class, pay attention to what surprises you in interactions.

- For example, when a classmate reveals something about their family of origin that seems very different than yours and that surprises you, note it. Previous to this information, what had you assumed about this person? Where did that assumption come from?
- As you gather these moments, paying attention to the surprise, you might start to see patterns. For example, perhaps you expect people who share some similarity to you (appearance, brand of computer, type of town you're from) to share other qualities with you. Or perhaps you are expecting certain people to be different. Be curious about where and when you are surprised.
- Pay attention to things that make you have strong feelings, whether they are frustration, fear, disgust, judgment, joy, jealousy, solidarity, or anger. Become more attuned to how your preconceptions are informed by your perception of difference.

The Social Construction of Awkwardness

SECTION **4.2**

If you take any social science course, you are likely to learn about socialization, social constructs, and the concept of *social construction*. This is a phrase used to explain things that have meaning because our collective society gives them meaning. So, for example, when someone talks about the social construction of race, they are saying that the significance of race in our society does not have any biological roots—rather, it is created by society. Social science also talks about the social construction of gender. For students who are starting to think about how society creates and assigns meaning, it's sometimes good to start with gender.

While gender is far more complex than this, we will use the example of society's constructions of the binary of male and female. As children, there is a distinct and obvious association between girls with the color pink and boys with the color blue. Can you think of any biological or inherent reason for these associations? This is an example of a social construction in which our society gives meaning to something it does not innately possess. It doesn't mean these associations don't exist or don't have power; they absolutely have wide-reaching effects and feel as real as facts. But the meaning of social construction is that this meaning did not exist until society breathed life into it.

One form of social construction that is prevalent in classroom spaces is awkwardness. For example, students will report that it feels awkward to talk to someone they don't know, or that it feels awkward to try to get a conversation started when they're not totally sure if they understood the reading that they're discussing. Students say they feel awkward when they struggle to understand each other's accents. This feeling of awkwardness makes many students avoid and shy away from these types of experiences, which is a common response, but is not a fruitful choice.

CRITICAL MOMENT
Student

The following are two critical moments from students' reflections on how they experienced difference in their first year of college. Read through them.

One student, Julie, had met a new friend, Sara, during the on-campus orientation. They seemed, according to Julie, to be totally similar and connected on multiple levels. On day five of welcome week, they got to tour different campus resources. Julie went to learn about the university recreation center. Sara went to the health clinic on campus. When they met after the programs, Sara was very excited because of all she had learned. As soon as Sara saw Julie, she eagerly held up a bag she'd received from the health center and opened it to show the contents to Julie. The bag was full of condoms. Julie was shocked. In her reflection on this, she realized that she was shocked not because it was so surprising that a university health center would give out condoms or even that this was in some way bad, but rather, her surprise was that Sara was so excited about this. Julie came from a religious background that shaped her ideas about sexual relationships, and because she and Sara seemed so similar, she had assumed that Sara would hold the same beliefs. Julie thought Sara would see that bag of condoms as more complicated and not something to be so psyched about.

The second story was written by a young woman, Sammi, who was placed in a small group in one of her classes. The instructor asked them to introduce themselves to their groupmates before launching into the discussion. As Sammi's group was doing introductions, one young woman in the group, Munira, didn't put her hand out to shake hands and explained that she doesn't shake hands because of religious reasons. Sammi was surprised, because she hadn't heard of that before and she was impressed by Munira's ability to explain it and hold true to her religion. In her reflection, Sammi wrote about how important her own faith and religion was to her, and yet in college, she'd hidden it from people because she didn't want to be judged. Here was Munira, wearing a headscarf and explaining that she doesn't shake hands and, according to Sammi, putting her faith at the center of her interactions. Sammi was surprised, and upon reflection, also inspired.

Where/when have you been surprised by an experience of difference or similarity within the space of college? This may be a big "Aha!" moment for you, or it may just be a "Huh?" moment, or somewhere in between. Write one paragraph where you tell the story of what happened. Explain who was there, what was happening, etc. Then, in the second paragraph, analyze the experience. What was the surprise (a difference, or, perhaps, an unexpected similarity)? How did you know this was a difference or a surprising similarity? What was your emotional reaction to it at the time? What is your emotional reaction to it now?

Is feeling awkward based in anything biological or chemical or physical? If you touch a hot burner, you quickly learn that is bad because it will burn you. If you are walking on ice, you need to be careful because it's easy to fall as ice has no friction for your shoes to grip onto. However, while it is true that talking to someone you don't know well about new ideas or concepts *is* hard; understanding one another when you have different accents can also be hard. But rather than avoiding what feels hard, try to assess *why* it feels hard. Are you avoiding an interaction because it's the easiest path and takes the least effort? Or are you avoiding it because your assessment determines that it doesn't feel okay for you? This is fair. You get to decide what feels okay for you, but we're asking you to make an assessment of the why and work to push through when your assessment shows it's more about feeling this awkwardness and less about actual danger.

This is something that needs to be done but may not come naturally, and so you must develop the skills for doing it. Sometimes instructors will require their students to learn each other's names, or engage in small talk before leaping into course content discussion, or practice ways to understand each other, and these approaches can ease some of the awkwardness. Even if your instructors aren't easing the awkwardness, you can still do it yourself through practices such as learning your classmates' names or starting conversations with them. This is a set of skills that are valuable to learn in college because they are going to be useful in every single future stage of life. Part of pushing through this feeling of awkwardness is paying attention to how you take risks and how you step outside of your comfort zone.

TRY THIS — 4.2

Here is an activity to help you reflect on your experience with leaving your comfort zone.

1. **Think of and write** about a time when you "stepped out of your comfort zone"—when you decided to do something that felt like a risk, a challenge to yourself to grow in some way: emotionally, intellectually, or physically. What encouraged you to take on the challenge? How did it feel to do it? How did your past knowledge or experience shape your decisions and choices once you were outside your comfort zone? Was there any old knowledge or any experiences that you needed to let go of in order to move forward? Did your past lead you to see or be aware of particular aspects of this new territory? Where did this new experience leave you emotionally, intellectually, or physically?

2. **Take a picture** of an object or image that represents this risk-taking choice you made. For example, if I were thinking about a time I spoke up despite my fear of voicing my ideas and having them ridiculed, I might take a picture of my own mouth, wide open, or of a person or object that brings me a sense of confidence or strength when I need support.

In Your Own Words

To synthesize and reflect on the Try This you just completed, do the following journal assignment. In a page of writing, explain:

▶ Describe the key moments or components of the risky event. What did it entail? What happened and how did you feel?

▶ How do you think you developed as a result of the risk you took? We usually take risks because despite the potential for loss or hazard, we believe we will grow in some way or make some gain (emotionally, physically, intellectually). Where did you begin and where did you end up after doing this risky thing? What did you gain or lose?

▶ How did you select your image and how does your image represent your risk?

▶ Be prepared to share both the image and your writing with classmates.

While taking a risk is the beginning moment of dismantling your feelings of awkwardness, engaging in the awkward also appears in many other forms, one of which is how you listen.

SECTION 4.3 ## Engage in Listening

Think about the last really interesting conversation you were involved in with your friends. Perhaps someone was telling a funny story and everyone was hanging on their every word. If something wasn't clear, questions were asked. If moments in the story seemed too crazy to be believed, more details were requested. Or perhaps it was a conversation about an issue that is impacting you and your life, right now—an upcoming election, current event, or a policy proposal at your college that directly relates to you but that your friends have mixed opinions on. Think about how much you listened in those conversations. You listened and you probably asked questions—specific questions, because that's how you learn something. You listened because, in wanting to share your ideas about the issue, you had to know what your friends really thought and why. Ideally, this kind of engagement is also present in the classroom, but too often the enthusiasm is absent. Try to recall or imagine a scenario where one small group is reporting their key points to the larger class, but no one seems to be listening, or the students keep looking at their phones as the professor lectures.

To help develop your own best practices for active listening (see **Figure 4.1**), think about situations where you have been listened to, and instances when you were ignored. How did you react in each situation?

Figure 4.1 Active Listening Strategies

COMMUNICATION SITUATION

"One moment when I felt really frustrated in class was (early on) within a group with two other girls. We were talking about a question that was given to us from the reading 'Umbilicus.' I was trying to get across how I thought this question was logically answered in the text. They could not grasp my thoughts (however). Although there was a bit of a language barrier between us, it was as if they just dismissed my thoughts completely and moved on to their own beliefs. I felt misunderstood and unimportant to my other two group members." (Student)

- What is going on in this moment? How would you characterize the listening that is happening in this interaction?
- What is the role of the narrator, and how do they feel? What are the roles of the other students, and how do you think they feel?
- If you were the narrator, how would you handle the situation differently? What about if you were the group members?

Margaret Montoya, a professor at the University of New Mexico, talks about listening in connection to silence, and introduces silence as a form of participation and engagement:

> "I explain that some students are prepared to answer quite rapidly, while others are slower in preparing a response. Despite the conventional wisdom that overvalues quickness, I announce that I will wait for those who do not think aloud and who need more time to collect their thoughts before speaking. My purpose is to give those who need more time the opportunity to pause and process their thoughts without having to fear that they will be interrupted by those who are quicker to speak (the "crowders"). I want to help the students hear each others [sic] silences and defeat the tendency to reach negative conclusions about pauses and hesitancy." (Montoya, 2000, pp. 297–298)

Like most things in life, listening occurs on a continuum. We can say, "I'm listening!" in instances where we are hearing noise but not distinguishing words on a conscious level, and yet we can still repeat some of it back if we had to (passive listening). This is something we might experience when sitting in the living room engaging in something else (TV, a videogame, a book) as an adult figure in our life is telling us to do something. We can also indicate "I'm listening!" when we're leaning in, hanging on every word of what the speaker is saying and trying to remember our follow-up questions, but not wanting to interrupt the speaker (active listening). Think about the celebrity or public figure who is being interviewed by a skilled journalist or interviewer. You see the interviewer lean in; perhaps they jot something down as they continue to nod to the speaker. Often, you can practically see the brain of the interviewer working as they take in the information and formulate the next question. That is active listening!

THINK ABOUT IT

When was the last time you noticed you were engaging in passive listening?

When was the last time you noticed you were engaging in active listening?

Listening is a skill, and reflecting on the different parts of it can help us develop it. Imagine a small group discussion in one of your classes. Many people think they are listening, and on some level they are, but how much of their focus is paying attention to what they are going to say when it's their turn? How much of how you interact in listening is based on norms from your culture or any identities you carry? How much of your focus is paying attention to the ticking clock and whether or not this information is going to be on the exam?

One interesting thing about listening is that, as a speaker, one can often identify exactly where our listeners are on the listening continuum. "Are you even listening to me?" is something commonly uttered in many households. When engaging with your classmates, you might often read their listening cues as you speak. On the simplest level, this is audience analysis. If they look confused, you restate it. If they look bored, you try to talk faster and get to the end of your idea. If they don't even look like they're listening, you give up. The struggle is that listening is hard; it takes energy. Also, as you already know, learning new material is hard. When you're tired and dreaming of a nap or an upcoming vacation, being asked to actively listen can feel like a lot. However, working with peers to talk through material that you're working to learn is shown to be an effective way to learn material—and part of that is due to the effort involved.

TRY THIS ──────────────────────────── 4.4

A Small Group Activity to Try Inside or Outside of Class

Students who haven't really paid attention to their listening skills benefit from going through some listening exercises. Grab some friends or acquaintances and give this a try.

Level 1: After forming a group of four people, choose a topic to share. Make sure it is something you all have something to say about—perhaps discuss what you did over the past weekend. Take turns and allow every person to have at least 90 seconds, uninterrupted, to tell their story of what they did last weekend. As listeners, pay attention to what they say and then think of follow-up questions. (For example, one person might explain that they worked 16 hours this past weekend. So, some likely questions might be where they work, how long they've worked there, what skills they learned from their job, or the craziest work story they have from the weekend.) But don't ask them these things as they pop into your head, let them keep speaking. After they are done, let the two others in the group spend time asking follow-up questions and listening to the answers of the speaker. However, for this Level 1 activity, try not to share your own similar stories. Save those for the Level 2 activity. After follow-up questions have been put to the speaker, it's the next person's turn to start and speak for 90 seconds. At the very end, spend some time reflecting on the questions that follow.

Questions to reflect on, first individually and later as a full group:

Speaker—Did you feel listened to? How did you know that your peers were paying attention? Were there times when you felt they were distracted (did they look at the clock, or at their phone, or perhaps their eye contact just shifted)? Were you surprised by their follow-up questions? Did those questions make you feel more heard? Or did the questions make you feel less heard (for example, you talked about how you had to work all weekend but the message you were really trying to communicate wasn't about your job but about how stressed you are trying to balance work and school)?

Listener—How active and engaged did you have to be in order to listen to your peers? On a scale of 0–10 (0 being very little, and 10 being an enormous amount), how hard did you have to work to listen? What were the external sources (phones, clocks, others in the room, outside noise) that threatened to pull away your attention? What were the internal sources (upcoming exams, worries, the ever-evolving "to do" list)? What did you hear as you were engaging in this focused listening that you might have missed had you not put the attention toward it?

Level 2: In a group of three or four people, choose a topic to discuss. This could be a topic that came out of a previous discussion that you can all relate to, so perhaps it's about the pros and cons of working different types of jobs while in college, or it could be about some shared knowledge (for example, a newspaper article you all read). For this activity, you will not "take turns" in the same go-around-the-circle manner, instead you will converse more naturally, allowing the conversation to jump around from person to

(continued)

person. When listening to your peers, you'll likely have to decrease your focus on them to formulate what you want to say, but try to keep it near the level of the most engaged listening you did in the Level 1 activity. Pay attention to what people are saying and be prepared to explain how your ideas connect to what they have said. Also, as you're listening to your peers, pay attention to how you know who is going to talk next. Spend 3–5 minutes in this discussion. Once finished with the discussion, spend a minute to reflect by yourself as both a speaker and as a listener. Then reflect as a group.

Speakers: Did you feel listened to? Where did the energy in the conversation come from? What do you believe you contributed to the discussion? What drew you into the conversation? Were you ever invited to share or contribute?

Listeners: How did the content of speakers shape what you added to the conversation? What did you learn from your peers? How were you drawn into the conversation? What motivated you to do so? If you didn't draw someone in, either by asking a follow-up question or by asking them their ideas, why didn't you? What held you back?

Everyone: Represent who talked in this conversation in a pie chart (literally, think of a pie or a circle and then imagine that each slice shows the percentage of who talked). How is it divided up? Was there a dominant speaker? If so, why? Did they have more to say (more opinions or ideas), or were they asked more follow-up questions? Or did they work to keep the conversation going as distractions started to creep in?

One option for the Level 2 activity, if there are four people in the group, is to have one person be a group observer. This person, because they are not preparing to speak/join in the conversation, is often able to take the balcony view on the conversation. An observer can often see someone formulating an idea and getting ready to share it only to be bulldozed by another person who is eagerly adding their own ideas. Observers also can see how a group deals with the natural pauses in a conversation and who takes on the role to keep the conversation going, and how this necessary steering shapes the group dynamic.

SIMPLE STRATEGIES _____

When you are in a conversation with anyone (a classmate, roommate, family member, anyone who you are talking to for more than 2 minutes), commit to engaging in active listening.

- Focus on what they are saying, which will require you to ignore your phone and other distractions, as well as ignore thoughts that pass through your head (like "I'm hungry" or "They always complain about physics class").
- Remain mindful throughout the conversation about how you are practicing active listening.
- Ask questions to make sure you truly understand what the other person is talking about.

CRITICAL MOMENT

Instructor

Michael Brown, an 18-year-old African American, was killed in August 2014 in Ferguson, Missouri, by a white police officer. This caused great unrest in Ferguson and throughout the nation. There was a grand jury investigation into the shooting of Brown, and news that the police officer was not indicted was released the morning of Monday, November 24, 2014.

This was my last class meeting with a group of first-year students before Thanksgiving break. I entered the classroom at 8 am just as students were getting the news and beginning to process it. Some students were devastated by the news, because they saw it as an injustice against Brown's community. One young woman was visibly emotional and told classmates sitting near her that she feared for her brother and his safety, as he was a young black male. Some students hadn't been following the case very closely. They were just learning about it now, once the decision not to indict the police officer was announced.

As an instructor, I start every class with an "attendance question." These questions are sometimes related to course content, but more often are just easy get-to-know-you type questions. (For example, "What is a strategy you use to get out of a rut?") On this day, I erased my preplanned "What are you most looking forward to for your days off?" and changed it to a more general, "What is on your mind?" My thought at the time was that students could share their processing of the Ferguson verdict.

The responses to this question represented the stark differences in how students' lives were impacted by this event going on a few states away. Some students answered the question "What is on your mind?" with weary, heart-heavy "When will the violence end?" rhetorical questions. Some students gave impassioned "We must act" responses. Other students talked about how excited they were to go home for Thanksgiving and have their favorite food, or see their friends from high school. As more and more students talked about apple pie, there emerged a real sense of tension and disparity in the room. Some students' positions in the world would not allow them to take a break from the implications of the Ferguson verdict. Whether they were worried for themselves, a family member, or their sense of racial injustice, this verdict was heavy. Other students didn't even have to hear of, or understand, the verdict, because it did not directly impact their life. This discrepancy felt stark.

Reading through the preceding Critical Moment, the instructor recognized that there were different emotions and responses in the room. The beginning of class offered an important opportunity to share and listen. But then there were some missteps and missed opportunities. What were they? What could they have done differently, and at what stages, to better support all of the learners in the room?

The Importance of Engaging Productive Discomfort

"If the wariness about discomfort is stronger than the desire to hear different viewpoints because engaging difference is uncomfortable, then the quest for diversity is hollow no matter what the demographic statistics on a campus reflect." (Liebowitz, 2014)

Not everyone comes to college expecting college classes to make them feel uncomfortable, and for many students coming to college, this discomfort is a real surprise. Many people entering college believe that learning should be a harmless intake of new knowledge. Often, however, the knowledge includes hard truths and inconvenient facts—things that are true, but that we wish weren't.

A Sense of Belonging

As illustrated in the preceding Critical Moment, the reality of engaging diversity in a university class is that the discussions and activities are unpredictable and incongruent, yet memorable. Oftentimes, the outcomes of exercises and projects are based on the interactions the individual students experience. Engaging diversity and paying attention to differences has an end result of helping you become aware that people react to the same information with different responses and emotions. Being in a shared space with these differences can feel confusing, uncomfortable, and unsafe for different students. It is useful to become aware of the multiple factors that affect our perceptions and that shape the roles we assume in different spaces.

THINK ABOUT IT

Now think through places on your campus. Where do you feel like you belong the most? The least? Somewhere in between? What makes these places different?

Roles We Assume

Insider: Where is a space that you feel like you belong? This is a place where people expect you to be present, either because they know you or because you are the type of person who is usually in that space. You know how to act in this space and feel so comfortable that you aren't even aware of how natural it is for you to be there. You understand the unstated rules of that space—for example, you know how to get permission to speak, and recognize whether permission is even necessary. You know where you sit and how to interact with the people around you.

Outsider: Where is a space that you feel like you don't belong? You feel like people are surprised that you're there. Perhaps people are staring at you. You are very aware of being an outsider and feel uncomfortable. You are also unsure how to act and what the rules are that you should follow.

The sense of belonging is not a static thing. It changes depending on any number of factors. In general, people are very sensitive to this feeling of being an insider or an outsider in any given space. Think back to a time when you were new to a school, neighborhood, team, or activity. The feeling of unease of entering a new space with new people is one example of that sensitivity.

How people respond when others enter a space can influence one's sense of belonging. For example, being greeted by name or being smiled at makes a difference. Someone moving their bag off a chair and gesturing that you can sit next to them signals belonging. Being stared at or ignored can make you feel unwelcome. You can pick up on very small, subtle clues about how people feel about you joining a space, whether it's a store, a restaurant, a place of worship, or a classroom.

THINK ABOUT IT

Identify ways you can signal belonging to someone else in your community, such as smiling at them, greeting them, using open body language that indicates they can join you, etc. How do you feel when you experience these signals from other people? How does it feel to do it yourself? Do these feel connected to belonging? Do you think this affects the community?

This feeling of belonging or not belonging is just the tip of the iceberg when it comes to discomfort. It's hard to enter a new space because of the anxiety about not knowing how to act, and most people choose not to return to spaces where this feeling doesn't dissipate fairly quickly. It is understandable that these situations are avoided, and yet in the context of learning and your college education, it is valuable to push through this discomfort.

Like all learning, engaging diversity requires a willingness to be uncomfortable. Encounters with dissonance around ideas or problems can work to break apart old notions and invite openness, but they also provoke an unavoidable increase in anxiety that can ultimately cause a person to strengthen their defenses and become entrenched in prejudice.

Humans are basically hardwired to seek out intellectual and emotional comfort zones—places and interactions where we meet little resistance and where our actions, thoughts, and attitudes are validated. Yet research shows that in a number of different disciplines, from the human sciences to the natural sciences, it is far more likely for change to occur after some disruption takes place.

This change state is absolutely necessary for intercultural development. It is work that cannot be done without examining preconceived notions or accepting, integrating, and finding space for other perspectives within your own frames of reference. Additionally, if the disruption itself is too drastic, it can have the opposite effect and push people further into their own comfort zones, while prompting harsh judgment of others and binary ("us" vs. "them") thinking. Therefore, the facilitation task is to try to create and maintain the change state—a place between comfortable and uncomfortable where the perspective shift can take place.

This facilitation task is known as "creating productive discomfort." In the classroom context, this means actively and intentionally supporting students as they process a disruption in their thinking about difference—and sometimes this involves crafting and introducing the disruption itself to start the process.

Takeaways

▶ Engaging diversity is an approach to a class or experience that includes interacting with your classmates and seeking their perspectives. Not doing this is a missed opportunity.

▶ Engaging with difference often exposes you to new ways of thinking, some of which may go against your values or perceptions of right and wrong.

▶ The social construction of awkwardness affects how you take risks and step outside of your comfort zone.

▶ Listening is a skill, and reflecting on the different parts of it can help you develop that skill.

▶ People react to the same information with different responses and emotions. Being in a shared space with these differences can feel confusing, uncomfortable, and unsafe for different students.

▶ The sense of belonging is not a static thing and changes depending on any number of factors. In general, people are very sensitive to this feeling of being an insider or an outsider in any given space.

▶ Change state is absolutely necessary for intercultural development. It is work that cannot be done without examining our preconceived notions or accepting, integrating, and finding space for other perspectives within your frame of reference.

Takeaways on Your Terms

▶ Were there any parts of this chapter that you felt didn't apply to you? If so, what were they? Why do you feel these things didn't relate to your experience?

▶ Productive discomfort doesn't really make sense until you've experienced it. When have you experienced productive discomfort? If you haven't, imagine a scenario where you might feel it.

▶ Think back to this chapter and notice what stood out to you the most, either because you felt like it related to you or because it was a perspective you hadn't considered.

In Your Own Words: Keep. Quit. Start.

Think about how you normally interact with classmates who you don't know. After reading this chapter, what would you like to keep doing the same regarding these interactions? Quit doing? Start doing, either through actions or in the way you think about these interactions?

Anticipate the next time you might feel awkward in class or in a social situation. What about your understanding of this moment of awkwardness would you like to keep? What understandings of this awkwardness would you like to let go? And what, given your new understandings of these awkward moments, would you like to start doing?

Think about how you listen to classmates and peers. What about your listening would you like to keep? Is there anything about the way you listen that you would like to quit doing? What would you like to start doing when you listen to others?

Chapter 4 Assignment

Goals of the Assignment

▸ Observe a group interaction (in your own life) with an eye toward what supports the group and the conversation, and also what derails or limits the group and the conversation.
▸ Take the lessons learned from the first group interaction and apply them to another conversation.
▸ Have a list of do's and don'ts for group interactions.

Steps of the Assignment

1. Reread the Try This 4.4 listening exercise in this chapter.
2. During the next week, choose a group conversation you are part of and observe it. This will require you to view it from the balcony, meaning you will take a metaphorical bird's-eye view. While you can still participate in it, try to keep an eye on what's going on in terms of who's talking and who's listening and how different conversational moves are impacting the discussion.
3. Pay attention and note: Who's listening passively? Who's listening actively? What body language do you see? Are speakers being interrupted? Is the conversation building as different people speak? (For instance, does a speaker say something and then the next speaker builds on it or relates their point to it?) Are there speakers who are trying to interrupt, but are struggling to get a turn?
4. What moves do you observe that promote understanding, engagement, and help move the topic forward? Which moves limit the conversation?
5. Choose another group conversation and utilize the moves you identified in the first conversation as positive. Does this feel natural for you? What's easy? What's difficult?

What You Need to Hand In

Write a list of 10 do's and 10 don'ts for engaging diversity through listening. Be prepared to share the why's with classmates.

Tools for Managing Assignments, Workload, and Projects

I n the Toolbox section of this book, we introduce some tools and strategies that might be helpful to you in your studies, project management, and learning. You might already use some of these, so this will be an opportunity to confirm what works for you, or to try out, adapt, and adopt new tools. If you try a technique or strategy and it doesn't work for you, that's fine. Just move on until you find one that does.

TB SECTION 1.1 Time Management

When we ask students in our first-year classes, "What's something you need help with?" the most common answer is "time management." This isn't just a condition of being a college student. Many people struggle to stay on task, figure out how to prioritize tasks, and find the time to complete all that the world is asking of them. Time can also simply disappear with the constant and unending supply of information and entertainment available at our fingertips, with our phones, tablets, and the internet full of possibility and designed to keep us tuned in. Time management can be a more pressing skill for college students to develop because it's necessary for engaging in challenging schoolwork and because college students are transitioning to adulthood and independence. It's not that we're all terrible at managing our time. There are a lot of things to do and the rhythm of college is unusual. So many students have said, "It's like my professors don't realize that I'm taking other classes!" This is almost always during midterm or final exam time, and the students have a good point. Because of the unusual schedule, what works one week, when you have readings due in two classes, a paper in one, and a lab report in another, might not work in the next week when you are giving a speech and really need to get your research question for a paper finalized, which certainly won't work when you have four exams over the course of three days.

When you approach time management with the thought that you can control your time, it tends to be overwhelming and often counterproductive. A way to start getting your head around "time management" is to develop discrete habits and attitudes that support you accomplishing your tasks on any given day. Before you even start thinking about new habits, however, take a moment to make an inventory of what you've done in the past that has worked.

TB THINK ABOUT IT

Did you effectively structure your time during high school? What parts of your day were within your control? Which were not? What's different now? What could be used again?

How have you balanced a part-time job and school in the past? How have you balanced your social life and school in the past? How have you balanced entertainment/relaxation and school in the past?

What was your internal motivation for completing assignments in high school? Was it a desire to get into a good college? Competition among your peers? Class rank? What's your internal motivation now?

What were the external motivators for you in the past? Parents? Coaches? Peers? What did they do that worked? Are there structures or rewards/punishments they used that you could use now? What or who are your external motivators now?

How you manage your time will differ throughout your life and life stage. There may be some consistencies but never hesitate to try something new and then reflect on whether or not it was successful. You can try different habits, different tools, and if they work, great, use them again. If they don't work, try another. (See **TB Figure 1.1**.)

Observe your peers and identify strategies you think would work well for you, or that you would be interested in learning more about. If someone is using a paper planner in an intriguing way, ask if they will tell you about it. Ask your peers where they study and how they manage distractions. People who are active and busy in many ways usually have had to learn to manage their time well and are a great resource, such as students who are athletes or artists, in ROTC, active in governance or activism, who are working full- or part-time, or who also have families. Sharing strategies and tips on how to manage your life is a great way to start a conversation that can support and improve your time management toolbox.

use a paper
or electronic
calemdar

set a timer
to complete
a task

make a to-do list
and cross things off

take 5 minutes
every day to set
goals for the day

schedule difficult
tasks at times when
you are more alert

TB Figure 1.1 Time Management Strategies

Time management is part using your time wisely, pairing the time that you have to an appropriate task, and part project management, identifying the individual pieces of any given project so you can prioritize and complete them as needed.

Managing Time + Task

You can do anything for 10 minutes. No matter how much you don't want to do a particular task, because it's hard, it takes effort, or it's not interesting to you, you can do *anything* for 10 minutes. Choose a task. Set a timer. And write, or read, or calculate, or prepare the graphs, or dive into the data analysis—whatever it is—and give it 10 minutes of your undistracted time. At the end of 10 minutes, assess what you got done and move on.

The idea behind the belief that you can do anything for 10 minutes is that you can. Settling into a challenging task for three hours is truly too much sometimes, plus it tends to get delayed until you have three consecutive hours. Ten minutes isn't so bad. Sometimes, giving a task 10 minutes and not asking yourself to do more is enough to chip away at the dread that prevents you from starting it in the first place. (Margaret Delahanty Kelly, one of the authors of this book, has assigned this challenge to her students. In one case, her students challenged her back: "One student, when I said that I could do anything for 10 minutes, challenged me to do a 10-minute wall sit. While I agreed that he was right, it's now three years later and I've broken seven minutes. So 10, I'm coming for you.")

Once you've started a task, you know more about what it will eventually require *and* you are setting your brain up to think about it even when you're not. It's like when you notice something about your friend that's different and you don't really think about it, and then a day later, when you're no longer with your friend, you suddenly realize what it was that was different. You didn't even know that you were thinking about it. When you spend 10 minutes on an essay or a problem set, later, while you're walking to class or unlocking your bike, an idea just might come to you. This is just how your brain works. But if you never start engaging with the task, your brain won't do this.

Do, Don't Dread

How much time do you spend dreading doing something that you could actually spend time doing? In college, Margaret was in a French class where she was supposed to keep a daily journal (in French). "I didn't do any of it until the very end of the semester. For the last two weeks of the semester, each night at dinner, I'd complain to my friend Annie about how much I had to do and how awful it was. I was totally overwhelmed by it. I spent a lot of time beating myself up for it and feeling so guilty for having not started it. Eventually, one night at dinner, Annie asked me, 'why don't you just do it rather than dread it.'" "Do, don't dread" is not a strategy so much as a mindset, but how much time do you spend dreading things? Could you just let that go and spend some of that time *doing* the actual activity? It's a finite amount of work, and anything you could do to chip away at it could be worth it.

Six Things for Tomorrow, Prioritized

There are multiple systems you can learn about via internet research for listing your tasks, determining their urgency and their importance, and then prioritizing what you should do first. These are worthwhile activities and you should look into some of the following resources if you're interested in learning about them. One of the simplest of them is the *Ivy Lee Method* (Clear, n.d.). In short, before you go to bed, you list out the six most important tasks you need to accomplish the next day and then prioritize them 1–6. The next day you start with number 1, do it until it's complete, and then move on to number 2.

Some version of this can work for college students. The idea of listing out six tasks before you go to bed helps you to 1) put your tasks aside and hopefully rest a bit easier, and 2) know what you're going to start working on during your first time block the next day. This allows you to use your time doing what you need to do, rather than dreading it or deciding between many tasks, because you've already made the decision.

 **TB TRY THIS** ⎯⎯⎯⎯⎯⎯ 1.1

What are the top six things you need to do tomorrow? Try to identify six finite tasks that are doable in a chunk of time, perhaps 45–90 minutes. List them out and then number them 1–6, 1 being the one with the highest priority. Look at your planner for tomorrow. At what time will you start task #1? Schedule it.

Identify Your Time Blocks for the Next Day

Most college students are juggling a lot of demands and may have a lot of variety in their schedules from day to day. From your class schedule, to working, to childcare or family responsibilities, it can be hard to find a routine. In the absence of routine, assess your schedule at the beginning of every week and at the end of every day. What's ahead? Where are blocks of time you can schedule to do school work? When do you have to go to work? When are there student club activities or social events?

Different Spaces

Some students can read Plato's *Republic* while in line for dinner at the dining hall. Other students need a silent library space. Some thrive in a coffee shop environment. Others need a desk with all supplies nearby and available. A fun part of college is experimenting with different study spaces. Most campuses have a variety of spaces available with different chairs, tables, whiteboards, and vending machines available. Play around with the different options. What kind of study space do you thrive in? Where are you less prone to distractions? Where are you surrounded by people and sound that either energizes you or motivates you?

TB THINK ABOUT IT

What study space has been most productive for you? What kind of assignment were you working on? What do you think supported your productivity in that space? What study space has been least productive for you? Why?

Getting Rid of Distractions

Ahhhh, distractions. Everyone struggles with distractions; it's part of the human condition. Distractions might be flashier these days though, and there are certainly a lot of dings in our environment luring us away from our tasks, but distractions, in and of themselves, are not new.

There are plenty of resources that block the internet for a time if that is what distracts you. You can also develop the habit of closing tabs on your computer so you don't see the rising number of notifications. Silencing your phone and studying in a space without a videogame console are ways to lower the risk of distraction. Much of managing distractions is controlling your environment. Your odds of eating M&Ms increase if you carry an open bag of them around with you and similarly, your odds of looking at your phone/playing a videogame/streaming something on Netflix is much higher if the device is just as close to you as your homework. If you're having difficulty resisting distractions, try to make one decision (leave the device at home when you go to study, or put it on airplane mode) that will control your environment. This would be instead of putting yourself into a situation where you are forced to make a decision "to check or not to check" every time your phone dings.

Pay attention to the very specific things that get you off course. If you say that your phone distracts you but you need it with you because of safety, or need it as a calculator, or use it to pay for things, you've not gotten yourself any further. Instead, what is it about your phone that wins out in the battle for your attention? Is that something you could either block (using its technology) or commit to not using for a given period? Part of this is mindset. If we keep telling ourselves, "I can't stop myself from using my phone!" chances are we will continue to be distracted by it. If, however, we tell ourselves, "I'm developing strong habits where I keep my phone in a different room while I study" or "I can spend 30 minutes studying without checking X app," we begin to actually develop that mindset and habit.

TB THINK ABOUT IT

What specific things are distracting you? What are some strategies you can try to overcome that distraction? When and how can you try this strategy? How will you know if it worked?

If you're someone who operates best when there's something external that blocks you from the app/website/social media that distracts you the most, search the web for "apps that block apps/websites/social media." There are tons of apps and other software you can use that will not allow you to view specific distractions for a period of time. These can be really helpful if you are struggling with setting up your own limits. Consider using the SelfControl app or actual self-control. The app will keep you from accessing social media sites like Facebook, Tumblr, or Twitter when you should be working. It is free and customizable so you can block any website you like.

Identify Easy Tasks and "Treat" Yourself to Them

Sometimes the desire to check our phone or read an article in a newsfeed is strong because the current task we're working on feels too tedious or overwhelming. What tasks must you do that are "mindless" or require a different type of attention? Perhaps you have an essay with a bibliography and you need to go through the bibliography and check its style compliance—for example, are the commas, periods, capitals, etc., all in the correct place? Or perhaps you need to look at that final assignment and assess which tasks you'll need to complete as you manage the project. These tasks keep the momentum going while providing some recovery from the harder undertaking. Marathoners who walk through water stations do something similar—they slow down, catch their breaths, rehydrate a bit, but they keep moving in the direction of the finish line.

Reassess Your Multitasking Skills

There are some actions/behaviors that we think are multitasking but that, in the end, don't actually allow us downtime. In other words, doing dishes while the rice cooks, or answering emails while waiting to be called into your dental appointment, this isn't multitasking. You're still only doing one thing at a time. You're just structuring your time so you're using it more fully. Multitasking, on the other hand, is more like stirring the pot while also doing the dishes, simultaneously. Or, if you're scrolling through your phone while talking to your mom and hearing about her day, that's multitasking. In those cases, your brain (and body) is trying to pay attention to two things simultaneously, and it can't, at least not effectively.

TB TRY THIS   1.2

Keep a chart for four days of your productivity during your study times. When are you most alert and focused? When are you most tired and unproductive? Use your energy peaks for your key studying times! Don't use those times for your downtime!

If you still feel like you need some help with your time management, search the internet for "time management strategies." There are so many sites offering free strategies. Some sites ask you to pay for a class or video, but most offer a few simple ideas or concepts at no cost. Take 10 minutes to look through a few and write down some strategies that resonate with you.

Allowing Quiet Time and Creativity

You can't always be productive, and often you need a break in order to be productive. Some time management systems encourage a five-minute break for every 25 minutes of work. If this approach works for you, go for it. If it doesn't work for you (only five minutes!), play around with different methods. Perhaps you want to use mealtime as a natural and necessary break time. Or, perhaps a phone visit or a load of laundry will do the same for you. Or, perhaps you just need to sit, without any distraction at all and let your mind wander. Don't beat yourself up about needing a break—it's all part of the process, and sometimes your greatest ideas will come when you're not trying to think.

Balance

Sometimes it's helpful to take a step back and notice where your time is going. We have 24 hours in a day. And that's it. Scheduling your time to try and get more done in a day than is possible is not helpful. On the flip side, scheduling your time in a way that leaves large chunks of time completely open will probably not help you get your schoolwork done. So, in the middle of these two extremes lies a balance. And this balance looks different for each person.

TB TRY THIS — 1.3

One way to consider what balance looks like for you is to create a pie chart. Start with the 24 hours in a day. How many hours will you sleep? Prepare food and eat? Attend class? Do homework? Draw these in a pie chart and take a step back to look at how one of your days might unfold. Are you surprised by how much time there is in a day? Or how little time there is? Are there any adjustments you want to make to your pie chart? Look at **TB Figure 1.2** for an example.

Managing Time via Project Management

Knowing What's Next

There is a push and pull in time management. You don't want to waste time on planning what to do when you should just start doing, but often there is power in planning, especially when the task ahead requires multiple steps. So, if you have an article to read for a class, just read it in a time block that you've identified as

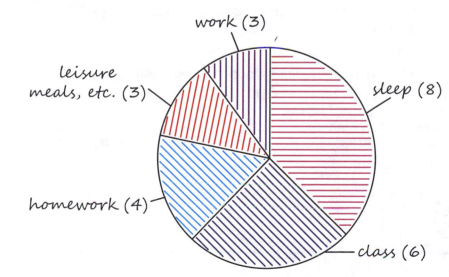

TB Figure 1.2 Time Well Spent

available. But if you have an annotated bibliography due in your writing course next week or if your final lab report in chemistry is due in three days, you'd likely benefit from mapping out the individual steps. When you have a sense of what tasks come next, your transition between the multiple steps of any given project is smoother and more efficient.

One challenge for students who are taking new classes every semester with different professors is that the assignments keep changing and the tasks for one type of assignment are different than for the next. While it can be difficult to develop systems when things are always changing, you can start to identify patterns that will help you figure out the tasks even when you've never done a certain type of assignment before.

TB THINK ABOUT IT

What was your last project or assignment in a class? How many finite tasks made up the completion of that one project? The following is an example that might help you see what we mean.

Annotated Bibliography for Research Paper To-Do List:

Brainstorm potential research questions

Narrow research questions

Peer-review research questions (done in class)

Online chat with librarian about good databases for research questions

Online library search for articles
- Find articles
- Check date of publication
    - If too old but relevant, see who has cited this article more recently
- Check relevance to question (read abstract, read findings)
- Check whether or not peer-reviewed

Choose 10 articles

Read first article, and write first entry for annotated bibliography
- Read and take notes (in margins)
- Summarize
- Connect to research questions
- Check the citation style that was autogenerated against style guide

Do this for rest of articles

Spell-check

Use Turnitin®

Reread

The annotated bibliography in the preceding example has three stages, as do many assignments.

- Stage 1: Gather and Prep
- Stage 2: Process and Produce
- Stage 3: Refine and Polish

You can see how the list can be divided into these three stages next.

TB THINK ABOUT IT

Annotated Bibliography for Research Paper To-Do List with Stages:

Stage 1: Gather and Prep

Brainstorm potential research questions

Narrow research questions

Peer-review research questions (done in class)

Online chat with librarian about good databases for research question

Online library search for articles

- Find articles
- Check date of publication
    - If too old but relevant, see who has cited this article more recently
- Check relevance to question (read abstract, read findings)
- Check whether or not peer-reviewed

Choose 10 articles

Stage 2: Process and Produce

Read first article, and write first entry for annotated bibliography

- Read and take notes (in margins)
- Summarize
- Connect to research question
- Check the citation style that was autogenerated against style guide

Do this for rest of articles

Stage 3: Refine and Polish

Spell-check

Use Turnitin®

Reread

We have included a template for these three steps that can be adapted for many kinds of projects that would benefit from being broken down into small steps. (See **TB Figure 1.3** for how one student uses the stages to plan.)

PROJECT:
DUE DATE:

stage 1:
gather & prep

deadline:
_____ due dates
brainstorm
narrow
research
choose

stage 2: process

deadline:
_____ due dates
make a plan
complete plan
seek feedback

stage 3:
refine

deadline:
_____ due dates
turn it in
reread
revise

TB Figure 1.3 Project Process Template

TB TRY THIS ─────────────────────   1.4

When you've received an assignment back and have a grade and, perhaps some written feedback, see if you can figure out which steps in your process need either revision or more attention. Also, was there something you spent a lot of time on in the assignment that doesn't feel "worth it" when the assignment is returned? So, for the earlier annotated bibliography example, a student might find they wrote great summaries but for the *wrong* articles, either because they weren't peer-reviewed or because they weren't sufficiently connected to their research question.

TB SECTION **1.2**

Understanding Reading and Keeping Track of What You've Read

The mark of a successful college student is the mastery of knowing not only what to study but also how to study it.
—Patricia I. Mulcahy-Ernt and David C. Caverly (Flippo & Caverly, 2008)

In this section of the toolkit, we will share and discuss a variety of strategies that will help you keep up with your reading, discuss ways to incorporate notetaking in your reading time as well as in your course meetings, and explore some study techniques you can apply as you synthesize the information from your readings and notetaking in classes so you can best study, learn, retain, and apply your knowledge.

There are a variety of methods you can incorporate to deal with your reading assignments. You should always try to read your course readings prior to attending class so you're familiar with the terminology, concepts, and theories covered in the reading material, so much so that you're ready to listen, apply, and act on the information.

How often you read something is immaterial; how you read it is crucial. —Virginia Voeks

Margaret's Take on Taking Notes

We asked Margaret Delahanty Kelly, one of this book's authors, to take the lead on this section because she teaches reading-heavy courses and has spent a lot of time thinking and working with her students on the process of keeping track of one's reading. Here's Margaret's take:

Likely, you learned a method of notetaking at some point in your K-12 experience. Some students have adapted a method to fit their own style, but many students haven't. The key is to find a method that works for you. How do you know your system works? It helps you stay engaged while taking in information and you can refer back to it as your knowledge and understanding continues to grow. It is useful when writing papers and studying for exams. If you have a system like that which worked in high school, great. See if you can adapt it for college. If, however, you have a stack of nearly empty notebooks from high school, now is the time to really dig in and figure out how you want to take notes in college. In my own experience, it wasn't until my senior year of college that I finally came upon a system that worked for me. I regretted all of those hours of color-coded two-column notes. A little more reflection along the way would have helped me find the style of notetaking that worked for me earlier. This section is intended to explain some of the factors that impact how and why you take notes, and offer some structure for figuring out what works for you as a learner. The big message is try, reflect, try again. The method I finally landed on in my senior year is the method I still use. It's a life skill.

What Does Our Brain Do While We Take Notes?

Taking notes, whether we're in class or out of class, forces us to process some of the information we're taking in. It engages our mind in summarizing, seeing causal relationships, comparing and contrasting ideas, etc. We evaluate the information as we read it. If we're taking notes in a way that only engages a small part of our brain, enough to highlight a line that seems important, or copy down a quote, we're not engaging sufficiently. Mindful readers engage with a text so that they can organize, evaluate, and elaborate on what they are reading (Rhoder, 2002). Even if you never return to the notes you take (although you should!), there is benefit in writing them.

Outside-of-Class Notetaking

The ratio of "time in class: time completing homework" in college is different than in high school. You have fewer hours in class and more time on your own, often reading. How you interact with texts outside of class impacts your learning.

Glossing a Text

Arrival at college usually means a shift in the quantity and rigor or demands of the reading you have to do. College instructors often use readings that are not written for students but for professionals. This is a great way to read the most recent research, but it is not always an easy read. The goal of the college reader becomes 1) completing the reading assignments, 2) understanding as much as possible, and 3) processing and recording it (notetaking) so you can return to it at a later time.

One of the least time-consuming methods of notetaking you can use is writing annotations (or notes) in the margins, which is called glossing the text. (See **TB Figure 1.4**.) While many students want to sell their textbooks back and keep them pristine, writing in the margins has its strengths. Here's the process: Read a paragraph, identify the topic, and write that topic in the margin next to the paragraph. This might seem easy. Often, the topic is spelled out in the topic sentence—the first sentence of the paragraph, so why do you need to write it down? You need to write the topic down in the margin because 1) doing so actually engages your brain rather than the more passive act of underlining or highlighting, and 2) when you return to the text in class or in the future to review materials, you can scan the topics you've written in the margin to locate the part of the text you want to pull from or review.

Just glossing the text does not take a huge amount of extra time, while the benefits are great—you're more mindful about what you're reading and you have something to go back to. If you're a reader (like most of us) who reads for 10 minutes before realizing you have no idea what you just read, it's a good idea to try glossing.

TB TRY THIS   1.5

Ten-minute practice: Gloss the following sample text as you read. For each paragraph, write one to five words in the margin identifying the topic of the paragraph.

Sample Course Reading

Wellness is about giving attention, care, and time to ourselves and our well-being. This means being in tune with how we feel, noticing what needs we have, and being committed to taking action to resolve issues. The basic pattern of attending to your wellness is such: understanding your past experiences and

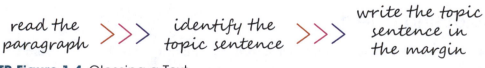

read the paragraph >>> identify the topic sentence >>> write the topic sentence in the margin

TB Figure 1.4 Glossing a Text

naming your habits, reflecting on whether these habits contribute to your wellness, then choosing to develop new habits if need be. It's important to maintain this in times when life is going generally well, just as it's important in times of challenge and struggle. Ultimately, the power of wellness is that it is a tangible way for you to take responsibility for yourself and show yourself care. It is a way that you can show up for yourself, by being attentive to your own needs, acting upon your feelings, and striving to build positive habits that make you feel good. The person who benefits from your wellness is you, and so it is a powerful and impactful choice to make.

Wellness is a complex thing made up of many factors, and therefore it's never as simple as being all good or all bad. There's no such thing as being perfectly well, or completely unwell. Each factor of your wellness will always be fluctuating based on events going on in your life, your decisions, and some things outside of your control. Maintaining your wellness is about paying attention to each of these factors, keeping them at healthy levels, and ultimately being forgiving of yourself when things don't go to plan. It will never be perfect, so don't punish yourself for not having it all together. No one ever does. The first step is choosing simply to care about your own wellness, which is powerful by itself.

TB THINK ABOUT IT

At the end of 10 minutes, reflect on the following questions:

- Did you feel more engaged in the reading?
- If/when you were distracted, was it easier to pull yourself back to the text?
- How do you rank your understanding of the material?

A step beyond glossing the text for topics is including your own thoughts in the margin. Students occasionally tell us that they don't have opinions about what they read; they are just reading for the information. While this is fine on many levels (this is one big reason we read—instructions, reports, etc.), reading in order to prepare for a debate is a trick that they can use to engage more deeply with a text. I ask students to read a text and come back to class prepared to challenge or affirm different parts of it. Where in the reading do they think, "This is totally true!" "This fits my experience" or "This reminds me of x, y, or z"? Where in the text do they think, "whatever," "this is bogus," or "I don't believe this"? Being critical while reading and adding notes to your margin annotations helps you prepare to discuss it. Underlining a few words in the text and then writing your reaction in the margin can be a simple approach. Writing words like "Really?" or "Not in my life!" or "This is crazy!" might not seem college-like, but it is evidence that you are reading, processing, and evaluating the information—which is mindful reading.

TB TRY THIS   1.6

Ten-minute practice: Take a course reading, and while you read, continue to gloss the topics of the paragraphs, but also react. Engage emotionally with the text. What do you agree with (affirm)? What do you disagree with (challenge)? It is easier to do this with a text from the humanities or social sciences. It's okay to exaggerate your reactions. You might not really have any strong feelings about the material, but engage with it like you do. Search yourself for reactions. If you have an inkling of doubt or excitement about an idea, run with it. Then, answer the following questions.

- Having reacted emotionally to the text and written those reactions in the margin, what do you remember about the text? Have you processed more of the meaning?
- Pay attention when you go back to class about how you take in the instructor's teaching about the text. Are you engaging differently with it?

Outlining

Many students learn how to outline in middle school and high school. This is a great skill—identifying the large ideas and then the smaller ideas that fit below it. Using the structure of the textbook (headings and subheadings) is a good place to start. You don't have to figure out what the big ideas are if the big ideas are written in bold or emphasized with underlines. If you take the time to transfer those headings to your notes, be sure to take the extra time to process the content below the heading. Just copying down the outline of the text for the sake of fulfilling the need to "take notes" does not get you much. You are not necessarily engaged with the text while doing that.

When it comes to outlining as a form of notetaking, don't let perfection become the enemy of good. It takes a lot of time to outline material. Students often don't know how much of the small detail is important to record and so they'll spend a lot of time and get overwhelmed by the task. I'll look at student notes and see incredibly detailed notes for the first five pages of a class reading and then nothing for the last 25 pages. The student simply ran out of time. It's about finding a balance. As you read and take notes, be aware of what part of the process is helping you understand the ideas, what part is helping you evaluate the ideas, and what part is creating something you can return to at a later time to review the ideas. This type of reflection while working with texts (and later going to class where the texts are used/discussed and being tested on the content) will help you to assess what's needed. In my own college experience, I was assigned a huge amount of text to read and I tried to take color-coded two-column style notes on them. I never made it through the entire text, nor did I understand and process the big ideas of the texts. What I created was not very useful either in class or in preparing for exams, and it also took a lot of time.

One way to use the power of outlining while not being derailed by it, is to use the organizational structure (the headings and the subheadings) as a way to take in the information *and then* spend some time thinking about why the author organized the information this way. For example, the following are the headings and subheadings from Chapter 10.2 of *Chemistry: The Molecular Nature of Matter and Change* (Silberberg & Amateis, 2015) and how you can use these headings to help give you direction in terms of recognizing and processing the important information.

THINK ABOUT IT

10.2 Valence-Shell Electron-Pair Repulsion (VSEPR) Theory

Electron-Group Arrangement
- Classifying Molecular Shapes
- The Importance of Bond Angle

The Molecular Shape with Two Electron Groups (Linear Arrangement)

Molecular Shapes with Three Electron Groups (Trigonal Planar Arrangement)
- Effect of Double Bonds on Bond Angle

Molecular Shapes with Four Electron Groups (Tetrahedral Arrangement)

Molecular Shapes with Five Electron Groups (Trigonal Bipyramidal Arrangement)

Molecular Shapes with Six Electron Groups (Octahedral Arrangement)

Using VSEPR Theory to Determine Molecular Shape

Molecular Shapes with More Than One Central Atom

If you don't have a lot of background in chemistry, this outline can be overwhelming because of the discipline-specific language. You can imagine writing down these headings and not actually knowing what they mean. Writing them down and then asking yourself why the author decided this was the best organizational structure might help you in decoding what it means and understanding the big idea. The next Think About It is a "talk through" of what that might look like.

THINK ABOUT IT

10.2 Valence-Shell Electron-Pair Repulsion (VSEPR) Theory—
I have no idea what this means but as it's the topic for this section of the chapter, hopefully I'll learn.

Electron-Group Arrangement—*Apparently where groups of electrons are in a molecule makes a difference.*
- Classifying Molecular Shapes—*There are different shapes of molecules and they need to be classified.*
- The Importance of Bond Angle—*Not only are there different shapes, but within those shapes are angles of the bonds and those are important.*

(continued)

THINK ABOUT IT

The Molecular Shape with Two Electron Groups (Linear Arrangement)— *One shape classification is when there are two groups. They look a certain way (and maybe act a certain way?)*

Molecular Shapes with Three Electron Groups (Trigonal Planar Arrangement)— *There is another classification when there are three groups of electrons.*
  • Effect of Double Bonds on Bond Angle—*Once we get to the three electron groups, double bonds impact bond angle.*

Molecular Shapes with Four Electron Groups (Tetrahedral Arrangement)— *There is another classification and shape when there are four electron groups.*

Molecular Shapes with Five Electron Groups (Trigonal Bipyramidal Arrangement)— *There is another classification and shape when there are five electron groups.*

Molecular Shapes with Six Electron Groups (Octahedral Arrangement)—*There is another classification and shape when there are six electron groups!*

Using VSEPR Theory to Determine Molecular Shape—*The theory helps me to figure out molecular shape (so this is why I need to understand the earlier sections?)*

Molecular Shapes with More Than One Central Atom—*All of the earlier configurations discussed are when there is only one central atom! Things are different when there is more than one?*

After reviewing this, I know there is a theory that helps me figure out molecular shape, and therefore how molecules interact with each other. And there are many categories that I have to learn and figure out. The number of electron groups, the angles of the bonds, and the number of central atoms are all important. The author took a large quantity of information and organized it primarily by *the number of electron groups* within a molecule. So, as I read, this should be my focus—what happens when the number of electron groups changes? If I notice this structure, I will pay attention to it as I read and structure my notes around it. Because I looked at the outline and asked why the author organized it this way, I am now focused on the number of electrons and how that impacts shape and characteristics. The task changes from an overwhelming "figure out what this means" to a more specific "How does the number of electron groups impact the shape and characteristics of molecules?" The more specific question helps me to limit what I need to write down under each subheading.

TB TRY THIS   1.7

Ten-minute exercise: Look at a course reading where the author(s) have provided an organizational structure with headings and subheadings. Write those headings and subheadings down.
• Why did the author organize it this way? What should be your focus in reading this?
• What is the question you need to answer under each subheading?

Bulleting

The last style of notetaking to consider as you launch your journey into finding what works for you is bulleting. An advantage of it is that you don't have to think about process or organization. You just have to jot down ideas. As you read, keep a notebook beside you where you list ideas from the text, reactions you have, connections to class material, etc., in bulleted form. By doing this, you are engaging with the text, the first goal of any notetaking. The disadvantage is that by doing this you are not necessarily processing the organization of the text (or the argument) or determining the most important ideas. However, you can overcome this by bulleting a section of the text (perhaps a chapter) and then taking a moment to process the information on a larger level. As you read, don't worry about outlining/Roman numerals or the argument; just read to understand ideas as they present themselves. Write them down and then, before moving on, reread your notes and add a final bullet point of summary or the big idea. Later, you can return to ideas to draw arrows, circle ideas to return to, etc.

TB TRY THIS ━━━━━━━━━━━━━━━━━━ **1.8**

Ten-minute exercise: Take a course text and read it while jotting down ideas on a piece of paper. Do not worry about form or organization. Include any kind of thoughts or ideas you take from the text or have in connection to your reading. At the end, look back over them and write a few summative ideas.

- How engaged did you feel while reading the text and bulleting your notes?
- Do you think you focused more on big ideas or small ideas? Could you recognize the difference while reading?
- Pay attention to how you feel and how you're able to participate when this text is being taught in class. Are your notes useful to you?

A Final Thought on Outside-of-Class Notetaking

You get to discover what works for you and what enhances your learning. Perhaps you meld together bulleting and outlining with the occasional margin note. Maybe you only write in the margins. Or perhaps you see what a classmate is doing with sticky notes and colored pens and you try that. Just remember to engage with the text *somehow* beyond moving your eyes across the words. And then reflect on how well that process worked for you.

In-Class Notetaking

The first thing to figure out when you are in any college class is what materials are available to you. For example, you may have an instructor who teaches from a slide show (e.g., PowerPoint or Google Slides) and makes the slide show available to students either before or after class. If it's available to you before a class, consider taking notes directly onto the slide show (either on a printed copy or digitally) or maybe simply refer to the slide show after the class to add their text to your notes. Regardless, if you have access to the slide show, consider whether or not your energy is best used writing down the words on each slide exactly as they are presented in class, or if creating a summary or shorthand based on the slides is a better way for you to take notes. Often, when teaching, I see students furiously trying to write down every word on my slides. And yet, that is not my intention as a teacher. I use the slides to provide an outline of any lecture component of my class. The words help me remember what to talk about and help the students know what topic I'm discussing if their attention drifts off for a bit. The slides can be really helpful study tools when preparing for an exam, and that is why I give students access to them. I provide the slide shows on the course website and they can see them before, during, and after class. Rather than copying down the content of the slide, I want students to listen to what I'm saying in order to understand *the meaning* of what is on the slide. Perhaps there is a concept on the slide, write the concept down as the header and then listen to the instructor. As you come to an understanding of the concept, write it down, using your own words and perhaps a form of shorthand. If there are moments in the explanation that stand out to you because they make sense (e.g., an example you can relate to), write that down. Or, if something is confusing to you, jot that down or draw a question mark. At the next opportunity to ask a question, you will remember what it is you didn't understand.

Other instructors might provide reading guides or discussion questions. Others base their class periods on a combination of lectures and the completion of problem sets. A perfectly reasonable question to ask an instructor during office hours is, "What do you think is the best way to take notes during class time?" Often, instructors have an idea of what their students *should* be doing in class and deliberately set up the class so that can happen, yet they never explicitly tell the students *how* to best use what they provide.

Notes During Small Group Discussion

Many instructors integrate small group discussion into their teaching so that students get a chance to really delve into a topic, practice a process being taught, and make connections between multiple topics. Students will often ask me, "Do we have to write anything?" and "Do we need to hand this in?" and "Is this being graded?" To me, the focus of these questions is off. They are focused on their grade rather than their learning. The answer is "Yes!" to all of these questions. Yes, you should be writing things down because that's one way you can more actively engage with the discussion. Yes, you want a record of this conversation and the quotes from the book you discuss because you will use it when writing your essay in a week. Yes, it is being graded in that there is a summative assessment in a month that asks you to take a larger view of our class content and you will need to review for it. Yes, you are about to interact with other students who think differently than you do and read this text differently than you did and whose life experience creates a different filter through which they understood the text. Capture as much of that as you can because it will benefit and deepen your own understanding. (Also, small group discussions are a great opportunity to see how your classmates take notes. What is their method and how does it seem to be serving them? Is it something you might want to try?)

Secret Teacher Language

A few years ago, I took a chemistry class because I'd never taken a lab science in college and wanted to see what it was like. I was a student, but I also had 15 years of teaching experience. Throughout the class, I often heard the professor use what I later deemed "secret teacher language," a language I was fluent in. These were moments when she'd drop huge hints about what would be on the exam. She'd point out certain exceptions to rules in the days leading up to the exam (around the time she was finalizing the exam problems) and I'd think, "Oh, that's totally going to be on the exam" and quite often it was. She'd also send out practice problems (in addition to the many problems assigned in the book) via email in the days leading up to the exam. Again, I paid attention because I figured that she had put some really difficult problems on the exam and wanted to give us more practice. Nearly identical problems would then show up on the exams. Immediately following the exam, I'd be surprised to overhear students complain about those tricky exceptions to rules that appeared on the exam or those really difficult problems. I didn't understand how they hadn't gotten the really clear hints that that was exactly what we were going to be tested on. Then I realized that they weren't fluent in secret teacher language.

While it certainly isn't universal, teachers often think that they are being very explicit about what is going to be on the exam. They give examples in class during a review session. They post study guides. They say, "and now this is really important" before explaining a concept. Or "be sure to write this down." To the teacher, this is like putting flashing lights on an idea or concept and screaming that it will be on the test. And yet for students, who are grappling to understand concepts and ideas, these big flashing lights often go unnoticed. You can, however, train yourself to pay attention to your instructors and identify what their "flashing lights" look like. Prime your brain to listen for phrases like "This is really important," or "this is an idea that students get confused by," or anything else that seems to mark one idea as particularly important.

Shorthand

When you're trying to write things down quickly, you often don't have the time to spell things out fully. As you dive into new subject areas, you'll find that different words are used time and time again. As you recognize what these *high-frequency* words are, develop a shorthand for them. These can be abbreviations (e.g., RXN for reaction) or symbols (e.g., using an arrow to indicate cause and effect). As you are developing new systems of shorthand, you can make a key so that you remember what abbreviations mean. It's also worthwhile to look through your notes while the ideas are still fresh to see if you can understand them. Add ideas/expand abbreviations that you might need in a few weeks to remember what you wrote down.

Pen and Paper vs. Computer and the Cloud

Ultimately, this is your decision, but keep in mind that there is research that the kinesthetic activity of writing your notes by hand may actually stimulate and support memory and cognition (Mueller & Oppenheimer, 2014). It's about what works for you, your access to sources of power (loose-leaf paper does not require charging) and what suits your personality. The students whose systems work for them are the students who have a system, know what it is, and maintain it. The key in any system is being able to retrieve what you need when you need it. A notebook with handouts jammed into it (some folded, some not) is not as effective as a three-ring binder with loose-leaf sheets that contain text notes, lecture notes and three-hole punched assignment guides. A Google Drive where you have to use three different keyword searches to find your most recent draft of a paper is not as effective as one with everything clearly labeled in a consistent way and stored in virtual folders. It requires maintenance, but the maintenance *always* pays off.

On a related note, as colleges are trying to reduce the cost of textbooks, more and more classes are going to ebooks and ejournal articles. This is great in terms of cost to students (often, although not always) and the cost to the environment. Electronic texts allow keyword searches, and readers can locate moments in the text with an ease that paper does not permit. However, it doesn't always work for notetaking if you've chosen the pen and paper route, especially margin annotations. While there are a number of good electronic annotation tools, some of them work differently with different types of scanned materials, and this can cause frustration. Just be aware that if one in-text annotation tool (e.g., Good Reader) doesn't suit you, find another. I have found that the people who know the best new tools for reading and notetaking are graduate students. If your class has a TA working with it, ask them if they use an ebook/etext annotation tool. With that being said, sometimes it's easier to just print the article out so you can annotate it with your pen.

TB SECTION 1.3   Organizing Tasks and Mapping Goals

Use a Planner

There are some amazing and fierce planner users in our classes. Whether it's a generational thing, the power of YouTube videos, or something else—wow!— some current first-year students really know how to use a paper planner. If you're one of those people, please share your method with others around you. If you aren't one of those people, pay attention to what your peers are doing and ask them. Your planner can be very personal to you, but you have to start somewhere and see what people out there are doing to get a sense of what will work well for you. Regardless, a place where you can bring together all of the tasks, due dates, and exam dates will help you show up to classes knowing what to expect.

Use a Digital Calendar

As your life gets busier and follows an ever-changing schedule, a digital calendar can help you keep track of where you're supposed to be when. Some instructors will use calendar invites as a way to schedule appointments and one-on-one conferences with you. Digital calendars can be great ways to find a shared free moment with groupmates who you need to meet with outside of class time. It's also a great way to find time slots for different items on your priority to-do list. If you have a two-hour time block, perhaps you could head to a library or another dedicated study space. If you have a 45-minute time block between classes, you could find a location between classes where you can review notes from the last class session. Once you put these in your digital calendar, you can set it up to send you a notification of what you're supposed to be doing when.

Google Calendar is probably the most popular calendar app available, because it is used on both iOS and Android platforms and is part of the Google suite. You can easily download the app to your mobile device and keep track of your tasks and deadlines.

ZenDay, another app that is available for iOS and Android, is considered to be one of the best productivity apps, because it provides you with a flowing timeline so you can see not only what you need to work on now, but also what you need to work on next. It also gives you a productivity grade, which may help you become a more organized student.

Read Syllabi

A course syllabus is full of important information. Course goals, required texts, and policies are all listed in the syllabus. Due dates and exam dates are also listed. Even though it might seem redundant, consider putting all of these dates on either your digital or paper planner. Knowing that you have two exams, one paper, and one lab report due within two days of each other, seven weeks from now, is going to help you know what to do today—or at least avoid the trap of "college is so easy" that many students fall into.

Figure out Your Folder and Naming Rules Now

Unless you already have an amazing folder and naming system for creating new documents on a computer, create one now. One of the greatest gifts you can give your future self is a system that allows you to find documents when you want them. Whether you use Microsoft Word, Google Docs, or some other word processing tool, name and organize them in a logical way. Students regularly hand in the wrong draft because of faulty labeling or are unable to find the Google Doc where they started their essay because if all docs are called "essay 1," it's hard to distinguish between them.

An example of a naming rule might be: year.course.assignment.draft. So, 2020. statistics.midterm.firstdraft and 2020.statistics.midterm.finaldraft might be a way you could label two drafts of a paper for the same class. And this naming rule lets you sort your files in the order of the year you handed them in, which can also be handy. Another naming rule might be date.course.assignment, so from this you might have the name 12/1.shakespeare.researchpaper. This will let you sort by date, which can keep your drafts in order. We also recommend you create a folder for each of your courses so you can keep your syllabus, assignments, drafts, and maybe even notes in the same place. No matter what organizational tool you decide to use, be consistent so you're able to keep your files organized and readily accessible. And if you do lose something, the search function on most computers and cloud storage services is very handy and helpful.

Map out Your Goals

Many people, textbooks, and websites will tell you that goals are critical to a person's success. This might be true, but it's less because without a goal you never achieve one, and more because having a goal helps you to structure your days in ways that get you going in the right direction. Goals can serve to motivate you. They can also help you make decisions. Knowing what you want to major in determines many of the courses you will take. Saving up for something you really want helps you to say no to other purchases. Goals can limit the seemingly endless options that are out there.

There is a downside, however, to the way our society often talks about goals. We are expected to have them, aim for them, and work for them, but what if we truly don't know enough to know what we want? Many students simply don't know what they want to major in or what they want to do professionally after graduation. We tell students that goals are essential for getting where they want to go, but many students simply need to engage in the transformational process of college in order to even figure out what their future goals are. Do not equate having goals with belonging in college. We sometimes hear our first-year students saying that not having a goal/a major/a career plan makes them feel like they don't belong in college. This is simply not true. The goal of college is, in part, to help you figure this out, so you are working on the goal of determining the next goal right now.

In this section of the toolbox, we will identify a number of future-oriented (goal) strategies so you can return to it when you're need to get yourself going in the right direction.

Isn't Being in College Enough?

First off, congratulations! You have a clear goal (college degree) on the horizon and you're actively pursuing it! This goal is going to do a lot to shape your upcoming years. In many ways, being in college *is* enough. Getting through your classes, choosing a major, determining the topic for any number of papers—these are all goals that are innate within your college degree. In addition to this big goal, there are some good reasons to pay attention to your other emerging goals. 1) Goals will help you stay the course even when it gets rough or when you experience some setbacks, and 2) goals can help you be aware of opportunities you might otherwise not pursue because future goals become a lens through which you see things. This occurs when you ask the question, "Might this _____ (class, internship, volunteer opportunity, public lecture, study abroad course, student group) help me get closer to my goal?"

Identify the Smaller Goals That Lead Toward the Bigger Goal

Big goals that exist far in the future require a series of small steps long before the big goal is achieved. Identifying the smaller goals gives you something to do now and can provide you with tiny wins as you go along. (See **TB Figure 1.5**.) Seeing the connection between what you are doing now and what you want to do in the future can help you persevere. Completing a challenging chemistry lab report when you see it as what you're doing today so as to work in the medical device industry in the future, makes a difference. Making these connections between the small goals and the larger goals also helps you to get the most out of the small goals. How might your mindset about the chemistry lab report change when you see it as practice for your future career, as opposed to just a daunting assignment?

You can work to identify the small goals that lead toward a larger goal in a number of different ways.

List what you already know needs to be done. For example if your goal is to be a mechanical engineer at a particular company, work backward to identify what credentials, degrees, courses, and experiences will need to be on your résumé to have the strongest application possible.

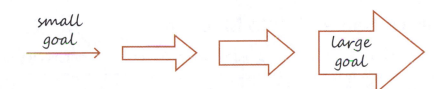

TB Figure 1.5 Small Goals Lead to Big Goals

Talk to people who've already achieved your goal. Informational interviews are great places to find out what the smaller steps are for achieving a larger goal. What is the background of the person you're talking to? Was theirs a traditional pathway to this career? What type of advice do they have for you as someone who is wanting to work in this industry?

Research. If you're a first-year student who is dreaming of writing screenplays and working in Hollywood, identify the screenwriters that you admire and read interviews with them. Listen to podcasts that interview them. What were their paths? What were they doing when they were your age? What patterns do you see between different screenwriters? If everyone is writing every day or taking improv classes or entering film festivals, then you can start to map out your own path of things to try.

Discover Your Template

What is something you wanted in the past that you achieved? It doesn't have to be something that was remarkable to others, just something that you set your mind to. So perhaps it was saving money for a big purchase, completing a particular physical feat, or maintaining a streak. What did you do? How did you motivate yourself to keep going when the going got tough? Did you always feel like you were making progress toward your goal or were there setbacks? If you take some time to reflect on past goals, you might start to see patterns emerge related to what works for you.

It might be even easier to think through goals you didn't achieve. What are goals you held at some point that drifted away? Were they too big and too far away and you couldn't see the smaller goals you needed to pursue first? Were they based on an idealized version of yourself? For example, did you want to be a professional athlete at some time in the past? Assuming you do not consider yourself still on track to be a professional athlete, what happened? How did you modify your goal when it became clear you weren't going to go pro?

If we make goals that require perfection (I'm going to go to the gym every day this week and workout hard for two hours) and then experience a setback, what happens to our goal? Did we fail or was the goal not a good one?

Our patterns around making and achieving goals *and* making and failing at goals can be very informative for us. What are the goals that have worked for us? What are the goals that have left us frustrated?

Goals as Something to Measure

Goals can provide a way to assess progress/achievements. For example, if you are aiming to enter a major that requires you to complete prerequisites, you likely have a list of courses you have to take. As you progress through the course-work, you can assess your progress as you check off the ones you've completed. Likewise, if your goal is to complete three informational interviews in the next month and those require you to first contact 10 potential people to meet with, as you check off those initial steps, you can see your progress. Many people find this kind of assessment very motivating and satisfying. Tracking your progress is a way that allows you to see both ups and downs, and lets you move on from the "downs," assuming you still see progress toward the goal.

Goals as Having Something to Do

Similar to some of the guidelines in thinking about time management, having goals gives you something to do. The transition to college removes a lot of structure from most students' lives. Many high schoolers have goals that come from both their stage of life (finish high school, get into college) and their activities (win the game, go to state tournament, plan the dance, manage the student fundraiser). When students transition to college, they have to seek out some of this structure. Being involved in student groups or volunteer projects uses your energy for achieving a collective goal. These goals can help you seek balance and well-being in your college experience. Whether it's intramural sports or organizing a dance-a-thon for cancer research, having a goal with a new group of people can help you get out of the personal goal malaise that we, alone, can sometimes fall into.

Are the Teachers Making Your Goals for You, or Do You Still Have to Do Some Goal Setting? Looking through your syllabi, you'll see that your instructors have mapped out quite a few things for you to do in the course of a semester. There are typically learning goals attached to those tasks. Many students struggle with uncertainty about their majors and ambivalence about where they belong in the world (even whether or not college is the place for them), and yet, if you look at the learning goals of the courses you're enrolled in, you can start to get a feel for whether something in this discipline or field draws you in.

Do You Thrive with Crazy Goals?

Are you a person who thrives on huge, seemingly unattainable goals? Many of us just get overwhelmed and discouraged by goals that seem impossible, but not everyone. Pay attention to whether or not you thrive on a challenge. We've had students who are writing novels while going through college or who are selling artwork online. They set these big goals and then go for it. If this is you, great! While this personality type is out there, it is not the norm. If you feel like you are surrounded by people with crazy goals and that you don't fit or that you are somehow a failure because your goal is just to survive, recognize that our culture encourages us to have these crazy goals. Many people adopt crazy goals and talk about them, yet they later abandon them. Just don't despair if you feel like you're at capacity with getting your homework done and paying attention to what interests and excites you.

Are You a Different Person at Different Times of the Day?

Do you find that your energy for a particular goal (I'm going to read all of the articles that are due tonight!) is really strong when you set the goal, but not as strong at the time you're supposed to achieve the goal? Many of us are able to imagine an idealized future self achieving our goals, but the real-time self isn't nearly as productive. If you recognize this trait in yourself, own up to it. All that it requires you to recognize is that if you *think* you're going to be a perfect version of yourself later (and therefore you can do something else right now), you're not. Owning up to the fact that your idealized future self is just that, an idealized future self, allows you to move onto a productive strategy for reaching your goals—like just spending 10 minutes, right now, trying to read your articles.

Are You Visualizing the Dream or the Work?

We have worked with multiple students who want to be an elementary school teacher until they volunteer in a third-grade classroom or who want to be a doctor until they shadow a doctor for a day. Gaining experience and exposure to different professions while you are still in college will help you discern what you want. If your desire to reach a particular goal is the prestige, the income, or just the idea of it, that does not guarantee you will enjoy the work. We've seen Elementary Education majors switch to Youth Studies because of a recognition that they want to work with youth, but not in the highly structured educational environment. Likewise, we've seen pre-med students set their sights on pre-pharmacy as they gained more knowledge about the actual day-to-day practice of medicine and what kind of a role they wanted in it. You need to start off with the general idea to identify a goal, but be open to modifying it, or changing it altogether, as you learn more about both the profession and about yourself.

A Final Note on Goals

If you have a goal but you hate the process of achieving that goal, pay attention to that. This is your life. Every day is precious. And you don't want to wish away any of the days. If the journey to your goal is making you crazy, consider the possibility that your goal is misaligned with what you really want to do.

TB SECTION 1.4   # Plagiarism

Academic integrity is extremely important both as a college student and as a professional. In a world that depends on creative ideas and the sharing of those ideas to solve the problems we face, it is crucial to have a code of ethics that reinforces the importance of attributing these ideas to their proper authors. This code of ethics is built into the foundation of higher education which is why your college or university has very strict policies related to plagiarism. In our experience working with students, there are three general categories of incidents of plagiarism:

1. *Intentional:* A student copies and pastes from sources and turns it in as their own work when they understand the concept of plagiarism.
2. *Unintentional (doesn't know the rules):* A student doesn't understand the rules of attribution (giving credit to the original author) and does it incorrectly. For example, often students will paraphrase an author and not realize that this still requires a citation.
3. *Unintentional (doesn't have the right habits):* A student has poor notetaking habits, and does their research without following a clear system. This student then writes a paper unsure of where the information came from and doesn't use proper citations.

Intentional

While there are some students who set out to find something online and copy it, or who seek out places where they can buy a paper (as opposed to writing their own), this is much less common, in our experience, than students who use the internet to do research/get ideas and then discover a source they end up copying from. Students are given a writing prompt or a problem to solve, Google it, and find that someone on the internet has not only written about it but that this writer's ideas are really good/smart/better than they think they could produce. And so they copy it. You must keep in mind that your instructors have the same access to the internet as you do. If they wanted to know what some random person on the internet thought about their essay prompt, they could Google it. They want to know what *you* think. It can be tempting to cut and paste from the internet. You may know people who do it and get away with it, but like all forms of cheating, you are really cheating yourself *and* the consequences of getting caught far outweigh any temporary benefits (the paper is done and you can go to bed). Starting your paper early and using campus resources are two ways to proactively lower the temptation to plagiarize. But if it's the night before something is due and you're feeling like it's the only option, know that the likelihood of getting caught is real and the consequences are not worth it. The consequences of asking for an extension or handing in a paper late are much lower than committing plagiarism.

How do you prevent this type of plagiarism? You make the choice not to do it.

Unintentional (Lack of Knowledge of Rules)

Plagiarism is one of those things that appears on most syllabi and yet many instructors aren't teaching it overtly. If your high school did a good job of teaching what plagiarism is and how to avoid it, email your former teacher now and thank them. If, however, you have a vague sense that copying something you didn't write and saying you wrote it is plagiarism, both read on *and* spend some time looking through websites that give more thorough explanations of plagiarism. (You can Google the names of most universities and the word *plagiarism* and you'll be brought to their page that both defines and gives examples of plagiarism.) It is also important to note that the culture around plagiarism can vary between K-12 school systems, different countries, and what you are now operating under in college. What may have been seen as okay in high school (or allowed to slide) could very likely not be okay in college.

How do you prevent this type of plagiarism? You learn the rules, practice them, and then check your work. Beyond this text, go to your school library or library website to understand which resources are available to you to learn more about plagiarism.

Definition—Plagiarism is when you take the words and/or ideas of another person and use them without giving credit to the source.

Different texts sometimes refer to the types of plagiarism by different terms (e.g., patchwork plagiarism is also called mosaic plagiarism), but in general there are three types:

- *Direct plagiarism:* The writer copies words of another author and does not cite the source or use quotation marks. It's also considered plagiarism if you *do* cite the source but don't use the quotes, or vice versa.
- *Patchwork plagiarism:* In this case, the writer might use some direct words, phrases, or ideas from another author but doesn't cite the source where they came from. Sometimes we see writers who take someone else's text and try to move things around, paraphrase here and there, and then present the work as their own. This is plagiarism. In general, everything that is not an original idea to you and is not common knowledge (e.g., Minnesota became a state in 1858) needs to be cited. For many first-year students, this makes them feel like they are citing every sentence of their paper. That is okay. As you develop your voice and refine your research methods to learn how you find the best sources (as opposed to finding and citing 30 not-that-great sources), this will naturally change.
- *Self-plagiarism:* Here a student uses previous work that they created for another course and either hands it in again or modifies it a bit and hands it in for a different course. Self-plagiarism also occurs when a student hands in one paper for two separate courses *without* permission of both instructors.

Unintentional (Lack of Good Habits)

This type of unintentional plagiarism is caused by messy, unorganized work and bad habits. For many students, this type is the most daunting because it feels like it's hard to prevent it. And while it's not hard, it does take some time and effort. Ironically, a number of highly regarded researchers have been guilty of exactly this kind of plagiarism. They, or their researchers, cut corners in gathering information from sources, don't give credit to the ideas they are using from the work of others, and they get caught. Accidental or not, this is plagiarism and there are consequences. Avoiding this accidental plagiarism requires both a level of organization and a commitment to following good habits.

In her classes, Margaret Delahanty Kelly, one of the authors of this book, walks her students through the following exercise. For each part of the assignment, the students are only given that part. In other words, they do Part A before knowing what Part B and Part C consist of, and then do Part B before knowing what Part C asks them to do, and so on.

THINK ABOUT IT

Mini Research Paper:

Research Question—Why is sleep important?

Part A: Spend 15 minutes researching why sleep is important. Try going beyond the surface answers that you've likely read online or in magazines in dental waiting rooms.

Part B: Write a paragraph that answers the question, "Why should college students get a minimum of seven hours of sleep per night?"

Part C: Write out the steps you engaged in while completing this research and composing your paragraph.

Part D: Read through the following definition of plagiarism and assess whether or not you used another writer's words or ideas (not common knowledge) without proper attribution.
  • Some questions to consider:
    • Did you cite any sources in your paragraph? If not, are the ideas in your paragraph original to you or something you learned in your research?
    • Did you paraphrase in your paragraph? Did you cite those paraphrases? Did you write those paraphrases while *not* looking at the original? If you wrote them while looking at the original, assess how well they are paraphrased. Are the ideas of the original source truly rewritten in your own voice and style? Or, are the ideas simply moved around a bit with some wording changed?

Discovering Plagiarism

Some teachers use Turnitin as a learning tool for students and allow students to submit a draft of their paper to Turnitin as a means of checking their work and their habits. This can be an effective way to get some feedback on how successful your paraphrasing and citing has been.

One of the most common ways an instructor discovers plagiarism is by reading a sentence and noticing a change in voice or tone in the writing or even just noticing language or conclusions that don't seem typical for that level of student. The instructor can then Google a section of the paper and easily discover what internet source it comes from. Teachers also have access to tools that do this searching for them. Many institutions use Turnitin, which is an online tool that compares student papers to everything on the internet in addition to previously searched student papers. It creates an originality report that says how much of the student paper was copied from internet sources. As papers are submitted online and teachers have these tools integrated into their digital classrooms, it's becoming much more routine to search for plagiarism as a matter of policy.

How do you prevent this type of plagiarism? Every source you go to needs to be recorded. Copy the URL before you copy any content. Put quotes around anything copied.

TB SECTION 1.5 Individual and Group Presentations

Often, instructors will give an assignment where you will need to put together an oral presentation that includes projected slides. Sometimes this assignment is given individually, and sometimes it's given to a group. Sometimes these projects last the whole semester. Sometimes a few weeks. You may have had some experience with these sorts of projects in high school or even in a work setting. While this sort of assignment may seem repetitive or time-consuming, or even incredibly frustrating, there are many reasons why instructors give this work. These sorts of projects:

- Give you practice working by yourself or with a group to produce a product
- Give you a chance to work on your oral presentation skills
- Give you a high-stakes opportunity to produce and present slides
- Give you the chance to improve your work based on feedback and constructive criticism

The following are general tips that come from years of teaching a first-year public speaking course.

Don't Memorize Your Speech

Students sometimes think the gold standard is to write out their speech word for word, memorize it, and then deliver it. Even if you nail it and recite it perfectly, it will likely have a canned vocal quality to it. Canned vocal qualities have a lulling effect on the audience. More likely, you will forget a word or a line and you'll be stuck wondering what comes next. Because you're reciting a speech, you are also not as responsive to audience feedback. If your audience looks confused but you haven't prepared a way to clarify or expand on your point, you might be inclined to just keep going with the script.

Aim for an Extemporaneous Delivery

We recommend you write out a fairly brief outline that you will speak from. Practice your speech multiple times from that sparse outline. If you need to refer to a fuller outline as you practice, this is fine, but resist using the full outline frequently for your practice, because you may unintentionally start to memorize it. If you're rehearsing from a sparse outline, you'll use different words every time to say the same thing. This is going to build a lot of potential ways to talk about your ideas when you give your speech. This will make you a more flexible and responsive speaker when you are actually giving your talk. Because you've said it a number of different ways when rehearsing it, your brain will have all of those ways to pull from when you are nervous and when your audience looks confused and you need to clarify something.

Rehearse

Rehearse in your room, as you lift weights, as you walk, as you look in the mirror applying hair gel. Rehearsing your speech 20 times is not too much.

Visual Aids

Yes, pictures tell a thousand words, but are they the words you want to be saying? Choose your visual aids carefully. Stock photos often read as stock photos, and might show up in a classmate's presentation or cause your audience to wonder, "Why is that family so happy?"

Be aware of the resolution of any image you use. It might look great on your laptop, but what will the resolution look like when it's displayed on a large screen?

Keep black slides between images if you want to draw your audience's attention back to you between images. Well-placed black slides keep you in control of what the audience is looking at. Unless you're planning on going from image to image, a black slide forces the attention away from the visual aid and back to the speaker. The most important black slide is the last one. When you're done with your visuals and are leading your audience into your fantastic conclusion, you don't want the bright light of the projector blinding you because you're slide show has finished.

Do not use blue-colored fonts on black backgrounds or any other color combination that limits your audience's ability to read what you put on the slide. Black and white might be super unoriginal, but it sure is clear.

Filler Words

We all use filler words. It's how we hold our turn in conversations. When you're giving a speech, it's always your turn, and filler words can be a distraction for your audience. The way you get rid of filler words (or reduce the number of them) is to rehearse with a peer and ask that peer to count your words. The first time through a five-minute speech, you might have 25 filler words. The second time through, once you're made aware of it, it will almost always be less. Think of those pauses as making your audience wait for it. They will wait and your next idea will be all the more powerful when preceded by a pause and not an "um."

Presentation of Self

Somewhere in the course of teaching FY speech, we stopped telling students how to dress for speeches. While you might feel most confident if you wear a traditional business look, you don't have to. What you should be aware of is how what you wear is "read" by your audience and how that might distract them. A speaker wearing a winter coat might distract the audience as they wonder "Are they really that cold?" A speaker wearing a baseball cap might be read by some as disrespectful if the audience members come from a tradition where taking off your hat is a sign of respect. As an audience member myself, I find that if the content of a speech is engaging, I don't really pay attention to how they dress.

That said, if you know you're going to work in a profession where a certain type of dress is required, you might as well practice in that type of clothing. How does it feel to be nervous during a speech and wearing a necktie? Knowing that now might help you in the future. Likewise, if you have a habit related to certain types of clothing (e.g., you keep your hands in your sleeves while you speak) that might communicate something you don't want to communicate (e.g., lack of confidence), avoid those types of clothing.

Finally, you can wear your hairstyle however you like, but do be aware that if you're using a paper outline or notecards and your hair falls into your eyes when you look down, you will likely want to push it back every time you look back up. This can be distracting to you as a speaker and to your audience. Rehearsing in the clothing and hairstyle you plan to wear during your speech, in front of a friend or family member, can help you discover some of these things before the actual delivery of your speech in class.

TB SECTION **1.6**

Online Learning

More and more learners come into college having some experience with online learning. Some students did online high school, others have completed one or two courses in an entirely online context. It was not until COVID-19 that all students were thrown into the online learning space. Likely, we will look back on this time and see how impactful it was in shaping higher education. Instructors will get better at effectively teaching in the online environment, and learners will learn more about what works for them in this environment. As online learning increases going forward, remember some of the following points, which outline ways to find out how you're most successful in online learning environments.

Create Structure

Many of us are dependent on the structure that our day provides. So, if we're going to college in a face-to-face setting, we know what time we need to leave to get to class, how long we'll be in class, how much time we have between classes, etc. It's all mapped out. Even if we're procrastinating about getting assignments started, we often still show up. And that counts. Online learning doesn't have that same structure. For many of us, everything seems like it could be done now or later. Later can feel compelling when one either doesn't want to sit at a desk in front of a computer or when the computer has so much more to offer than challenging subjects to master. Another thing that tends to be missing in an online environment is the informal conversing/checking in with classmates or the instructor in order to get clarification on an idea or an assignment. There are ways that we, as learners, can create structure, routine, and spaces for informal exchanges within the online environment.

Our minds love having decisions already made. While a big open day (think about a Saturday when you don't have classes and you don't have to work) can feel exciting and full of potential, it can also feel overwhelming. When you're enrolled in an online, asynchronous class, you face that big open day every day. Put structure into your day by doing the following:

Think about your online classes as mirrors of face-to-face classes. (See **TB Table 1.1**.)

You can see from TB Table 1.1 that requirements 2, 3, and 4 are usually structured for you because they occur in class. When you engage in online learning, you are less constrained by a narrow class time, but you also need to complete the work in a timely manner so as to stay caught up.

What you need to do:	How you do it: Face to face	How you do it: Online class
1. Preparing for class	Read, do problem sets	Read, do problem sets
2. Taking in information from instructor	Go to class	Watch recorded lectures, watch videos on own schedule
3. Engage with material with peers	Work in class with peers	Participate in online discussions, complete online group activities on own schedule
4. Show what you've learned through assessment (exams)	Take exams in class	Take exams on own
5. Show what you've learned through assessment (homework and essays)	Complete homework, write essays	Complete homework, write essays

TB Table 1.1 Online vs. In-Person Classes

TB TRY THIS   1.9

Look at your online classes. How many credits are they? For each credit, you need one hour of "instruction" per week. Requirements 2, 3, and 4 from TB Table 1.1 fit into that instruction time. Put a time on your weekly calendar for when you will "go to class," and for when you will complete the tasks of requirements 2, 3, and 4. For a three-credit class, you need to find three hours for 2, 3, and 4. For a four-hour class, you need to find four hours.

For each credit, then, you need an additional two hours to complete requirements 1 & 5. So if you have a three credit class, you should plan on spending six hours reading, completing problem sets, completing homework and writing essays. For a four credit class, you will need eight hours. Put a time on your weekly calendar when you will complete this.

One benefit of online education is that you can structure it with more freedom because you aren't constrained by someone else's schedule. If you want to watch lectures while you eat your breakfast, you can. If you want to do all of your reading at a time when you are most alert, you can figure out that time and do it. The disadvantage is the big open space of time where one day bleeds into another and one week into another. There is also an inclination to overschedule other activities because there is more freedom. In general, you're less likely to schedule an extra shift at work during a face-to-face class meeting time. Before you do this in the online schedule environment, be sure to weigh the costs and benefits of making this choice.

Seek to Reframe Your Mindset

During COVID-19, a number of our students reported that they didn't like or weren't good at online learning. This made sense. Students had left for spring break and classes never resumed. They missed their friends, classmates, and the independence that came with being on campus. Having access to technology and a conducive space for learning was challenging for many students. The online learning, though valiantly put together in four days' time, was not exemplary. But all of that aside, simply believing that they did not like, or weren't good at, online learning had hints of a fixed mindset. A growth mindset in this situation proves to be beneficial.

TB THINK ABOUT IT

Think about online learning experiences you've had in the past. List five things that worked for you. This might include having a more flexible schedule that allowed you to pick up desirable shifts at work or share childcare responsibilities. Or perhaps you liked being able to pause lectures to take notes at your own pace. Also list five things that didn't work for you. This might include the lack of structure or the inability to interact with classmates and have occasional moments of social connection.

When you look through your list of what didn't work, how could you either modify your own behavior and where could you seek support from others?

Like most things in life, we have to learn how to do online learning. We have to figure out how our own set of skills and preferences work within this context. When you find yourself dreading taking a course because it's only offered online, or feeling a sense of doom because you're not good at online learning, honor your feelings and then challenge yourself to 1) pay attention to what works and what doesn't work, 2) be intentional about how you respond, 3) reflect on how your response shifts what works and what does not work.

Seek Connection

Finally, what tools is the instructor providing to help you connect with each other? It may be that the space is only in formal spaces—like a discussion forum or a Q&A module in the course learning platform. Or, perhaps there are informal spaces available to you. This might be a class "Slack" that allows for quick questions. If you have an idea of ways that an instructor could facilitate some of that informal connection, let them know. During COVID-19, we got our best ideas from students who knew of some technology that we didn't know about.

Conclusion

Through the use of these strategies, we hope you will gain more confidence in yourself as a student, and feel prepared to take on any assignment or project. Every student is unique, and the better you understand your own strengths and habits as a student, the more equipped you will be to adjust to new situations and take them on with confidence. In order to do this, be mindful of your habits, and be open to trying new methods or strategies to find the ones that work best for you. Have confidence in yourself as a student by having a wide variety of tools in your toolbox, and feel free to refer to this resource throughout your college career as you evolve as a student.

Collaborating and **Communicating**

Collaborating Effectively

> " *Collaboration is always tough. It requires a lot of rumbles, circle backs, and constantly utilizing the powerful tool of 'the story I'm telling myself.' And, when you can stay brave, it produces something far more powerful than you could ever do alone.* —Brené Brown
>
> *Collaborative learning combines two key goals: learning to work and solve problems in the company of others, and sharpening one's own understanding by listening seriously to the insights of others, especially those with different backgrounds and life experiences* —George Kuh "

In Your Own Words

5.1

For this journaling activity, think a bit about teams you have experienced, and spend 15 minutes or so answering the following questions. What does being a team member mean to you? How does it make you feel? How do you act when on a team? What is positive about being on a team, and what is negative?

Throughout college, you will be asked to participate in, and contribute to, many different types of groups in a variety of ways. Nearly all jobs now rely on some kind of collaboration or teamwork. These experiences provide you with the opportunity to build skills that you cannot build when you work alone. This chapter focuses on developing your self-awareness as a team member by reflecting on past collaboration experiences and the habits you've developed and practiced as a result. We present research and examine the characteristics of effective groups, while introducing strategies for fostering these practices, including a list of questions that you and new groupmates should answer when initially establishing your group norms. Ultimately, our goal is to help you develop a mindful and intentional approach to collaboration in order to experience it as a transformational part of learning.

Reflecting on Your Experiences in Groups and Teams

Working with people toward common and shared goals can be energizing and motivating. Groups and teams are about collaboration, where a group works together to achieve something. You practice this all the time and have developed collaboration skills, experiences, and habits, whether you realize it or not. As you dig into this chapter, challenge yourself to identify your habits as a collaborator and to assess whether those habits serve you well.

Think about an experience when you have been part of a team—maybe in a club or on a sports team, maybe at a job or volunteer opportunity, or maybe at mealtime in your home. Think about an experience where everyone has a role to fill and needs to stay out of the way of others so as not to prevent them from fulfilling their role. Perhaps you have experience as a team, where you've been adaptable and able to deal with setbacks as they arise, such as with customer complaints or technical difficulties. Or perhaps you've been on a sports team or in a musical group and through extensive practice your group figured out how to perform collectively at a much better level than you ever thought possible, where you elevated each other.

TRY THIS _____ 5.2

1. Look at the following table. Open up your journal and either re-create the table or record your answers however you prefer. Identify five teams or groups you have been a part of. Think about your extracurricular activities (sports, music, theater, robotics, etc.) and your jobs, as well as study groups you may have been a part of. It can also include personal ones, such as a group of friends or your family. For the sake of this reflection, define a team or group as three or more people working toward a common goal.

Group or team	Your attitude toward the common goal or activity (1–3) 1= negative 2= neutral 3= positive	Did your teammates/groupmates make your experience better or worse? (1–3) 1= made it worse 2= no impact 3= made it better	Choice to join? Yes or No
1.			
2.			
3.			
4.			
5.			

Table 5.1 Your Group Experiences

2. Considering the five groups you've identified, rate your attitude toward the common goal. Give a 1 if your attitude was negative, a 2 if your attitude was neutral, and choose 3 if your attitude was positive. For example, if you love badminton and were on a badminton team where you got to play a lot, your attitude was likely a 3. Make a note about it in your journal.
3. Spend a minute reflecting on whether your teammates/groupmates made the experience better or worse. Write 1 if they made it worse, 2 if they had little impact on the experience, and 3 if they made the experience better. Make a note about it in your journal.
4. What kind of control did you have in these situations? Did you get to opt in to joining the group or was it required of you? Did you get to choose your groupmates/teammates or did someone else? Make a note about it in your journal.

By looking at these aspects of a group, you can see that there are many factors affecting the success of, and experience in, a group. If you have a 3-3 example, you have a situation where you love the task, and the people on your team make it better. Or perhaps you have a 1-3, where you are not invested in the task, but because of the other people, it's actually a positive experience and you do a better job. Then, of course, there is the 3-1, where you really want to do well and invest yourself in this goal or task, but your teammates bring you down and make it difficult.

People often tend to see group situations as clear-cut. Either you get a good group or you get a bad group. Either you're good at this, or you aren't. As you know, however, from previous material in this text, you need to recognize multiple perspectives and factors in every situation, and you need to develop an awareness of everything that is going on in a situation and what you have control over. Things aren't always as they seem. As you resee yourself and assess the skills you already have to engage in teamwork, you can start to ask yourself: Who am I in a group? How does my attitude shape the experience? What skills do I already have, or have I seen in action, that make a collaborative activity successful?

THINK ABOUT IT

Return to your answers in Table 5.1 and identify the one you rank as the most positive group experience. Try to identify five aspects of the experience or five different elements that made it positive. Think about the people, the shared goal, the setting, the leadership, what you felt you were contributing and learning, etc. Try to be as specific as possible, so rather than thinking, "I loved my teammates," and stopping there, push yourself to figure out why you loved your teammates—for example, "They always encouraged me and helped me to improve and learn."

Group Type:

What made it so great? (Be as specific as possible.)

1.
2.
3.
4.
5.

Notice which of these "made it great" qualities were under your control, and which were not.

Many factors affect how each member of a group feels within it, and the dynamic of a group can be fragile. You've likely been part of a group or team where someone made a scene and ruined the experience for others. Or perhaps someone new joined the group and the dynamic totally shifted. Sometimes, a shift gradually occurs with the passage of time. Or a group that was your favorite as a 15-year-old becomes something that you dread as a 17-year-old. What changed? Was it you, your passion for the activity, the coach, or some other factor?

In school, groupwork tends to get a bad rap. Those of us who teach undergraduate courses often hear a collective groan when we introduce a group project. Students often self-identify as the person who had to do all the work because everyone else flaked out. Other students explain that no one listened to their ideas, so they gave up. Students frequently describe a group where one person dominated and didn't seem to leave space for anyone else to participate meaningfully. Other students, on the other hand, just prefer to work on their own. Then there is the fairness part of it. For instance, is it fair to be graded on something you cannot entirely control? Overall, students tend to have a negative view of groupwork in school, and to view collegiate group experiences as completely different from those outside of it. In reality, however, they are just different versions of collaboration.

THINK ABOUT IT

Think for a moment about a negative group experience. What made the experience negative? Which of these things were in your control (your attitude, your effort) and which were outside your control (number of groupmates, time given to complete a task, directions given by the professor)?

As we've already discussed, when students think about collaboration for a group project for school, they place it in its own separate category: as a dreaded activity, and one that is different than sport teams or extracurricular, or work teams they have been involved in over their careers. All of these experiences really aren't so different: Both environments (inside and outside school) include a random group of people with a shared goal that requires working together. Factors like working for a grade, collaborating with peers with whom you socialize outside of school, and stress outside academia can make groupwork in school feel like a completely different experience.

THINK ABOUT IT

- Think about a positive group experience in comparison with a negative group experience. How are these experiences different? Now compare collaboration done outside of school with a collaborative experience inside of school. How were these experiences different?
- Do you have different attitudes, expectations, and anxieties about them?
- Do you see an overlap of skills, so that something you learned about in one group setting worked for you in another?

Many people approach groups or teams mindlessly, just letting the experience unfold. This can be problematic. If you think back to the positive experiences of a team or group you worked on, chances are there were structures and/or roles in place, as well as some incentives and disincentives for certain behaviors. There might have been appropriate rules or norms to consider. In a group for a class or work project, you might be given a task and timeline without any structure, so it is important to know how to create and maintain a structure. The rest of this chapter will discuss some strategies, or structures, for effective groupwork that you can apply to make your future groupwork experiences the best they can be.

TRY THIS ———————————————— **5.3**

The next time you have a different way to approach a project than one of your collaborators, or perhaps the next time you have a different point of view than what is presented by your instructors or in an article or text you read, try pausing and focusing on active listening first. Don't rush to formulate or share your perspective right away; just carefully listen to them or read their text to comprehend more fully their perspective. Then, give yourself time to consider what you heard and to reflect on it. Take 10 minutes to write or speak into a voice memo about it (some people find this a great tool for capturing creative and free-flowing thinking) and respond to the following questions.

1. What is the opposing point of view?
2. What is everything that supports this point of view?
3. What is your perspective?
4. What is everything you can think of that supports your point of view?
5. How can you respectfully point out this difference in a way that honors everyone involved?
6. What have you learned from this exercise? How might you approach multiple perspectives differently next time?

Laying the Groundwork for Effective Groups

SECTION **5.2**

As the call for, and value placed on, collaboration in the workplace increases, more people are trying to figure out the secret sauce for a good group dynamic. Some of the most exciting work comes out of Google, with their attempt to review the extensive research on functional collaboration and groups, as well as collect and crunch data from their experiments with teams and groups. (Duhigg, 2016) As a result, they have identified factors that influence functionality, satisfaction, and effectiveness in collaborations. Their research, collectively called Project Aristotle, determined that effective groups share a few characteristics:

- People in the group *talk in equal amounts*—there isn't one person always dominating or one person who never says anything.
- Groups share norms/rules, so they have *clear expectations* about how things are going to happen.
- Members are *attuned to each other* and pick up subtle cues about how others in the group are feeling.
- Members *feel safe enough* to put their ideas out there without risk of being mocked or belittled.

These are useful conditions or characteristics to keep at the forefront of your thinking as you enter collaborations. But how do you create these conditions in a group with peers? The rest of this chapter presents specific strategies and practices that help promote conditions that support effective collaboration.

COMMUNICATION SITUATION

Whether passive or active, intentional or spontaneous, how a group begins communicating with one another will definitely impact the sense of belonging, or lack thereof. As you read the following Critical Moment, think about it as a communication situation and prepare to reflect afterward.

CRITICAL MOMENT
Student

When we first got into our lab groups, we just stood there. The TA was busy doing something else and didn't give us directions as to what to do. Eventually, we started to talk about where we were from and what our majors were. Because I was a returning student, I was a lot older than my three groupmates. It was obvious that I didn't fit in the group. I figured that this wasn't that big of a deal, but soon it was clear to me that it was a big deal to them. Two of us were from Minnesota, and two were from Wisconsin. In those first 10 minutes of being in a group, my three groupmates talked about the Packers and the Vikings and which team they liked. I was all ready to tell my story about how I married a Vikings fan so I had to commit to being one (even though I had reasons to be a Packers fan), but they never asked me which team I liked. It was really odd to me that they didn't include me in this part of the conversation. It made it really clear to me that because of my age, I didn't belong in this group.

- What is going on in this moment? How would you characterize the communication happening between the group members?
- What choices were available to the narrator? What was in the narrator's control?
- What might you have done differently in this scenario as the narrator or group member?

Effective Groups Listen to Each Other

In order to support multiple perspectives, effective groups include members that listen to each other. What are the group norms in regard to distractions (such as phones, updating social media, online shopping, homework for other classes, checking email) and what are the stated or unstated norms regarding side conversations? What are the group norms for dealing with the consequences of someone not being engaged and not actually listening?

Fostering an environment where everyone is listening means a team in which people feel they belong, that their ideas matter, and that they will be heard when they speak.

Listening to each other requires being attuned to how others are reacting. Listening involves hearing, but it also involves attention to nonverbal cues. Asking clarification questions or seeing if you can restate ideas that group members have contributed are important in ensuring clear communication.

If you are in a group and haven't had a chance to complete the active listening activity in Chapter 4 ("Try This 4.4"), now might be a good time to do it. Pay attention to what real listening feels like.

THINK ABOUT IT

What does it look like when the entire group is paying attention to the speaker? What does it look like when people aren't? How does each of those experiences feel as the speaker?

Do a Google image search for groups of people working together and make a bulleted list of what it looks like to be actively engaged in work, and also what it looks like to not be engaged. Include tiny moves that speak volumes, such as a person's posture or when people glance at a clock or their facial expressions. Be prepared to both share and report on your image and list them.

Effective Groups Have Members Who Feel Like They Belong

In the chapter's first Critical Moment, many things are going on. There is a lack of structure or support from the TA in those first few moments. Because the students weren't given specific goals or provided with group identity building tasks, they didn't know how to start. As the conversation evolved, three of the members did find something they could talk about, but for some reason they didn't include one of the group members—the narrator of the case—in the conversation. Maybe the writer was correct in her assumption that she was excluded because she was an older student. We typically assume that how we are treated is a result of a perceived difference that we have, whether it be age, race, sex, class, ethnicity, language, gender identity, etc. If she feels "different," it's hard to imagine her feeling like she belongs in this group.

When a new group forms, there are some key things that create a sense of belonging.

- *Names:* It's very important to know the names of the people in the group. It's really hard to talk to people if you don't know their names. Whether you use name tents or play one of those name games, effective groups support group mates in learning each other's names, and in regularly making sure that names are remembered and pronounced correctly.
- *Access:* You need to be able to hear and see the people in your group. You know that you don't belong if your voice (literally) can't be heard or if your eyes can't be seen. If you look around a classroom where students are working in groups, how the students are sitting says a lot about their group dynamic. A student who is sitting off to the side is going to have a difficult time contributing to the conversation. Students who are not facing each other have a difficult time even getting a conversation started. In trying to create a sense of belonging, everyone should pay attention to how they are sitting and invite all the groupmates to physically sit around a table where they can easily see each other.
- *Identity:* Finally, as a group, it helps to have some sense of a group identity. Some instructors have student groups come up with a team name or play an icebreaker game (like finding out everyone's favorite food). While this might feel silly to some, it can create a group identity. It is usually a low-stakes task that requires a newly formed group to brainstorm and then come to a consensus. Another way to build group identity is to have a conversation, a kind of a warm-up. Rather than launching into complicated discussions of course material, a warm-up question like, "What's your favorite place to study on campus?" or "What's your guilty pleasure TV show to watch?" allows the group to get to know each other on a human level before the work of the team begins. This is the beginning of building psychological safety within the team.

THINK ABOUT IT

What does it take for everyone in a group to feel like they belong? What steps does the group have to take? What steps can you take as an individual? Give an example.

TRY THIS   5.4

People often have expectations that group members, including themselves, display a willingness to participate in a group and do the work by behaving in an outgoing and gregarious manner. Yet research shows that one-third to one-half of the population consider themselves introverts. Susan Cain is a writer on the topic of introversion. After she received her law degree from Harvard Law School and worked in law for seven years, she left to write. She had something to say about being an introvert in a world that placed such a high value on extroversion. She is the author of the book *Quiet: The Power of Introverts in a World That Can't Stop Talking* (Cain, 2012) and gave a TED Talk where she addressed how our society is more and more geared for extroverts and how we should pay attention to what both introverts and extroverts bring to the table when it comes to creativity and productivity.

For this assignment, watch the Susan Cain TED Talk "The Power of Introverts." (Cain, 2012) (Note: Visit Ted.com to find her lecture.) Then, answer the following questions:

- Do you consider yourself an introvert or an extrovert? How do you know?
- What do you see as the strengths of introverts in collaboration?
- What are some of the dangers that Cain points to by relying on groupwork in all settings and by always deferring to the extroverts in the group?
- How can groupwork be structured to support the strengths of all its members?

Write up your answers to these questions and be prepared to discuss them in class.

SIMPLE STRATEGIES

- When you are working in a small group in a class, make sure everyone can see each other.
- Adjust yourselves so you are in a circle, not a straight line.
- Lean in and show interest in the conversation.
- Put away all distractions.

Effective Groups Have a Shared, Stated Goal (Short-Term and Long-Term)

In many business settings, when a group is formed, employees are given a *charge*, in the form of a clear outcome, or set of outcomes, that they are asked to achieve. If you get a job at a coffee shop, you may know that the goal is to make quality coffee drinks and get them to the customer quickly with a smile. Even though that goal might be obvious, training for the job will likely include an explanation of how your role on the team works to achieve this goal.

When you are put in a group in class, sometimes there are discussion questions or a problem to solve, but beyond that you may not know *why* you are in a group rather than allowed to just work on your own. Your thinking might then spiral—if you wonder why you can't just work on your own, you might just move forward without your group and try to get the task done without their input. Or you might wait for someone else to do the work for you. On the simplest of levels, the goal of some groupwork is to "talk about the ideas." Having this as a goal creates the reason to be collaborating with others.

Groups that share a stated goal have stronger incentives to collaborate effectively because everyone understands what they are working toward. It gets everyone on the same page about the work being done, and it also gives the group an identity, because people now share a concern for, and an interest in, that goal.

Effective Groups Have Norms/ Rules That Are Agreed Upon

While group norms are important for all groups, no matter how small or short-lived they are, they are essential for groups that are going to work together on larger-scale projects over a longer period of time. It would be inefficient if every time something new happened, you had to figure out how to respond. It is also true, however, that if you don't actively establish norms that you discuss and agree upon, those norms will be formed anyway, but likely not in a purposeful, or useful, way.

THINK ABOUT IT

Think about a group you've been a part of in the past. What were some of the rules you followed, whether they were explicit (discussed) or implicit (followed without talking about them or being named). Were you happy with these rules? Which ones served the group well? Which ones didn't serve the group well?

In the classroom setting, there is more flexibility when it comes to the norms a group sets. Often, that flexibility gets confused with an "anything goes" attitude. Students resist creating rules that others have to follow, but if they are created with a consensus, it's much easier to deal with unexpected situations when they arise.

CRITICAL MOMENT

Student

Once we began the capstone project, I began to dislike the class. It only got worse from there. Once I started to realize the situation I had gotten myself into with my group members, I began to dislike the class even more. I got into a very unlucky group, with two girls who apparently do not care as much about their homework as I do. As we worked through each step of the project, the girls continued to not hold up to the part they said they were going to do. Almost all of our steps got turned in late, and a couple of them didn't even get turned in at all, even though they told me that they were turned in. I tried so hard to keep our group together by sending emails to confirm that things were getting done, but I rarely ever got responses to them. One of the girls just stopped coming to class and made no effort whatsoever to help us. I got even more discouraged when I talked with other students in the same program who told me that their capstone project steps were much easier and much less work than ours were.

Upon reading the preceding Critical Moment, it is hard to know what was going on from the perspectives of all the group members, but you can see how the writer interpreted these events. From her perspective, her two groupmates did not care about their homework as much as she did. One fellow student was so disengaged with the class that she eventually stopped coming. Clearly, this was stressful for the writer and, in the end, seems to have ruined the class for her.

While the problems that this group faced are multilayered (For example, was the groupmate who stopped coming to class otherwise disengaged and actually dropped the course?), a discussion early on that would have established some baseline group norms could have helped the writer. She would have had a road map to direct her on what to do when the difficulties first arose.

Considering the following questions may help you establish group norms.
1. What are our goals for this project?
2. How much time do we have to spend on this project?
3. What does it look like when the group works together? (For example, can phones be out?)
4. What should we do when someone is absent from class or a group meeting?
5. How should we divide the work outside of class?
6. What are our expectations for meeting outside of class?
7. How should we set deadlines? What should we do if we can't meet a deadline?
8. How should we communicate and share tasks when deadlines are approaching and more work needs to be done?
9. What's the best way to discuss conflict in our group? Face to face? Email? Text messages?

10. At what point should we seek support from the professor?
11. What should be the primary mode of communication for our group? Is this the *most effective* mode of communication, or is it simply the most convenient?

Effective Groups Recognize the Value of Multiple Perspectives

In the Google research, they found that successful groups have equal participation from all group members. In the field of sociology, researcher Gordon Allport describes this as group members having *equal social status.* (Allport, 1954) If someone takes over a group or believes they have the right way to mold the group's norms, and that their way is the only way, other group members will likely disengage and limit their participation.

In groups, usually one or two people tend to emerge as leaders or organizers, and it's absolutely helpful to have people fill this role. But this does not mean those people get to make the decisions and have free reign without consulting the group. In a successful group, everyone feels their contributions matter.

To put this into practice, it is important to encourage members who seem reluctant to participate. Asking them about what they think during groupwork or being encouraging when they speak can make a difference in their participation and improve the dynamics of the group.

In Your Own Words

5.5

For this journal exercise, ask yourself the following and write down your answers. How do you usually show up in a group? Do you hold back and speak less than others? Do you take charge? If someone saw you in a group and asked you *why* you participate at the level you do, how would you explain it?

TRY THIS

5.6

A useful activity to determine the roles individuals will assume in a group is the "cartoon activity." You can do this with a group of friends or in a class. You'll need one multi-panel cartoon, cut into individual panels. Sunday comics usually have the most panels and therefore the most complexity. They are available online, so you don't have to actually have a paper or wait until Sunday. You also need as many group members as panels, plus one additional member who will observe.

Directions:

- No one should have read the full cartoon before the activity begins.
- Everyone gets one panel and does not show it to anyone else.
- Individuals can look at their panel, but should keep it out of view of the others.
- Participants explain the picture that they see and any accompanying text.
- The goal of the activity is to put the panels in the correct order. Participants should place their panels, cartoon-side down, once they have decided upon an order.
- The observer should pay attention and take notes during the activity.

After the panels have been placed in order and then flipped over, consider these reflection questions.

- Was there a clear leader in your group? Did someone take charge in terms of how best to complete this activity?
- Did multiple leaders arise at different stages of the activity?
- Was everyone's voice heard?
- Were groupmates ever talked over or were attempts to take a turn by some group members ignored? If yes, what was the impact of that?
- Were groupmates attuned to when others wanted to talk or to disagree? What did this look like and sound like?
- Did the participation feel equal?
- Does the observer agree with the assessment of the participants?

Students who do this activity often reflect on how different it feels to be in a group where they literally cannot complete the task without hearing from everyone. This is counter to the perception that some students hold, which is: When completing groupwork, they *don't need everyone's* ideas, they just need *enough* ideas. The belief that you just need enough ideas means that one or two people can take over and generate sufficient work for the stated goal. This, by its very nature, ignores the maxim that effective groups value multiple perspectives and that its members contribute equally.

THINK ABOUT IT

What are some of your assumptions coming into a group about who has something to contribute or what it looks like to have something to contribute? For example, does a groupmate sitting slouched in a chair communicate, "I have nothing to contribute"? Is there a way to challenge your assumptions?

Effective Groups Support Each Other and Foster Risk-Taking

It's really hard to put your ideas out there. There are natural fears of being laughed at, ignored, or misunderstood. This is especially true when you're in a group with people you don't know and may not trust yet. It's also true when you have been given a challenging assignment, or when you're asked to explore topics you may not know much about.

CRITICAL MOMENT
Student

I remember when we were numbering off for groups. My heart was racing. I looked at the people ahead of me who would number off first and counted to figure out what my number would be. I was afraid that I'd say the wrong number.

Creating an environment in your group where you reward each other for just putting yourselves out there is a great first step. Subtle cues communicate that you aren't engaged or supportive—trading looks with a friend, looking at a watch or a phone, moving on after someone says something without acknowledging you heard them by either building on their idea or explaining how yours is different. But other cues reward the bravery and vulnerability that you, along with your classmates, are undertaking: nodding as they speak, asking them to repeat themselves if you can't hear them, or to tell you more if you're not following their idea, asking follow-up questions, sharing your own ideas (see **Figure 5.1**). These are the ways you communicate that your group is supportive.

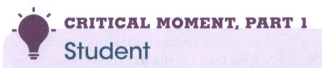

ask thoughtful questions

share your ideas

disagree respectfully

work towards compromise

Figure 5.1 A Few Ways to Support Your Group

In Your Own Words   5.7

How can you foster risk-taking as an individual in a group? What can the group do to support your comfort in expressing ideas? How can you work to support group members so they feel comfortable?

CRITICAL MOMENT, PART 1
Student

An incident that occurred due to my involvement in the FYI class was having issues with working in a group. The whole class revolves around our capstone projects, which are done in groups. Groupwork for this class was quite difficult for me because I am someone who likes to have everything planned out before doing work, and then getting the work done quickly and efficiently. The majority of my group members are much different than that. They are more easy-going with the work and procrastinate a lot. It was hard when we'd get together for group meetings because we'd always get off topic for the majority of the time, which was a waste of time. Also, our writing styles are very different, and so when people wouldn't be done with their part of the project until very close to the deadline, I would get stressed out because I wouldn't be able to look over our work and try to make it flow together. At first, groupwork was quite a challenge to me because of different work ethics of the members.

THINK ABOUT IT

Take a second to put yourself in this student's shoes. If you were in this situation, how would you handle it? What do you think you could learn from this?

CRITICAL MOMENT, PART II

Student

I am glad this happened though, because it has helped me learn how to work with a group better. I have never really liked groupwork, because it seems like one or two members of the group usually put forth most of the effort for the project, and this is how I felt at the beginning of this course, but I have learned that groupwork is also a very good way to do projects because everyone's skills and abilities are different, and work together to make the project good. Also, I have learned that groupwork is nice because everyone has different ideas, and combining three good ideas can make one great idea. All in all, I am very glad to have experienced groupwork within this class.

THINK ABOUT IT

Do you relate to this student's feelings about groupwork? Are these benefits that you've seen in your own experiences of groupwork? Does this make you think of groupwork differently in any way?

The student who shared their reflections in the preceding text did not have a single turning point or a lightbulb moment. Instead, she had a slow move from her first point of view on groupwork to her later one. In Chapter 8, you will read case studies of students looking back at writing assignments they had done earlier in college, reflecting on their approach and on what they would do differently. This student is also looking back and realizing that it took working through the discomfort to get to the productive outcomes that group experiences can offer. She hasn't necessarily changed her outlook completely; she might still prefer to work on her own if given a choice. But she can see the value in collaboration now, as well as what it takes to achieve the value and not just the hassle.

Diversity is about all of us, and about us having to figure out how to walk through this world together. —Jacqueline Woodson (Kirch, 2014)

Sometimes different points of view or approaches to a project can be harnessed into a stronger, collective whole. Other times, different perspectives and approaches to a process can instill tension and competition with one another, and then you need to do some navigation, coordination, and decisions. In other words, difference can produce tension. It is up to you whether you can create generative results from that tension. Your ability to navigate conflict across differences through clear communication, active listening, an understanding of implicit and explicit bias, and privilege will make you an invaluable member of a team, an employee in a company, a leader, or an innovator.

🔑 SIMPLE STRATEGIES

When in a group, make a point of integrating everyone's viewpoints.

- At different moments, ask "What do you think?" to other people in the group, especially those who have been quiet or uninvolved.
- Practice really listening to their responses, and making sure they feel heard.
- Notice the effect this has on the group dynamic, and stay mindful of the feelings and thoughts of all people in the group throughout the process

The next chapter will walk you through the different group formations you're likely to encounter in various college classrooms and offer some strategies for turning these collaborations into effective groups where you can take risks, be brave/vulnerable, and do the work necessary in college.

This chapter provided you with knowledge about the characteristics of effective groups and strategies, which are key to fostering them. In the following chapter, we will build on this by leading you through case studies to practice these strategies, as well as examining common pitfalls of ineffective groups.

Takeaways

▸ You have experience collaborating and have developed habits in your collaborative practices.

▸ Recognizing multiple perspectives and factors in your thinking about working in a group develops an awareness of everything that is happening in a situation and what you have control over.

▸ Recognizing differences in group experiences can help you better understand yourself as a collaborator.

▸ Understanding how to create and maintain a group structure in situations that are presented with less structure is an important aspect of groupwork.

▸ Recognize that every time you practice collaboration skills in college, you are gaining knowledge and capacity that you can use in future, higher-stakes environments.

▸ Effective groups have members who feel like they belong, have a shared, stated goal (short-term and long-term), have norms/rules that are agreed upon, recognize the value in having multiple perspectives, listen to each other, support each other, and foster risk-taking.

▸ The behaviors you focused on in Chapters 3 and 4 about engaging diversity (active listening, humility, perspective-taking, being able to engage productive discomfort) will also be essential for effective collaboration.

Takeaways on Your Terms

▸ Name one or two of your *strengths* when working in a group. Why are they strengths? Name one or two of your *weaknesses* when working in a group. What makes these weaknesses for you?

▸ From your perspective, what are the benefits of completing tasks in a group?

▸ Choose one or two aspects of effective groups that seem the most important to you. Why did you choose these?

In Your Own Words: Keep. Quit. Start.

Using your journal, write about some of the habits you've developed in group settings in the past few years. What role do you typically fill? After reading this chapter, which of these habits would you like to keep? Which would you like to quit? And what new habits would you like to start developing?

When you get into a group for an assignment or class discussion, what are some specific things you feel and do at the very beginning of the experience? As you move forward toward cultivating skills and habits that support your way of participating in groupwork, what are some of these first impulses you can keep? Which of these would you like to quit? Any new actions or mindsets you would like to start?

Think about the way you see other people in your group. Do you really see them? Do you stick to a surface level of understanding and listening? Or do you go deeper? What aspects of how you see your group members would you like to keep? Is there anything you would like to quit doing in the way you acknowledge your groupmates? Is there anything you would like to start doing in how you interact?

Chapter 5 Assignment: Collaboration in the Workplace

Goals of the Assignment

To learn about collaboration in a workplace setting. To better understand how the skills of groupwork and collaboration are utilized in the workplace.

Steps of the Assignment

1. Identify someone in your circle who spends time collaborating with others in a non-classroom setting. This could be a family member, a friend, an instructor, an adviser, or someone else.
2. Ask this person if you could have a 15-minute conversation with them to learn more about collaboration in their work life.
3. In order to be prepared, write down some questions you want to ask about their experiences, perspectives on, and challenges with collaborating. For example, what conditions or strategies do they believe support effective collaboration? Undermine collaboration?
4. Interview the person. Your first question might be something like, "Are you asked to work in groups at your job?" Then you can let the conversation unfold naturally.

5. Write up a summary that's 500–750 words, including the final reflection of your conversation to be handed in. Your writing in this assignment should be conversational, informational, and descriptive. Keep in mind the following when you write your summary:

   • Include a brief introduction and conclusion in your final reflection.

   • Be sure to document who (the contact person is, including their title and work and their relationship to you), what (the specific goals for the conversation are), why (you chose this contact), where (you had the conversation), and when (the date and time) of the conversation.

   • Include details that will help the reader be there with you, such as brief descriptions of the room and the contact person, and perhaps your initial feelings as you first sat down with them.

   • Try to synthesize your interviewee's responses, and write about the major takeaways you have from this conversation, rather than the specific answers they give. Consider: What have you learned? What stands out? What surprises you? How will this influence your approach to groupwork in the future?

If their response to a question is lengthy, and it would be beneficial to cut down its length, you can edit it down and make it readable, but make clear where you are cutting out information by adding ellipses (…), and add any words you might need by putting them in brackets [ ]. Remain true to the content and intent of their comments.

What You Need to Hand In

Your final report on your interview (500–750 words).

Collaboration and Teamwork in College

> ❝ *Things which don't shift and grow are dead things.*
> —Leslie Marmon Silko
>
> *Individually, we are one drop. Together,*
> *we are an ocean.* —Ryunosuke Satoro ❞

In Your Own Words

Set your timer for five minutes. Free-write in your journal on the following scenario:

You are a new student in your second week of class, and suddenly the professor says, "Get in groups of three. This will be the group for your final project and presentation."

▶ How do you feel? Anxious? Excited?

▶ How do you choose your group members? Do you immediately look to the person next to you? Do you wait for someone to ask you to join their group? Do you scoot over to students who seem like they know what they're doing? Do you drop the class?

▶ Once your group gets together, how do you feel? Are you nervous? Excited to get started? What will you notice or watch for in your group? What will make you stressed about working with others? What will put you at ease?

▶ What do you plan to do in this group? Do you start organizing the group right away? Do you sit back and wait for others to get things going?

In the previous chapter, you were introduced to general principles that characterize effective teamwork and collaboration and the value and purpose of doing it. You were guided to reflect on past experiences with collaboration, in or out of school, and how those experiences shaped your current attitude and approach to collaboration. In this chapter, you will prepare for and practice some of the specific types of collaboration and group projects you are likely to encounter in college. Your professors will regularly invite or expect you to work with others, whether in informal or formal, short- or long-term, low-stakes or high-stakes ways.

As we discussed in Chapter 5, collaboration isn't simply natural or easy. There are a lot of factors and interpersonal dynamics involved, especially when the stakes are high or the team members are strangers to one another. It is important to have a growth mindset when it comes to each new collaboration and some strategies ready to help you approach it effectively. As in previous sections, we will close with case studies.

☁ THINK ABOUT IT

Go back to the *In Your Own Words 6.1* journal prompts at the start of this chapter and reread your written responses to the prompts and the scenario. What adjectives would you use to describe yourself as a group member? Would you want to be in a group with you? Are you satisfied with your habits and mindset about groupwork? What might you want to improve or modify?

SECTION **6.1**

What Collaboration or Groupwork Might Look Like in Your Classroom

For the sake of this chapter, think of groupwork as *any time you engage with someone else around content within a class*. In order to get the most out of these interactions, you need to understand the different ways collaboration is used in the classroom. For each method of collaboration ask yourself: Why is the professor asking me to do this? What do teachers think is the benefit of it? What might derail it? What might support it?

"Turn to Your Neighbor and Discuss"

In Chapters 3 and 4 on engaging diversity, we argued that not talking to your classmates and hearing their ideas on the course content is like buying a textbook and never opening it. Sometimes instructors will use the "think-pair-share" framework, where you have a moment to reflect on a question, then turn to a neighbor and exchange your ideas and eventually join another pair (or in some cases come back to the full class) to share your ideas further. Other instructors might follow a less formal setup and just ask you to turn to your neighbor and discuss a concept or problem for two to three minutes.

COMMUNICATION SITUATION

"My professor told us to number off and get into groups for the final presentation. My group had five people in it. One of the students immediately took over the whole thing, deciding how we were going to organize things and assigning us roles without asking for our input. The rest of us kind of just sat there, even though I know we didn't agree with everything he was saying. I think we appreciated that he was showing leadership, but leadership doesn't mean taking over and ordering people around, and it felt like he didn't care about our input at all. I am someone who needs time to think about things a little before speaking up or acting and I didn't get to do that."

- Imagine yourself in the role of the narrator. How would you feel? What might you have done to change the communication here? What choices would you have and what risks/rewards would you see in each of those choices?
- Now, try putting yourself in the role of the student who took charge. How do you think that student felt and why did he communicate that way? What other choices could he have made?

THINK ABOUT IT

What is your emotional reaction to being told to discuss something with a partner in class? Are you excited for a break from the lecture? Are you concerned about who you're paired with? Do you reach for your phone, email, notebook, or material from another class because this feels like wasted time? Are you nervous about not knowing what to say or that you may be confused by something? How does your reaction to hearing, "turn to your partner and discuss" shape the quality of the exchange?

Why Is the Professor Asking You to Do This?

Typically, an instructor wants to give you time to process something or connect it to your previous knowledge. Thinking for a moment about something shared in class and then comparing your thoughts with a neighbor requires you to be active. You have the opportunity to understand, apply, and analyze. Active learning helps students both process and retain information, and it helps students recognize what they don't understand. Sharing what you don't understand when you are paired with a classmate gives you an opportunity to ask for clarification. Peer-to-peer instruction is both efficient and mutually beneficial. Having to express your ideas to someone outside your perspective who won't automatically know what you mean forces you to refine and more deeply understand your own thoughts.

In his book *Transformational Learning Theory* (1997), sociologist Jack Mezirow argues that people operate from deeply engrained habits in thinking and point of view. These are formed and reinforced over time, and they eventually constitute one's "frame of reference" (Mezirow, 1997). Mezirow argues that productive discomfort is necessary to disrupt one's own preconceived notions and "to encounter different perspectives and to accept, integrate, and find space for those perspectives in our own frames of reference" (Lee, Poch, O'Brien & Solheim, 2017, p. 119). (**See Figure 6.1.**)

SIMPLE STRATEGIES

Choose a class where you have been asked to discuss ideas with a partner in previous class sessions.

- The next time you go to a class meeting, sit in a different location.
- Observe how the room looks and feels from that location and what is similar and different.
- Does your experience of the class change when you interact with different classmates?

CRITICAL MOMENT

Student

So far, this class has helped me to realize that everyone's contribution is important, because we all come from diverse backgrounds. It helped me realize that what I have to say isn't any less important just because I don't have a cool past or come from a different culture. What each individual brings in their different perspective to the table, may end up shining a light on something that others haven't thought of yet. As an individual, I've realized that what I have to say is important, but I should make sure that I've thought it through before I just go blurting things out in discussion.

"Number Off and Get into Groups"

The type of groups that require you to pick up your backpack and travel to a new location in the classroom typically involve more complicated problem sets or discussion questions than "turn to your neighbor" assignments. The groups also

Figure 6.1 An Illustration of Productive Discomfort

usually have more than two members. Because there often is not a grade associated with these group discussions or completions of this type of problem set, these can be a sweet spot for students. If done well, it's a low-stakes way to both practice your collaboration skills and learn from your peers.

In Your Own Words   6.2

Take a minute to reflect in your journal on different small-group discussions that have been productive and positive, and on others where you've felt disengaged. What was the difference? The course material? Who was in your group? How was the groupwork structured? What were the instructor's directions? Try to identify one aspect of either a positive or negative experience that was in your control. (For example, you started off by clarifying the names of everyone in your group and this made it feel less awkward.)

Write up a short description of the groupwork. What was the task? How many students were in the group? How did it go? What issues arose? Share this description with classmates in order to hear their perspective and analysis on why what worked was successful and why there may have been challenges. How would they advise you to do things differently going forward?

Why Is the Professor Asking You to Do This?

The opportunity to work through materials and ideas with others, and to listen carefully to peers, can help you reflect on and refine your own thinking and approach to a problem or task. Approaches to this type of collaborative learning range from study groups within a course, to team-based assignments and writing, to cooperative projects and research. Research shows that this type of collaboration in the classroom increases students' opportunities to engage in multiple levels of thinking. On one level, students can build their comprehension by working through their ideas with classmates whether from course text, a lecture, or an experiment. On another level, students can connect new ideas to both previously discussed ideas and concepts outside the classroom. Often, groupwork in class asks students to apply a concept or theory to a new problem. Consider the student (perhaps you) who is uncomfortable raising his or her hand in a large-class setting. Small-group discussions allow more students to be more active in the processing and application of course content.

🔑 SIMPLE STRATEGIES

This sort of groupwork can be tricky, because you may have a limited amount of time to learn about each other and do the task at hand. It requires you to keep the best practices for successful collaboration at the forefront of your thinking.

- View it as an experiment. How quickly can you get to know your groupmates and their work styles?
- Remember to make sure everyone speaks. This will help you understand how everyone works.
- If anyone volunteers to lead, let them lead the discussion.
- If your mind starts to wander regarding how the group is or isn't working, try to let that go and move on. This type of group assignment is often too short to reflect on group dynamics.

💡 CRITICAL MOMENT
Student

I find that, since being in the class, I am more outgoing and find it easier to talk to new and diverse people. In high school, I stayed with one group of friends the entire time. Everybody in the school had their own cliques, which they stuck to. Since we are a diverse group of students, and we are put into situations of groupwork in large discussion groups, I find I am able to talk to new and different people. I believe this skill will really help me be successful at the university.

Long-Term Group Projects

In some of your courses, you will have long-term groups, established on the first day or in the first week, which will be in place throughout the semester. The strategy behind forming long-term groups is that:

1. It mirrors how professionals work—in teams, over longer periods of time.
2. It provides a manageable way to complete a large or complex assignment when there is more work to be done than one person can do on their own.

Long-term groups provide consistency. You are able to develop an understanding of how group members operate. With a longer time frame, the group can recognize mistakes and make the adjustments necessary to address them. Group norms and structures are established from the beginning so you get to hit the ground running when it comes to completing an assignment, producing a product, or working through an experiment.

THINK ABOUT IT

Have you ever had a class where you were placed in a long-term group for a semester? How did it go? What do you remember about this experience?

If you haven't had the experience of a long-term group project, how does this type of project sound to you? Chaotic? Powerful?

Why Is the Professor Asking You to Do This?

While lots of higher-level learning can occur in the other group and individual formats, long-term groups that have multiple class periods to complete a task have the potential to achieve meaningful learning outcomes. Higher-level learning is when you're able to apply new knowledge to a variety of situations and go beyond understanding and into application and analysis. Whether you are determining the chemical makeup of an unknown compound or creating a digital story based on an oral history, you are taking multiple, discrete pieces of knowledge and using them to apply, analyze, evaluate, and even create. Long-term groups that exist over some extended duration have a chance to build rapport and a sense of belonging.

SIMPLE STRATEGIES

In this situation, students often start off being disappointed at being placed in a group that they deem less desirable. Remember that part of transformational learning comes from experiencing discomfort and new situations.

• Be patient and open to the process of developing rapport as a group.
• Get to know each other early on and set goals.
• Make time and make it a priority.
• Discuss group member preferences and maintain contact/communication throughout the duration of the project. These are key aspects of having a successful group.
• Invest the time to create a positive group dynamic to ensure group members learn to collaborate and meet the goals of the assignment.

Peer Review or Critique

Each of us needs information and perspective from others at particular points in a project, whether it is a lab experiment, essay draft, painting, or research question we are developing. You will need to bounce ideas around, or seek help pulling apart something you know isn't working but you can't figure out why. Or you just want to observe how someone else experiences what you are creating. Part of learning and growing requires input from others, whether they are readers or viewers, who bring different perspectives. They see your work and encounter your ideas with different lenses.

THINK ABOUT IT

THINK ABOUT IT

Have you ever been asked to critique someone else's work? Has anyone ever critiqued your work? If so, how did it go? Did you have any preparation before critiquing or being critiqued?

Why Is the Professor Asking You to Do This?

Each of your classmates offers a particular perspective that can serve as a new lens through which to see what you are doing. These different perspectives, and your substantive interaction with them, can help you steer your work in a way that is true to you instead of simply trying to please a professor. The process of actively listening, of absorbing someone else's input, is extremely valuable in learning more deeply. Remember that active listening isn't simply *not talking*. It is about opening space in your mindset to take in, engage, and reflect on different ways of thinking, experiencing, and interpreting. You have an opportunity to practice active listening when others provide feedback or input about your work or ideas, and also when you take in their work or creation.

SIMPLE STRATEGIES

Peer review can feel very vulnerable and sensitive, depending on the people involved. It can be very difficult to put something you created in front of other people and have them speak about it. And vice versa: It can be very difficult to articulate your feedback in a way that is supportive, yet constructive and honest.

- If you are the creator/writer/composer, try to outline a framework for the feedback you would like. This will help steer your audience to the parts you feel unsure about, so you can receive critiques that will move your process forward.

- Remember, you are you. Your work is a part of you, but not all of you. If someone doesn't like your work, it does not mean they don't like you. The same holds true for the other role: If you are the one giving feedback, do your best to be honest and clear, and to answer the creator's questions/ prompts.

- Remember that thoughtful feedback helps everyone grow in the ways they write/compose/teach/create and think about the ways they write/compose/ teach/create. (In the Toolbox: Tools for Managing Your Writing Process and Projects, included after Chapter 4, you will find suggestions and tips for giving feedback.)

Now, some of you might be thinking, "Yeah, this all sounds great in an ideal world." Of course, we realize we don't live in an ideal world. *Groupwork, and collaboration of any kind, is messy.* It requires stops and starts, lots of communication and questions, as well as productive discomfort. Dysfunctional groups do exist, both at the college level and in many workplaces. The skills of groupwork include figuring out how to accurately see where the group is, predict where issues might arise, work to prevent dysfunction, and when it occurs, address and treat it. Section 6.2 will focus on cultivating habits that will keep your group functioning despite imperfections.

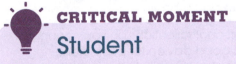

CRITICAL MOMENT
Student

I've also learned that, as a member of a group, everyone's opinions are vital in receiving the best education or getting the most from a class. Hearing other students' views on the different topics gives me a new perspective that I may have never considered. The course has helped me realize each student plays an integral role in the larger group because of the difference in opinions and what we can learn from them. Without speaking up or sharing your experiences, you're stopping your classmates from learning something new.

As you read the student's words, what comes to mind? What is a key takeaway or observation you make as you read this? Can you think of a time when you felt like this after working with a group?

Some Common Stumbling Blocks   SECTION **6.2**

Just as active listening and promoting belonging can impact groups in a positive way, there are other types of behaviors that can impact groups negatively. Some of these are internal, having to do with attitude and mindset about the task, the group, or a member's confidence. Others are external, having to do with behaviors or communication practices that diminish or detract from groupwork rather than contribute to it. Many of us exhibit these behaviors or attitudes unconsciously or mindlessly. Being a strong and productive collaborator means generating awareness about your way of being present in the group and becoming confident and comfortable with directing the group in productive directions.

TRY THIS

On a sheet of paper or in an online document, spend 10 minutes free-writing about your attitude toward group projects. Start by thinking about your most recent participation in a group project.

1. What is your general attitude about group projects in class? What part of this attitude serves you well? How does it serve you well? What part of this attitude doesn't serve you well? What would it take to change it?
2. How would you rate your willingness to work with everyone in the group? Is this a typical behavior of yours when working in a group? If yes, does this behavior serve you and your group well and should you continue it? If it's not a typical behavior, would it be worth doing again?

In a small group of students, share your personal reflections on your group work experiences. Use these to generate a list of good advice for people entering into group work. Think about group norms that can apply to the individuals, as well as the overall group structure.

Practice Applying What You've Learned

Let's look at some potential issues that could derail you or members of your group.

As you read through this section, reflect on which aspects of groups feel familiar and which ones you have yet to encounter.

1. Awkwardness of initial conversation:

   When you are first asked to talk with one or more classmates, it can be awkward. Asking their name or confirming that the name you call them is correct is a good way to start. Then, even a quick, "How are you?" helps reset your minds and get the conversation started. An authentic "How are you?" can produce responses that are actually useful: tired, super-excited for the weekend, hungry, nervous about an exam, etc. As a partner, this information helps you gauge what's genuinely going on for your partner.

2. Not being prepared for class:

   We encourage students to share whether or not they've done the reading or prepared for class with their groupmates. An honest disclosure is respectful to your groupmates. If you didn't do the reading, own up to it. Presumably if you've been in class that day, you have some context and some ability to contribute. Really listening and asking good follow-up questions to the answers your peer provides can be a way to make the time worthwhile for both of you. If your partner hasn't done the work, you can share your ideas and encourage them to offer thoughts they have as they listen.

3. Multitasking:

   Some students are in a constant pursuit to check things off their to-do list. You might be sitting in a lecture or seminar, while completing work for a different course. After all, if you don't have work to complete for the class you are sitting in, so why not work on something else? You came to class, presumably, in case something happened that you need to be there for. The moment you are asked to partner with another student is the moment to put away the distraction of other coursework, because this partner/groupwork is why you came. This is what you need to be present for, because you can't get it elsewhere. Developing the habit of limiting distractions during partner or groupwork is one that will serve you well throughout your life and career.

4. Not understanding/hearing what the instructor is asking you to discuss:

   If you don't understand/remember what the task is that the professor has assigned, look around for clues. (What are others doing? Is there a slide with discussion questions on it?) If you still can't figure it out, ask for clarification. It is very important to learn to ask questions without worrying about being wrong. For some students, that is a risk and it takes practice to feel comfortable with it.

5. Wanting to work with someone you know rather than a less familiar classmate:

   Groupwork can be intimidating, and people like familiarity. If there is someone in the class that you know, your fears related to being misunderstood or shamed are often less. That said, if you always find a way to do groupwork with someone familiar to you, you're missing out on learning from all of the differences in the classroom. The discomfort or awkwardness of collaborating with someone you don't know has great potential benefits. When you stretch by engaging or discussing with a new person, you are giving yourself the chance to gain a new way of viewing something.

6. Not feeling a sense of belonging:

   Contributing to each person's sense of ease and worth in your group will serve the purpose of benefitting you and your education, but it will also lead to a more engaged, enjoyable experience for all. If the instructor does not have you start off with a get-to-know-you style icebreaker, try to initiate some of that on your own. Some students do this naturally, wanting to know people's majors, backgrounds, dream jobs, or spring break plans. For others, it just feels awkward. But think about how hard it was to order in a restaurant for the first time or to check yourself in for a doctor's appointment—It was hard only because you hadn't done it before. It's not that the behavior in and of itself is difficult or will be perceived as strange. This is a low-stakes moment to embrace your "beginner-ness" and give it a try. In these situations, chances are that everyone in the group feels this awkwardness, and it's just a matter of one person breaking the ice by pushing through this discomfort to start the discussion.

If you are feeling "othered" or ignored by members in the group, identify one potential ally in the group and see if, as a duo, you can do something to reset the group identity. Students report that sometimes they don't feel the sense of belonging until the group bonds over the final push of the assignment. While it's better to find it later than never, reaching out to your professor when you first start feeling ignored or othered and asking for some support and guidance on building a group identity might help.

TRY THIS   6.4

Start a groupwork journal/doc/voice memo/folder. Whenever you receive a group assignment during the next few years of college, keep track of how it goes. Pay attention to how you feel about your role within your group, the work you put into the group, the way communication flows (or doesn't), what works for the group, and what doesn't work for the group. At the end, talk about your major lessons learned or takeaways from the experience. Over time, this will become an amazing resource for you to see how you have grown and developed as a collaborator. This archive of your groupwork will be important to review before interviews in the future.

SECTION **6.3**

Case Studies in Collaboration

As was discussed in Chapter 5, these skills of collaboration are highly relevant to many parts of life outside school. Many of us enter group projects mindlessly, and without an intention on how to establish positive communication, ensure all members feel a sense of belonging, and develop a shared process explicitly as a group. A take-charge person who jumps right in and begins organizing and directing the team is likely working from good intentions and sees himself as a leader, but it can also be domineering and overpowering to move into the work or to declare how a group will approach a task.

Groups function best when they make some time for their process of working and communicating together, being intentional and discussing how members want to approach the task and assess their work, and how they will distribute and delegate the work. It takes practice and reflection to develop your mindfulness as a collaborator and to hone agility that will enable you to enter into a range of collaborations in ways that support your engagement and the group's effectiveness.

The following are some case studies that illustrate collaborations going off-track. In this chapter and in Chapter 8, we present illustrative case studies to help us step outside the immediacy of our own experiences and habits of thinking or action, because they invite us to study a moment from a distance. In doing that, we can cultivate discernment and reflection about that moment and the factors that contributed to the dynamics. Practicing reflection in case studies can support a habit of reflection that you can apply to your own experiences, thus supporting your engagement and understanding in the moment.

THINK ABOUT IT

What's your favorite memory of working with a group? Why? What's your least favorite memory of working with a group? Why?

Case Study 1

Maria is in a General Chemistry lab, and students are in groups for the whole semester. Maria's group includes five people, none of whom has ever met each other before. When they first meet, people are pretty quiet and deferential to one another. They don't communicate much unless made to by the instructor. Once they start working together, it is clear they have different work styles. Some group members leave their assigned tasks until the very last minute, which results in a scramble of other people nagging them and then even sometimes taking over some of their work for them. Maria is frustrated and worried because she will be in this group for 15 weeks and there is already tension by Week 3, with members blaming others for not doing enough, some students finding others too domineering, and some students wanting more time to process their answers before talking about them immediately.

1. What are some derailing factors of this group?
2. If you were part of this group, what could you do to resolve some of these issues and help the group move forward?

From our perspective, there are two major stumbling blocks in this scenario:

- *The lack of sense of belonging.* Your group needs to make sure that everyone gets to know each person's name, major, and some other personal information, such as where they're from. By creating a setting where everyone has to speak at least a little, you can have a jumping-off point for connections and communication.
- *The differences among the group members in how they get their work done.* It is really important to talk about and establish group norms and expectations. It is never too late to bring this up or ask for clarification. If your group goes into a task without talking about what you want your approach to look like, there is no way that every person will feel good afterward. At the beginning, establish rules such as "Complete individual tasks 24 hours before the due date, so we can all look it over before submitting" or "Text the group chat any time you are confused and we will all commit to being attentive to each other's questions." No group will ever function perfectly, so it's worth the time to talk about what people want and need from each other in order to have the best function possible for all.

Case Study 2

Ray's English teacher assigns everyone to a group of six people for the semester to work on writing and performing a scene in the style of one of the authors you've been studying. The first two sessions are great! The group is focused on generating ideas and brainstorming. Everyone seems to really get along. Class periods fly by. Then, by the fourth and fifth classes, it's like the reality of the semester sets in. Everyone seems heavier with all of the work they are doing for this class and their other classes. Ray sees his group members getting more and more frustrated with the writing process. He observes some members getting more easily distracted, and spending more time on their phones or laptops during the meetings. Ray is worried about the final project. It feels like the group now has two subgroups: those who are working and present and those who are distracted.

1. What stands out to you in this case? What is important to notice?
2. What strategies could Ray use to help get this group to work together more effectively?

From our perspective, there are several stumbling blocks at work here:

- Being distracted by phones and computers during group time/class. Our societal norms are still evolving around phone and computer usage and they vary by age and place. Overall, cognitive and learning science have disproven the belief that "multitasking" is possible. It turns out that our brains cannot fully engage in two tasks (especially two complex tasks) at once.
- A lack of established norms about the use of devices. Perhaps you want to chat with your professor about creating some norms for the class surrounding electronics. A few simple rules can make all the difference. (For instance: If you need to text someone quickly, let your groupmates know. Also, while the group is working, no screens are allowed to be on.) Part of learning to live with our technology is learning to manage it. And part of managing it is developing good habits and communication that can head off any distraction before it happens.

 **TRY THIS** ──────────────────── **6.5**

There are a number of apps that track phone use and reward users for NOT using their phones. Try searching for "apps that reward you for being off your phone" and check out a few of these apps. Then, try using one for a week and journal about the effects.

Case Study 3

In Seungmin's sociology class, the instructor assigns a group project that piggybacks off a course reading. Each group has three weeks to find articles relating to the subject of the course reading and create synthesis and connection between the outside reading and the course content, which is demonstrated in a 10-page essay and a 10-minute presentation. At the beginning, one student takes charge and starts assigning work to each member. The group barely keeps in touch during the process and works separately. When they come together with one week left, each person has written completely different amounts of the paper and the styles of writing aren't consistent.

1. What has led to the derailment of this group?
2. What were the key problems the group faced in this scenario?
3. What could the group members have done to refocus their group on the group task and salvage the paper and presentation?

There are at least two factors contributing to the derailment of this group project.

- It is critical for all group members to know and be able to step into a leadership role, and also know when to step back and let others lead. In this scenario, it might sound like a good idea for one student to take charge and divvy up the work. However, when he or she blindly assigns work without taking into account the strengths and needs of each group member, the project is destined to fail.
- Second, there is a lack of equity in the amount of work each group member did. The lack of a group discussion about norms and expectations left each member with different expectations for their work and without any feedback from one another during the process.

To overcome this situation, the group needs to return to the initial stages of functioning as a new group, which includes learning about each other's preferred work styles in groups, establishing some group norms, and then agreeing on how the tasks should be split up. Norms around communication are important to avoid this situation, in which a lack of communication leads to disconnects in work accomplished.

Working with other people, either by choice or by requirement, is bound to be a part of your career and professional life. We tend to talk more about competition and individual achievement when talking about job markets and career development, but the reality is collaboration, cooperation, and teamwork are going to be present and valued in just about any line of work you choose.

Fun Fact

A Stanford University study found that people who perceived that they were working as a group stuck at their task 64% longer than those who thought they were working alone. (Parker, 2014) In addition, they felt less tired, more motivated, and more successful. There are research-proven benefits to collaborating with groups, which means you should seek out groupwork and embrace the opportunity to reap the benefits from collaboration.

College will present you with many opportunities to work with people you don't know very well or don't choose to work with, on tasks both vaguely explained and highly detailed and defined. All of these involvements are valuable. Use all of the experience your undergraduate career provides to work on teams in order to help prepare for your future. If you pay attention, you will learn about your style and preferred approach and roles when it comes to collaboration. For example, you will learn if you tend to take the lead or prefer to receive direction, or when that might vary for you. You can learn how you like to communicate, how you like to break down a task, and how you feel about who gets credit for what. All of this is available to you to start to figure out now, so you can be articulate and clear when it comes to working in a group or team for your work. And while each of us has a kind of default setting that we develop, we also need to develop the capacity to be flexible and take on different roles on different types of teams and projects.

Takeaways

▶ Collaboration is an important skill to work on in college, because you will use it for the rest of your life.

▶ Collaboration can take many different forms, structured and unstructured, big groups and small.

▶ When you are assigned collaborative tasks in school, it is important to consider what the benefit is of doing this in a group and what you can gain.

▶ Identifying derailing issues in a group and seeking to solve them can transform a dysfunctional group into a successful one.

▶ The beauty of a group is that each person fulfills different roles, so it's important for you to learn what parts of groupwork you feel most confident and comfortable in. (See **Figure 6.2.**)

NAME	ROLE/ RESPONSIBILITY	DEAD- LINE	TIME TO COMPLETE		NOTES
			ESTIMATED	ACTUAL	

Figure 6.2 Task Chart for Groups

Takeaways on Your Terms

▶ Which attitudes and behaviors that can hinder collaboration feel familiar to you? Why?

▶ Which strategies discussed in this chapter feel like they could work for you in the future? Why? Do any feel like they won't work? Why?

▶ If you could apply any of these strategies to past group experiences, what would you use and why?

In Your Own Words: Keep. Quit. Start.

We've covered a number of ways that groupwork can derail, as well as ways for you to work with your group to resolve the difficult situations you may face. What are some of the ways you work in a group that you want to keep? What are certain behaviors or habits you want to quit? What do you hope to start doing when participating in collaborative work in the future?

So much about groupwork is seeing and participating in your part in the group, but groupwork is also about seeing the larger picture of the group and how it works. As you move into groupwork in the future, what strategies have you used in the past that you would want to keep? Are there any strategies you see as unproductive that you would like to quit doing? Is there anything you would like to start doing after reading this chapter?

Think about some group norms—named or unnamed—you have experienced in past collaborative work. What group norms would you like to use in the future? Are there any you would like to never see again? Are there any group norms you would like to consider using next time?

Chapter 6 Assignment: Help! I Need Help!

Goals of the Assignment

To think through building a hypothetical dream team to help you accomplish a goal, so as to show how a team is essential for certain tasks.

Steps of the Assignment

1. Identify a situation you need help with. This does not have to be academically oriented, although it can be. It can be a task like preparing for an exam or creating a documentary film. It can be creating a weightlifting routine, or developing personal goals, or organizing your schedule, or identifying personal habits. Find something where one person helping you would be good, but a team would be great.
2. Identify why it would be more successful to accomplish it in a group.
3. Identify what strengths you bring to the group. Identify strengths that need to be brought to the group by other members. Be sure to consider both concrete skills (knows how to use a saw) and soft skills (helps others stay on task).
4. Assemble your hypothetical dream team. How many members? What skills do different members bring? Think of real people you know who could be on your team. If necessary, you can include one imaginary person, but this imaginary person cannot have strengths beyond the typical human (no superheroes).
5. Think through how you would structure this group. What are the "guidelines" for participation? How much time do you expect would be needed to accomplish the goal? What's the goal? How do you know when the goal has been met?

What You Need to Hand In

Write up a report with the Who, What, Where, Why, When, and How explained. At the report's end, spend 100 words explaining why this dream team (as opposed to you by yourself) is necessary for this task.

Being a Writer

> " *Talent is insignificant. I know a lot of talented ruins. Beyond talent lie all the usual words: discipline, love, luck, but most of all, endurance.* —James Baldwin "

In Your Own Words

7.1

Take a moment and then picture a writer in your journal. Take three to five minutes and draw or sketch or write the scene you envision when you picture a writer writing. Who are they? Where are they? What is around them? What is their expression? What is the mood of the scene? List five to ten words, phrases, or adjectives that come to mind when you think of writers.

In "Being a Writer," our goal is not to teach you the best and ultimate way to write. Writing does not work that way, for one thing. But seeing yourself as a writer; practicing some of the habits and strategies that professional writers use; and rethinking how you approach academic writing will be an opportunity to transform the course of your development as a writer.

Interview between George R.R. Martin (Game of Thrones author) and Stephen King (Atkins, 2016):

George R.R. Martin: How the f@!% do you write so many books so fast? I think, "Oh, I've had a really good six months, I've finished three chapters." And you've finished three books in that time.

Stephen King: The way that I work, I try to get out there and I try to get six pages a day. So, with a book like *End of Watch*, and … when I'm working I work every day—three, four hours, and I try to get those six pages, and I try to get them fairly clean. So if the manuscript is, let's say, 360 pages long, that's basically two months' work… But that's assuming it goes well.

George R. R. Martin: And you do hit six pages a day?

Stephen King: I usually do.

George R. R. Martin: You don't ever have a day where you sit down there and it's like constipation? And you write a sentence and you hate the sentence, and you check your email and you wonder if you had any talent after all? And maybe you should have been a plumber? (Laughs) Don't you have days like that?

Stephen King: No. I mean, there's real life, I could be working away, and something comes up and you have to get up... but mostly I try to get the six pages in.

George R.R. Martin and Stephen King are award-winning, extremely prolific authors. Yet, as they discuss here, they have developed different habits and approaches to their writing. As a first-year college student, you will often be asked to produce writing of different forms, for different purposes and audiences. With the right tools and mindset, you can grow exponentially as a writer in just this year. In this section of the book, our goal is to awaken and inspire the writer in you. For some of you, this may mean unlearning how you've learned to think about writing or yourself as a writer in the context of school. People come into college with a variety of relationships to writing, some with low confidence or a lack of interest in writing, and others feeling passionate about it. Regardless of where you sit on that spectrum, you can use this chapter to take ownership of your writing.

As we keep saying throughout this book, there is no single recipe for success. There are, however, essential ingredients. In this chapter, your attention will be focused on the essential ingredients of effective writing and a writing process. The essential ingredients are not formal or stylistic elements, but rather habits of mind and attitudes that specifically enable you to see yourself as a powerful writer.

We're All Writers

You will probably take a writing course in college, and it is likely to focus on formal elements of style and the writing process, and to promote your attunement to different writing situations. We are dedicating a section of this book to writing because writing and the writing process are fundamental to your success in college. Writing is not just the form or product you create to demonstrate what you have learned or done (in a paper for class or a lab report). Writing is also a way to *figure out what you know*; writing is a means to discover ideas, not just express them; writing is a means to refine and hone your thinking and develop a deeper understanding of various subjects.

Writing is part of a basic human drive to communicate, to form meaning, and to be understood. Like any form of art, writing is a means of externalizing thoughts, feelings, questions, and impressions that humans have as we encounter and interact with each other and the world around us. Writing as an act of creative expression is something people all do from an early age, whether in scribbles or actual words. But from this early age, one's writing is often judged or evaluated (Is it neat enough? Did we copy the letters exactly?) and not celebrated or cheered. Therefore, it's understandable that people form ideas about their worth or skill as writers very early on—whether they are capable, confident, and effective, or not—and those messages tend to take hold and become difficult to shift.

Unlike verbal speech, however, writing doesn't involve body language, facial expressions, pitch, tone, or pauses. Instead, there are words and white space on the page, which can at first appear limiting but can also be powerful. The reader gets to hold the written word in their hands, hold it captive and unchanging, and return to it. This is part of what makes writing so difficult to do and yet so exciting and powerful.

THINK ABOUT IT

Look back at your Scene of Writing sketch or free-write for In Your Own Words 7.1. What does your scene tell you about how writing makes you feel? Who you picture as a writer? Did you draw yourself? Was it someone like or not like you?

Early conditioning influences your thinking about writing, as well as your attitude about whether or not you are or can *be* a writer. Similarly, you develop habits as a writer that may be productive and help you be successful, or that may actually inhibit or undermine your confidence and effectiveness. Many times, people don't realize the habits they have developed. They adopt them mindlessly, by default. College and this book are an opportunity for you to take stock and reflect, and be intentional, strategic, and make plans about *how you want to be, who you want to be, and what you want to be confident in*. Journaling can be part of your strategy. Regular writing, in the form of journaling, gives you a space where you can practice self-reflection, practice writing and being a writer, and create new beneficial habits.

Professional writers develop habits and processes that *work for them*. One of the difficulties for those who teach writing is that there is *no one way* to be a writer or to approach a writing task. Different people have different ways that work best for them, which sometimes depends on the situation, the amount of time, the complexity and scope of the task, and what else is going on in their lives right then. But as we said, one thing professional writers do cultivate and leverage is an awareness of what works for them and what doesn't. This includes knowing things about themselves and their process, such as:

1. Why do you write, and on which occasions? (In other words, what gets you to write?)
2. Where do you write?
3. Who do you write for?
4. What is your internal definition or sense of "good" writing?

THINK ABOUT IT

Reread the opening conversation between Stephen King and George R.R. Martin. Do either of these approaches sound like yours? Does one resonate more with how you would like to be as a writer? What is surprising to you about Martin's feelings about writing? Do you find anything surprising about King's approach?

People come into college with a variety of feelings toward writing: many having low confidence or a lack of interest in writing, while others feel passionate about it. As a college student, you will often be asked to produce writing of different forms, for different purposes and audiences. With the right tools and mindset, you can grow exponentially as a writer in just this year. As we discuss throughout the book, everyone develops certain attitudes, frames of mind, and habitual ways of doing tasks that they undertake regularly. Sometimes, people aren't aware of their habits and aren't able to see where there is room for strategic changes to improve the results or the efficiency of these tasks. So, in this chapter, your job is simply to do some deeper and more extended free-writing and reflection to help you take stock of your habits regarding writing, both in and out of school.

TRY THIS   7.2

The following is an assignment, but rather than handing in the free-writing you produce, the final product you will hand in will be five pieces of advice for a teacher on how to support you as a writer. Your instructor may also want to collect your free-writing to reward your effort, but the primary product your instructor will gather is the advice you give in prompt #4.

Plan to spend 15 minutes free-writing about each of the following prompts. Remember: free-writing is literally free writing. Don't stop writing. Don't think about what you're writing. Turn off that inner judgmental voice. Just go. Or let go.

1. Think of a school writing assignment that you were proud of or satisfied with. What aspects of the process, assignment, or experience led you to feel that way? Did you have a connection with the topic? A passion for the form or subject? Was it the teacher who inspired your positive experience? If so, how?
2. Now think of one that you aren't proud or satisfied with—and answer the same questions shown in question 1.
3. What are you expecting will be different about college writing?
4. If you were to give advice to a teacher about how to both support your writing and you as a writer, what would it be?

After writing about these prompts, what have you learned about your mindset regarding your writing?

Ultimately, the goal is to learn from your past experiences and the impressions you have formed, while also realizing that college can be a fresh start in terms of developing a writer's mindset. No matter what experiences you have had with writing in the past, whether discouraging, boring, or confusing, you should see college writing as a new horizon for you. There are ample resources in this book, and on your campus, to help you grow as a writer in a way that makes you confident in, and proud of, your writing. Don't be defined by your high-school experiences in writing, or any one experience you have had with it. College writing is a new and different challenge that you can face with openness and confidence.

Those who don't believe in magic will never find it.

—Roald Dahl (Dahl & Blake, 2019)

Writing isn't magic. But believing in yourself and your ability can feel like magic. Writer Roald Dahl helps you imagine what's possible if you're willing to believe in yourself, your writing, and what can come of it, wherever your starting place may be. If you don't think you can be a writer, it is unlikely you will get very far in improving your writing. But by taking the simple step of believing in *you the writer*, you are opening yourself up to quite a lot of magic.

TRY THIS ——————————————————— 7.3

Close your eyes and imagine you are about to begin an assigned writing project.

1. What is the scene? Think about the space you are in and the details in terms of noise, sounds, and smells. What tools have you gathered to set about this task? Your laptop? Books? Paper? Pencils? Where are you located? What is going on around you? What is your state of mind and body?
2. What are your current thoughts and feelings?
3. If you could observe yourself and this scene, what would you think about how this person is going about the task?

If you think about *anything* you love or like to do, and have gotten better at and invested time in it, chances are you did not learn it the way many people learn to write. In school, you might learn to write, but you don't learn to see yourself as a writer. A writer is someone who uses words to explore and create meaning, feelings, and ideas, and to connect with others and understand the world, their life, or a given subject more than they did before they wrote. Writing is a mode of thinking, expression, and communication. It is like making music—creating a way to explore, experiment, express, connect, produce, and experience. But often writing is taught more like it's cleaning a bathroom—a process of steps to produce an end product.

In Your Own Words

7.4

In your journal, write about a critical moment that shaped how you see yourself as a writer? Who or what has had the most influence on your understanding about writing and about your sense of self as a writer?

Many people, when first learning to talk, are praised as soon as they utter a word (or even a word fragment). It is a *big* moment when a baby utters his or her first word. By the time a few words are strung together, it is a really really, really big deal. People around the baby applaud, comment, celebrate the words being spoken, and this goes on for some time. Babies also fail as they begin to speak. But their failures are supported and congratulated as well. Here, risk and vulnerability are celebrated, praised, and recognized as good and positive effort. This encourages the baby to keep trying new things. People do not usually begin to have someone "correct" their speech until later in life, at a point when they are pretty fluid and fluent at uttering lots of words. And at a time when they know they are successful communicators, they can see the impact of their words in the actions of others around them. When babies first begin to utter sensible words, and then utter more words in a row and combine them in ways that communicate thoughts, wants, needs, and emotions, they get a lot of praise. They are usually given a lot of room to mess up and just utter words without any correction or rules or thoughts about grammar and diction.

For many, the experience of learning to write is very different from learning to speak. Children typically begin speaking early and by choice, but many don't really begin learning to write letters, thoughts, and sentences until they go to school. Most early writing experiences take place in school, and that is where our sense of self as writers is formed. The experience of writing for school may feel compulsory, on demand, pressured, absent of creativity or passion, or lacking a deeply felt need to communicate.

THINK ABOUT IT

Did you see anyone writing while you were growing up? If so, who? Why? What associations did those early images bring you? What early impressions did you form of writers? How does this still influence your perception today—of writers generally, and of yourself as a writer, or not as a writer?

Amy, one of the authors of this book, often asks her first-year writing students what they have learned about writing and writers. Mostly, those conversations focus on a lot of rules, and on dos and don'ts. For example:

1. Don't use the first person.
2. Craft your paragraphs to be a funnel (general to specific).
3. Craft your paragraphs to be a triangle (specific to general).
4. Don't express your personal opinions.
5. Do express your opinions and analysis.
6. Restate your introduction in the conclusion.
7. Do not restate the introduction in the conclusion. Instead, share the significance of the paper.
8. Don't end sentences with prepositions.
9. Vary your sentence lengths.
10. Don't start sentences with "because."

Through the emphasis placed on all these rules, students learn to write by having their writing demanded and corrected. For many, writing—unlike speech—occurs due to an external demand, not an internal drive or need, and is shaped, evaluated, assessed, and graded, and you are told early and often to do it in a certain way and *not* to do it in other ways. Something to note about the rules of good writing that many of you learn and internalize is that they don't *really* get at what makes writing powerful even if they cite what makes writing "correct." Composition, like music, speech, or another art form, involves discipline and rules and norms. But beyond correctness, there is the question of whether or not the writing *speaks to* you as a reader, whether or not it expresses a feeling or articulates an idea or animates an intuition in a way that creates not an impression of *correctness* but of *connection*. Of course, not all readers will connect to the same form or piece of writing, just as people have different musical or artistic tastes and preferences and things that move us.

The point is, correctness and form are essential ingredients, but they aren't the only essential ingredients. When learning to write, rules and correctness are often valued over all the other elements of composition. This may lead you to neglect the real purpose of writing, which is to communicate with the reader. You may forget that it's not about checking certain boxes of grammar, or utilizing certain long words, or containing our thoughts within a structure that will earn us full points. The true purpose of writing is to make the reader understand and feel what you are communicating to them. Think about this as you proceed through this next activity.

TRY THIS

This activity is adapted from an assignment Amy Lee (one of this book's authors) uses with her first-year writing students (Lee, 2000). The categories and the excerpts that follow are all taken from an actual National Assessment of Educational Progress (NAEP) exam and student responses to that exam.

Imagine you are one of the graders for the fourth-grade Writing Task, part of the national standardized educational progress exam this year. Read the responses of the fourth graders and put each into one of the following categories/ratings:

- Unsatisfactory
- Minimal
- Adequate
- Elaborated

The Prompt:

In 17 minutes, identify a specific kind of animal and present relevant information about its qualities or characteristics.

Example #1   Bear's can Be mean But They won't Bother you if you don't Bother Them. Bear's are Defferent in many ways for instance Bear's sleep ontil spring and many other ways.

Example #2   Rabbits. Rabbits are very fuzzy soft animals (I love them). They eat carrots. Do make a mess. Some people do not like rabbits. Some people don't like animals but I don't know why! If I had a ribbit I would name it Fuzzy. That's a nice name, I think. Rabbits are different because they have tiny little noses and because their animals. They are speashal. Rabbits are very unuseual animals. It's funny but I hve a hard time eating a carrot. Rabbits are so small and they can ate carrots, they must have very strong teeth because carrots are hard for some people to bite. It's funny to think but how do rabbits get all that fur and what do they do all day??? If you have a ribbit your lucky.

Example #3   We went to the zoo and seen a tiger. It was orange with black dots. It was fun. We also seen a loine. It was ugly. We seen a ape. We also seen a zebra. It was brack white. It weit 2,0000 ponds.

Example #4   The Arctic Fox is a very tough animal. It thrives through long and cold winters. It reproduces more when there is more food. For instance, the average number of kits in one family is 10. Last year scientists studies came out 14 kits a family. The arctic Fox ranges from Northern America Eurasia and the northern islands. Sometimes the Arctic fox is white sometimes is a brown color. It really depends on the breed. Usually the Fox only has one breed but when one breed mates with another breed they sometimes have mixed breeds. The fox usually hunts small rodents like mice or sometimes whatever it can find. Arctic fox's take care of there young and the father leaves the mother soon after mating, but the arctic fox mother teaches her kits to hunt.

Which categories did you put each response in, and why? What factors did you consider most? For example: spelling, structure, style, voice, content, organization, development, topic sentence, imagery, vividness, tone/feeling, etc. Why did you value some qualities over others?

What if the categories were: dull, boring, impersonal, exciting? Which writer would you most want to hang out with? Why?

While most students articulate their awe at the "knowledge" and writing ability demonstrated by the fox writer, they don't choose that writer to hang out with, which means they value a type of writing but not the "persona" it conveys. However, as many of them point out, their own experience with school writing has shown them that form is inevitably privileged over ideas, and they describe moments when they felt they'd written an important or thoughtful essay only to be dismissed for lacking the "proper" structure or having grammatical errors. It is worth noting, then, that they value the fox piece because (and in spite of) the fact that it exemplifies the very style of writing they associate with their failures and frustrations as writers.

What are your takeaways from this exercise about the elements of writing that you value? That you don't value?

One of the difficulties for those who teach writing is that there is *no one way* to be a writer or to approach a writing task. Different people have different ways that work best for them, sometimes even depending on the situation, the amount of time, the complexity and scope of the task, and what else is going on in their lives right then. What is important is developing an awareness of what works for you and what doesn't.

🔑 SIMPLE STRATEGIES

The next time you have a writing assignment you don't feel like starting, try setting a timer for 10 minutes and spend that entire 10 minutes free-writing. Don't judge any of the words coming out. Even just putting words down on paper and putting the effort into thinking about the subject can help you greatly toward getting a start. If you're on a roll after 10 minutes, keep going!

The importance of you seeing yourself as a writer cannot be emphasized enough. It means you are taking responsibility and ownership for what you write, and it means you are giving yourself credit for the work you put into producing writing. Ownership of your writing means that you recognize the power of it—you are putting into words your ideas, with the intent to communicate those ideas to an audience. While this is powerful, it also means you must seek help. You can't see how your words are understood by your audience until you engage with others to see and hear their responses and questions. Throughout this book, we reference many different ways to utilize resources at your college to your benefit. Writing is a perfect example of this because all writers need help, end of story. Every single writer, which includes you, needs and deserves help to improve their writing. The simple act of asking a person who is outside your brain to look through your writing and survey a number of different factors will elevate your writing.

Debunking Myths About Effective or Successful Writers

THINK ABOUT IT

When you think of a "good writer," what type of person comes to mind? How do they write? Why do they write?

Through learning about writing in school, you build an image over time of who owns the title of "writer." You typically see this person as a mythical figure, uniquely suited to doing a task that so many people struggle with. Let's talk through some misconceptions that we might have about people who write. We believe that these misconceptions, or myths, as we will refer to them, perpetuate the idea of writing as an activity for only a select group. We aim to show you that writing is something we can all partake in, improve upon, enjoy, and maybe even love.

Myth #1: Writing is only part of my life when I have an assignment and the only purpose is to get a grade and fulfill the requirements.

Reality: You write every day, and you write to create meaning, to express yourself, and to connect with people.

It's important to understand that you are practicing writing every single day through a variety of platforms. You text your friends, send emails to professors, jot things down on your notepad, caption Instagram photos, send tweets, and have a million other uses for the written word. You already have probably more than five different platforms where you practice different forms of writing via the internet. All this writing you do is just in a different form than the writing you do for school. You have a variety of purposes, mediums, and modes of using this writing. Getting better at your academic writing isn't a whole new skill. It's more a way of flexing your muscles, that you do all the time in a new and different way.

TRY THIS _____ 7.6

Dig through texts you have sent that included a meme or an emoji. Cut and paste a screenshot of the text into an online document. Write a summary of all that is wrapped into that image. What did you intend for it to communicate?

Because you already write every day, we want you to begin to pay more attention to it. Daily writing practice is like practicing scales on a musical instrument or practicing dribbling a basketball. Practicing consistently is a great way to gain confidence and skill as a writer. It will help you experience and adjust to the flow of your writing.

In Your Own Words

7.7

1. Notice WHY you write and what inspires or motivates you to write. Do you write by choice? Regularly? When you write by choice, to whom or for whom do you write? (Yourself is a fine answer!) If you never write by choice, why not?

2. What do you think is the hardest part or stage of writing? What do you dread or avoid? What was a time you broke through—what was going on? How did you break through? How did it feel? How did you know you broke through?

TRY THIS _____ 7.8

For the next seven days, integrate daily writing into your routine. Decide when it will work best and make it easy. Keep a little notebook next to your bed? Use the voice memo app on your phone? What time will it work? During your commute? Maybe seven minutes before sleep each night? Or 30 minutes first thing in the morning? (See **Figure 7.1**.)

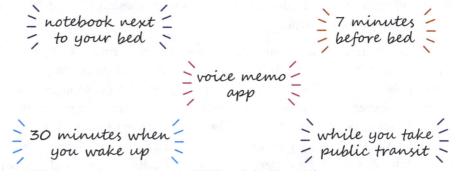

Figure 7.1 Ideas to Incorporate Writing into Your Life

Seeing your writing as only a means to receive a grade is an incredibly limited view, because your writing can, and does, do so much more. Writing is a unique way to express your feelings and thoughts in an external way, in order to connect with other people.

🔑 SIMPLE STRATEGIES

Start writing. Yes, that's it. Just start writing. Maybe write about something or someone that inspires you. Or, something that is worrying you or a decision you face. Or just start on one of your assignments.

Myth #2: Real writers don't produce bad writing or need many drafts.

Reality: Writing is revision. Professional writers produce and discard a lot of bad writing to get to their final drafts.

> *Writing is easy. All you have to do is cross out the wrong words.* —Mark Twain

> *I started a second novel seven times and I had to throw them away.*
> —Amy Tan

Amy Lee's (one of the authors of this book) actual reaction upon reading this myth was to snort with laughter. As she described in Chapter 1, when she started writing this chapter, she got squirrelly and had trouble sitting still and getting to work. She and her coauthors estimate that they wrote about 30,000 words that no one will ever read just to get to the 9000 or so that actually appear here. Writing for public consumption is rewriting. All writers, no matter how accomplished, renowned, or well-published, experience something Anne Lamott calls a "s@#ty first draft." (Lamott, 1995) Lamott explains that no writer can sit down and simply type a well-written piece to be published. Getting to a final draft requires countless previous ones full of errors, poor wording, and total chaos. This is important to remember because it means that the compelling, life-changing, beautiful texts that people love are not the product of pure genius. Rather, they are the product of a s@#ty first draft, plus a lot of revision, new ideas, outside input, and more and more revisions.

If you remember that writing is both a skill and an art, and you consider musicians or athletes, for example, to be an inspiration, you understand that there is no perfect concert or winning game without a lot of bad notes, missed shots, frustrating moments, failure, and determination beforehand. There is also a lot of experimenting and trying things to see what happens before you settle on a final result. Think of a cancer researcher in a lab, messing around with factors in the experiment in order to record, observe, and manipulate the results. This is what happens when writers write.

Writing is making meaning. Not just presenting already made meaning. You literally *do not* know what you are going to write until you write it, whether in an outline, or a journal entry. Early drafts inevitably have an element of improvisation in the early stages; it's like riffing in jazz or freestyling in hip hop. Does some pretty amazing stuff come out in improv and freestyling? Yes. But not the first time someone does it. It is awkward and not very good at first. But have patience with yourself.

The more you exercise the process of improvisation and condition yourself to get into the flow, the better your early drafts will be. But they won't be final drafts, just ones that are ready for editing. Sometimes, revising is moving things around in order to resee the relationships between the parts of ideas in a piece of writing. Sometimes, it is about deleting a lot. Revision involves different processes and tasks depending on the type of project you're working on and the context (audience, purpose) of the writing. We offer many ideas to motivate and support your revision in the Writer's Toolbox. Here is one to try:

TRY THIS 7.9

Print out an old paper and cut it into paragraphs. Shuffle the paragraphs around and then start resequencing them in the order that makes the most sense. Chances are, it isn't in the order you had it. A lot of times, we write how ideas come to us, but when we are putting them into the form/shape that helps someone else understand the ideas, a different sequencing is more effective.

Writing is not only a way to communicate meaning, information, and knowledge to others. It is also a way that one can create meaning, information, and knowledge. You can't really know what you think until you put words to it. When you put those words to paper (or screen), you begin to not only express yourself but to make meaning. Many times, however, you learn to approach writing as though it is a vessel and not a tool, and then perhaps you make the mistake of trying to polish and edit it too soon. Or you become too attached to your first draft because you don't see it as a kind of brainstorming and creative expression, but as the baby version of the final paper.

One of the most powerful things you can do as a writer in your editing process is show it to another person for feedback. When writing, you often don't even know what you're writing because you are just channeling your thoughts and feelings onto the page in the form of words. One of the best ways to remedy this is to give it to a person with a fresh outlook to read it, whether you use your writing center, schedule a consultation with your professor, or do a peer edit with a friend. The writing center is a very, very valuable tool for you as a student writer. This is free access to an expert consultation; if you were to hire a professional writing consultant, you would likely be paying in the range of $50/hour. Students who come to writing conferences with something, anything on paper, always get more concrete feedback than students who come to conferences with verbal ideas.

CRITICAL MOMENT
Instructor

I used to have writer's block or procrastination. I could never start the paper until the night before it was due. I literally couldn't force myself to do it. I would stay up all night writing my paper, every single time. This worked ok when the papers were pretty short, under 10 pages. But as I got older, my papers got longer and more complex and it didn't work to do that. There literally wasn't enough time. The first time I went to a writing center was when I had my biggest paper so far due and I couldn't make all the pieces fit together. I was nervous to make an appointment and to go because I felt like it was something you shouldn't actually NEED to do. I remember feeling kind of ashamed of what a mess my thoughts were and that I brought scraps of paper with half outlines and jumbled thoughts because I just couldn't get myself to formulate paragraphs or a thesis or anything. And I remember the relief and the freedom I felt when I left, after the tutor patiently asked me some really simple questions, such as: Why do you care about this? What is the foreground and what is the background? How does this fit in, or why does it seem connected to that?

As I talked it through, they took notes, and then at the end it was like I had a map of my paper and a path through what had seemed a thick jungle of half-formed ideas and connections. From that time on, I always asked myself those questions and I went to the Writing Center at that stage of my writing.

CRITICAL MOMENT
Student

My class partner had an inspirational story about their mother as their role model and their struggle through life and finally their move to America. As they read this, I couldn't help but be amazed by their story. They had a lot of grammatical errors because English is not their first language, but as they read we corrected and they caught many of their own mistakes. After they finished, I told them how amazing their story was to me and how they should just focus on the grammatical errors, but their story was heart-wrenching. They were taken aback by my comments and their confidence seemed to have risen greatly. I think just my positive comments reinforced how they felt about their essay and allowed them to feel confident turning in a final draft.

I think this in-class assignment allowed both of us as two young women to become closer as classmates and as human beings. We both learned a lot about each other in a small amount of time that probably wouldn't have happened in just an academic conversation within class.

For me, without a doubt it was one of my most life-changing moments in a classroom setting. They taught me so much about their history and their life as an immigrant family and I told them about me and my relationship with this little girl, and without this conversation this would have been lost within both of us and never talked about.

In this case, these two young women demonstrate a powerful and meaningful result of sharing writing. This gets at the most basic, immediate benefit of writing: communication.

COMMUNICATION SITUATION

Your professor tells you to swap essay drafts with a classmate and give each other feedback. When you receive their essay, you see there is a lot of room for improvement, and so you provide them with a lot of what you think is constructive criticism to help them with their paper. When they see your feedback, they confront you and say that your feedback hurt their feelings, and they didn't think their essay was "that bad."

- How do you react to this, and how does their communication make you feel? How do you think your classmate feels, and why might they feel this way about your feedback?
- How do you communicate with your classmate? Do you seek to understand where they are coming from? Do you feel the need to defend yourself, or to make your classmate feel better?
- Put yourself in the shoes of the writer who was hurt by the peer review comments. Why might they have reacted this way? Could they have communicated this in a more productive way?
- Is there a way the instructor could have framed the exercise differently to prepare and coach people for what was expected and included the concept of constructive criticism?

Myth #3: Once you are a "good" writer, you always produce good writing.

Reality: Good writers never stop producing bad writing, because it is the nature of the creative process, especially as you take on new and more complex writing and contemplative tasks.

> *Perfectionism is the voice of the oppressor, the enemy of the people. It will keep you cramped and insane your whole life, and it is the main obstacle between you and a (s@#ty) first draft. I think perfectionism is based on the obsessive belief that if you run carefully enough, hitting each stepping-stone just right, you won't have to die. The truth is that you will die anyway and that a lot of people who aren't even looking at their feet are going to do a whole lot better than you, and have a lot more fun while they're doing it.* —Anne Lamott

Sadly, for many students, the world and school teach them to be really harsh critics and to have little confidence in their writing. You might think of "good" writers sometimes in ways that really have nothing to do with what makes writing powerful. Error-free writing, for instance, doesn't necessarily move someone. Research on adult learning and on how writers develop establishes that, because improvement and skill development doesn't happen in a straight line with only forward progress. When you challenge yourself—whether as a mathematician, writer, pianist, or something else—to take on more complex and challenging tasks, you are likely to start making mistakes you wouldn't make if you took on a simpler task. This is simply the nature of learning and human development.

The point is, getting better at writing and growing as a writer often results in messier or worse writing along the way. Just like anything, if you are taking risks and challenging yourself, you're going to stumble a bit. A toddler doesn't start running laps after their first few steps across the kitchen. But from an early age, writing for school is judged as a product and students don't always get a lot of coaching or guidance on the writing process. They are asked to *produce* writing on demand, and then are graded and evaluated on it. They often don't understand exactly why they got the evaluations they received or what they did that led to those results. It also is sometimes unclear as to why some writing is evaluated as effective and some is not.

Sitting at your computer, writing an opening line and then deleting it because "it doesn't sound good" is a great way to never get started on writing your ideas. Seeing writing as something more complex than a formula or a set of perfectly executed rules is one way to relieve yourself of this self-imposed expectation to create something "perfect." It is also essential to remember that there are many stages to writing, and "getting started" takes different forms, depending on the project at hand. For example, gathering and organizing resources, reading and synthesizing information on your topic, and outlining your ideas as they develop are all important parts of the writing process, and they all count.

In Your Own Words

7.10

Reflect on one of your top writing experiences. What were you writing (a letter, an email, an essay, a poem, a group project, a grocery list, a to-do list) and what made this writing experience a positive, rewarding, or pleasurable one? Next, reflect on a negative writing experience. What was it and what made it frustrating or otherwise unpleasant? What do you know about yourself as a writer, drawing on these experiences?

SECTION **7.3**   # You Are a Writer

I need an hour alone before dinner, with a drink, to go over what I've done that day. I can't do it late in the afternoon because I'm too close to it. So, I spend this hour taking things out and putting other things in. Then I start the next day by redoing all of what I did the day before, following these evening notes. When I'm really working, I don't like to go out or have anybody to dinner, because then I lose the hour. If I don't have the hour, and start the next day with just some bad pages and nowhere to go, I'm in low spirits. Another thing I need to do, when I'm near the end of the book, is sleep in the same room with it. That's one reason I go home to Sacramento to finish things. Somehow the book doesn't leave you when you're asleep right next to it. —Joan Didion (Parker, 2018)

Joan Didion had her first novel published in 1963 and has had something published in just about every form and genre of writing since then, from news articles to memoir to fiction to screenplays. She has fashioned a routine that maximizes her productivity, as well as her peace of mind and the quality of her work. Along with where and when, it is important to be aware of what type of environment helps you write, or prevents you from writing.

The key to being a confident and capable writer is taking charge of your writing process by developing routines that work for you, and knowing when and where to seek support. This requires knowing yourself as a writer and developing your own habits rather than adopting someone else's process. For some writers, absolute isolation is important. For others, music or noise is necessary. For others, having people around is really key even if not to talk with but just as company in the background as the writer writes. Some writers need particular types of pens or notebooks. Others need specific reference books around them. It is also really helpful to know what kind of routine and rituals help you focus and relax, so you can write. (See **Figure 7.2**.)

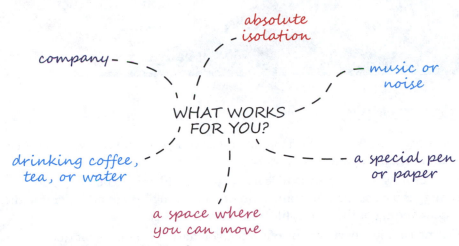

Figure 7.2 What Works for You?

In Your Own Words

7.11

In the next couple of days, using your journal, try writing in three very different locations and at different times of day. Maybe a busy café, at night, in your bedroom, when you're angry, at a park, right when you wake up, etc. Reflect on how each of those places/times/states of mind worked for you as a writer. Be prepared to hand in or share with a peer your three What's, Where's, When's, Why's, and How's (computer, phone, pen and paper, etc.) and the success/ failure of these three writing attempts.

Takeaways

▸ College writing is a new horizon for you as you grow and become confident in, and proud of, your own writing.

▸ A writer uses writing/words to learn, explore, and create meaning and feeling, as well as ideas to connect to others through them and increase their understanding of the world, life, or a subject or idea.

▸ Writing isn't just part of your life when you have an assignment due. You practice writing every day through a variety of mediums.

▸ Writing is a process that requires time and effort and involves writing what Anne Lamott calls a "s@#ty first draft," seeking feedback, and revising in order to make it the best it can be.

▸ You are a writer.

Takeaways on Your Terms

Describe one critical moment and one sticking point in this chapter for you. That is, when did you have an "A-ha!" moment of insight? Also, cite a moment or idea that you didn't quite connect with, or want to hear or talk more about.

In Your Own Words: Keep. Quit. Start.

Having read this chapter, what are some things about your mindset concerning your writing that you want to keep? Quit? Start? These "things" could be habits, actions, mindset/ways of thinking, activities, rules, or structures. Write all these down in your journal.

Right this moment, think of yourself as a writer. What about yourself will you need to keep believing in regarding your abilities? What about yourself will you need to quit believing? What about yourself will you need to start believing?

If you were to zoom in on a few of your past experiences as a writer, what are some things you would keep? Quit? Start? You may want to consider the steps you used to start writing, the ways you revised (or didn't revise) your writing, the ways you asked for feedback, or even the place you chose to write.

Chapter 7 Assignment: Written Communication in the Workplace

Goals of the Assignment

To broaden your understanding of what type of writing occurs in either your major or in a potential future work setting. To connect with a person in your major or potential future work setting and interview them on the type of writing they do.

Steps of the Assignment

1. Identify a person who works in either the department of your major (or potential major) or a person who works in a potential future work setting.
2. Reach out to that person, asking if you can have 15 to 25 minutes of their time to ask them about the types of writing they do in the context of their work life.
3. Have a conversation with your contact person about the kinds of writing that occurs, as well as strategies to be successful in these types of writing. This will include the different kinds of writing found in the workplace, such as emails, memos, grant applications, newsletters, donor letters, protocols, as well as web content, social media, etc.
4. Write up a summary and final reflection of your conversation. Your writing in this assignment should be conversational, informational, and descriptive. Please include a brief introduction and conclusion to your final reflection.
5. Be sure to include where (you had the conversation), when (date and time), who (the contact person was, including their title and work or faculty relation to you), what (the specific goals for the conversation were), and why (you chose this contact).

What You Need to Hand In

Your final report on your interview (500–750 words).

Writing in College

> " *How do you write? You write, man, you write, that's how, and you do it the way the old English walnut tree puts forth leaf and fruit every year by the thousands... If you practice an art faithfully, it will make you wise, and most writers can use a little wising up.* —William Saroyan
>
> *You don't start out writing good stuff. You start out writing crap and thinking it's good stuff, and then gradually you get better at it. That's why I say one of the most valuable traits is persistence.* —Octavia E. Butler "

In Your Own Words

8.1

Using your journal, spend 10 minutes reflecting on your impressions of college writing. What are your concerns, hopes, expectations, and worries regarding it? In what ways do you feel prepared, and in what ways do you feel unprepared? Why? What is your reaction to Octavia Butler's description of the writing process shown at the beginning of this chapter—that persistence is critical in writing and that crappy writing is part of the process? Do you feel confident in your writing process? What do you hope to improve about your writing in college?

Introduction to Writing in College

An important aspect of writing, not only in college but in your future career path, is understanding the writing style that is appropriate for a given writing task or situation at hand. For example, you may be writing a report, giving presentations, applying for a job, or corresponding with collaborators via email or social media. Why not start a practice of awareness of how you currently use the written word in order to be better prepared once you graduate?

You can practice this now by noticing how the writing differs in the texts you read from one class to another, in terms of style, tone, form or format, voice, language, use of evidence, and the types of evidence. Notice how credibility is established and how arguments are constructed. For example, the style of lab report writing is not narrative—it is about clear, direct description. The more you notice the style used, the more you will be able to steer your communication into that style and change between styles easily. This concept is known as *attunement to audience and context*.

You are practicing written communication when you send emails to your instructors or messages via social media to your friends or peers. You implicitly adapt your communication style to that particular context and you strategize how to compose your communication effectively given the audience and form. For example: Is your message formal, with greetings and salutations? Is it informal, with abbreviations and emojis? Do you go through multiple stages of writing when you communicate person-to-person in this way? Do you go back and read through the message before sending it to be sure it says what you want it to say? You have already learned to strategize as a writer when working in different media and contexts. This may be something you now naturally do in your daily writing tasks, and it isn't something you even notice yourself doing.

All of these are learned strategies. You have learned how to attune your communication through trial and error. We will ask you to bring awareness to the strategies you use so as to discover new strategies, deepen existing strategies, or even let go of unnecessary strategies to better your writing.

College assignments often ask you to do hard things, with topics you are not an expert in—and, quite honestly, professors don't always present the information in the clearest way.

This chapter presents two Case Studies of critical moments that were experienced by first-year students as they tackled real writing assignments during their initial year of college. The first Critical Moment Case Study involves a paper from a history survey course; the second Critical Moment Case Study is a research-based project from an introductory science course. We will first look at what the student did, and what her thoughts and processes were. Then, we will look at how she would have changed her process after looking back on the assignment.

Illustrative case studies do not present exemplary or best or worst models. Instead, they present typical ways that things happen, and then situate those examples within some background, reflection, and postexperience analysis. In this chapter, we offer these Case Studies to explore, analyze, and compare with your own experiences of academic writing. Part of writing in academic settings is being prepared for whatever is given so you can take it and run with it, and successfully complete the assignment.

These case studies also illustrate the value of revisiting and evaluating one's learning process. This is a step that is often overlooked by instructors and students, but it is critical to developing competency and retaining skills. It can apply to tests (i.e., reviewing them afterward and planning for future tests based on what was learned), as well as papers or written projects, which are modeled here, and group projects and other activities.

THINK ABOUT IT

When you receive a writing assignment, what is the first thing you do? What aspects of your process are consistent? Which vary? Which parts are you most proud of? Which do you want to work on?

No matter what people tell you, words and ideas can change the world.
—Robin Williams as John Keating in *Dead Poets Society* (1989)

Case Studies of Critical Moments with Writing Assignments

CRITICAL MOMENT
Student—Case Study 1: History Paper

This first case study comes from a student in an introduction-level history class; the assignment is a medium-length paper. As you read the case studies, write little stars or make a note next to important, relevant, or useful ideas. Later, review your marks to get a sense of what stood out to you and which ideas you want to use for your next writing project.

The Assignment

Everyone must turn in the paper by *noon* on Monday, April 24. Papers should be turned in by sending them to me as attachments to emails in Microsoft Word format. The paper is 1500–2500 words long (5–8 pages). The paper's font should be no greater than 12, and margins no more than one inch per side.

Your paper will answer the question: How has there been continuity and change in history since the era of *Muller v. Oregon*? This is actually a very big question. To refine it, you will focus on one aspect of the reading we do in the *Muller v. Oregon* book (or perhaps one reading) and trace how that aspect plays out in one *state-level* case (trial or appellate level) that you find from the years 1920–2019.

The assignment has three dimensions: 1) historical research using a legal database to find an appropriate case; 2) historical interpretation using documents from two different periods to make claims about how things change and how they stay the same; and 3) historical writing—making an argument that is based on historical sources and that informs readers about the past in interesting and engaging ways.

THINK ABOUT IT

What stands out to you in this assignment? What words stick with you or seem important? Does anything confuse you? Is there any key information missing?

Student's Notes About the Context of the Assignment

Returning to look at this assignment is honestly kind of harrowing for me. I wrote this paper only a few months ago, and I still not only remember but *feel* how stressed it made me and how much I disliked the process of writing it, as well as the final product I turned in. One of my goals in college is to feel responsible for, and proud of, all my writing and only turn in papers that represent my best effort. That goal was not met with this assignment. That's how writing is sometimes— no matter how hard I try, sometimes I'm just not able to feel great about every assignment.

This was a class in my major that I was excited to take because of the subject and the professor. There were only 20 students in the class and I went in expecting an interactive and challenging class. But the professor's style of teaching was one of lecturing for most of class, which left little room for student questions or interaction. This isn't my preferred or optimal way to learn in a small class, especially because the readings were dense, complicated, and interesting. So I wanted an opportunity to break them down with people and to hear different perspectives. The lack of opportunity to discuss the ideas and readings meant we weren't held accountable for paying attention in class or doing the readings. This made for a disengaging environment for me.

In terms of my own context that semester, I was really busy. I had a full schedule of classes, plus work, sports, and some activities. I had multiple other assignments due around the same time as this one. I also was struggling with a bad habit of pushing the work I was least interested in or confident about to the bottom of the heap and saving it for "later." "Later" usually translated to some major procrastination and ignoring this essay until closer to the deadline than I should have.

Student: Looking Back at the Context

Now I see that sometimes the projects you want to do the least are the ones you need to make sure you start first because they will take extra time and will be hard to mobilize yourself to work on. (See **Figure 8.1**.) If I could go back, I would force myself to take even just one hour to jot down ideas immediately

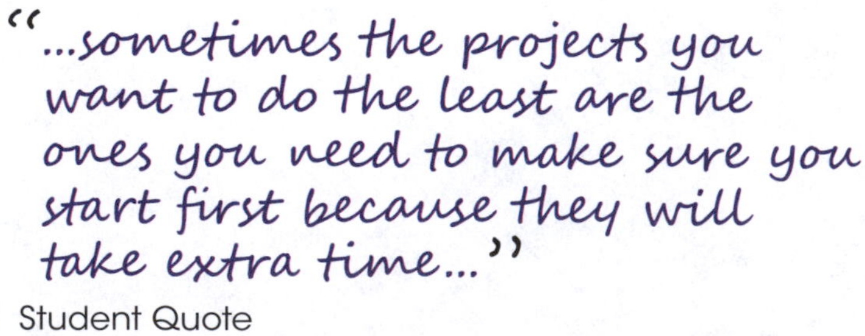

> "...sometimes the projects you want to do the least are the ones you need to make sure you start first because they will take extra time..."

Figure 8.1 Student Quote

after it was assigned, in order to get any brainstorming, writing, or ideas down on the page. Forcing yourself to do any of this type of thinking and start eliminating possibilities makes writing the actual essay much easier and less overwhelming.

Student: My First Reaction upon Reading the Assignment

I learned a long time ago that essay prompts can vary quite a lot. Some are clear and direct, some have a lot of text and instruction but don't make things clear, and some don't have enough information and instruction, which leaves you guessing. When I receive an assignment, the first thing I do is force myself to actually read through it to make sure I don't miss any information. Phrases like "use MLA citations" or "must be at least five pages" are integral aspects of the product you will be delivering.

I began by reading through and annotating it, circling and underlining important information. (See **Figure 8.2.**) This is helpful so that when I refer back to the prompt for clarification while writing, my eye is immediately drawn to the most important information. It's important to at least get down the basic parameters such as prompt, length, and type of argument. This essay clearly had one question to answer, I knew I needed to use a court case of my choosing to prove my argument, and I had approximately 2000 words in which to do it. Even

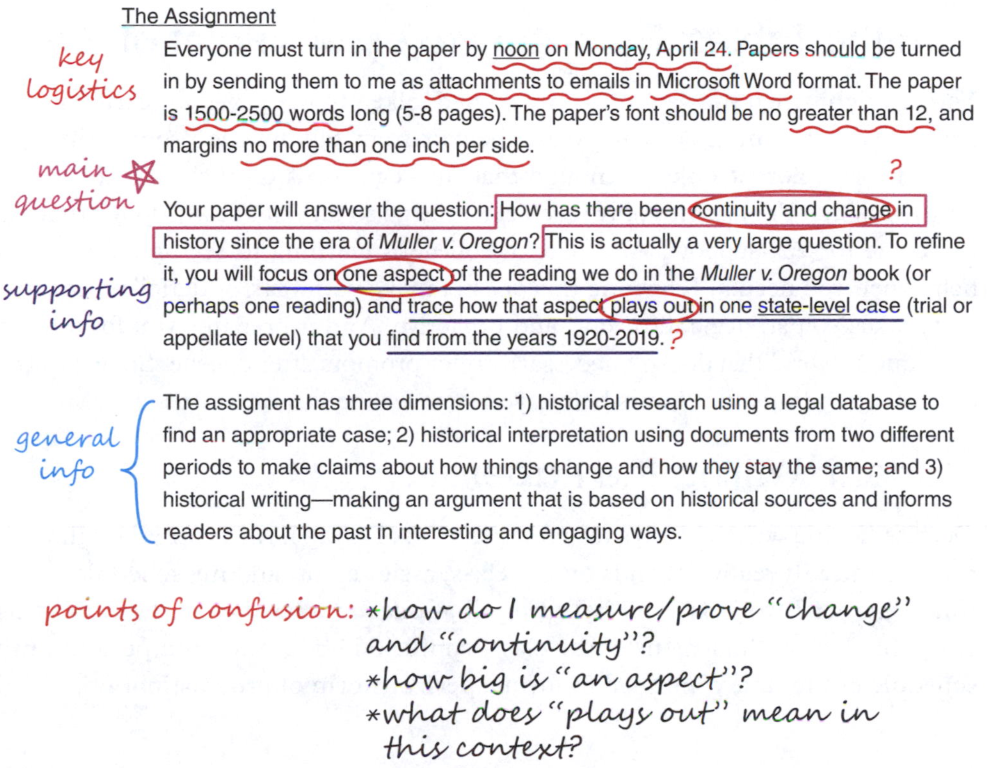

<u>The Assignment</u>

key logistics — Everyone must turn in the paper by <u>noon</u> on Monday, April 24. Papers should be turned in by sending them to me as <u>attachments to emails in Microsoft Word format</u>. The paper is <u>1500-2500 words</u> long (5-8 pages). The paper's font should be no <u>greater than 12</u>, and margins no more than one inch per side.

main question ★ — Your paper will answer the question: How has there been continuity and change in ? history since the era of *Muller v. Oregon*? This is actually a very large question. To refine it, you will focus on one aspect of the reading we do in the *Muller v. Oregon* book (or *supporting info* — perhaps one reading) and trace how that aspect plays out in one state-level case (trial or appellate level) that you find from the years 1920-2019. ?

general info { The assigment has three dimensions: 1) historical research using a legal database to find an appropriate case; 2) historical interpretation using documents from two different periods to make claims about how things change and how they stay the same; and 3) historical writing—making an argument that is based on historical sources and informs readers about the past in interesting and engaging ways.

points of confusion: *how do I measure/prove "change" and "continuity"? *how big is "an aspect"? *what does "plays out" mean in this context?

Figure 8.2 Example of Annotated Assignment

when there's a lot to read, it's important to remember that the professor put all this information in for at least some reason, so even if it doesn't look important, I make sure to give it at least a once-through read.

In addition to circling and underlining, I put question marks throughout to signify that I need to either ask someone, consult a resource, or think about it and work through it myself. The prompt left a lot of room for confusion and ambiguity. The main question was very vague, and I didn't know exactly how this question was meant to be answered. Additionally, I was unsure on what type of support I needed to employ in order to back up the answer to such a broad question.

Student: Looking Back Now at My First Reaction and First Steps

Looking back, I know that I should've gone to the professor's office hours early on to talk about this essay. As a general rule, confusion about the words used in the prompt would be best fixed by talking to the person who not only wrote the assignment but would also be grading my essay. But I kept telling myself that I would seek feedback once I had done work on the essay. Ultimately, I felt embarrassed and intimidated to go to the professor's office hours because I felt like I should have done more work on the assignment at each point. If I were to redo this, I would have set a goal like "choose court case and draft basic thesis to present to professor three weeks before the deadline."

Turn the Tables: From the Professor's Point of View

You are right when you say you wish you had talked to the professor earlier in the process, because most students really benefit from talking the prompt through a few times before it sinks in enough that they can focus on their argument and writing. When I'm teaching, my reach can only go so far—it's really up to students to decide to seek support. And part of college is learning to seek guidance and help when you need it. Knowing this doesn't make you weak or deficient. It actually makes you strategic, efficient, and proactive. And it prepares you for a more ambiguous world that doesn't necessarily offer prompts after college. So, get in the habit of attending office hours before you start feeling lost or confused.

Student: Writing the Paper

Despite having written essays for multiple years, I don't have a formal method or process I use. It really depends on the class, assignment, and my schedule at the time whether I work on it bit-by-bit or all at once in a few hectic days. For this essay, my lack of enjoyment of the class, confusion about the prompt, and busy schedule at the time combined to form a perfect storm of procrastination.

COMMUNICATION SITUATION

Visiting a professor's office hours can be intimidating because it's so unlike other communication situations we find ourselves in. Unlike going to the doctor's office or even going for a job interview, there is no standard script that we are familiar with that we can follow. Also, you'll need to take the lead in terms of topics to cover because it is based on your questions and concerns. Before you go to office hours, have a couple questions ready, know what your goals are, and take a moment to think through the event as a communication situation.

- How is this different from an impromptu conversation with a friend or classmate? What do you need to keep in mind?
- What do you want to communicate to the professor about yourself as a student and person? What do you want them to know?
- What questions about college or specific classes can they help you with?

In class, our professor encouraged us to utilize the freedom of the prompt to write about something we found really interesting and tailor it to what we would enjoy learning about. In theory, this definitely sounded like a nice idea and a great opportunity, but for me this generated so much stress as I struggled to rein in my ideas and settle on one. I really just wanted him to say "write about this and make an argument about this" so I wouldn't have to do so much brainstorming and narrowing of ideas. I successfully used the resources provided by the professor to find a number of cases which seemed like I could write about them. My actual interest in the cases took a back seat as I tried to discern which would give me the easiest to write or most straightforward argument. I took much too long to narrow down my ideas and kept second-guessing which one would work the best.

Student: Looking Back Now at My Writing Process on This Paper

Looking back, I should've just chosen one and started writing rather than spending so much time trying to get my choice "just right" to support an argument that would be easiest to make. Sometimes, you just need to make a choice and go with it, which will either go well and be the final choice, or will be enough of a disaster for you to be forced to choose something else. But either outcome is better than spending too long weighing pros and cons and being paralyzed by choice.

I put this essay off until close to the deadline because I had been just plain avoiding it, partially because the prompt was so general that it didn't inspire any thoughts or excitement for me. Because of this, none of my ideas from brainstorming really spoke to me, so I found it hard to find the motivation to write. A rushed writing process is the worst kind, as I have repeatedly found out, because you keep having to make choices like "Do I have time to switch to this new idea or is it too late and I need to settle?" which never yields the writing you'll be most proud of.

Making at least some choices about the paper—whether it's the topic or approach or a rough idea of your argument—soon after the essay has been assigned makes a huge difference! Maybe even doing just a little research right away will give you a sense of where you might want to go. Or going to your professor's office hours right away to discuss some of your ideas could get you started in a productive way. Then, even if you give yourself a less-than-optimal amount of time to work on it, you will at least have a basis from which to start.

I made the mistake of showing a draft of this essay to my friend from another school a couple days before it was due because I needed some last-minute help. This ended up being a poor choice because I had to explain the prompt and my argument for context so much that I felt like I was wasting my time when I should've been working on the essay. Her feedback was hard to take because a lot of it seemed like the wrong ideas to me, but I didn't know whether to trust hers or my own ideas, which was a conflict I didn't need when I was already stressed about completing the essay at the last minute.

Turn the Tables: From the Professor's Point of View

Your instinct to show someone the draft was a good one, but unfortunately they learned what happens if you don't choose the reviewer or the timing of the feedback carefully. The writing center would have been the *perfect* place to go when you got stressed and pressed for time. Writing center consultants are trained in and skilled at working with assignments from around the university, and you don't usually need to spend a lot of time explaining the prompt to them. Students are often self-conscious about seeking help or support close to a deadline. Many feel like they have not done enough, started early enough, or reached an adequate stage to "get help." But *any stage* is a good stage to seek input if you want some input. (See **Figure 8.3**.) Writing Center consultants are trained to work with writers at various stages from brainstorming to organizing to research to final edits. The Writing Center is also a place where you will get zero judgment and really helpful advice from seasoned writers and writing coaches. They know how to help you pull something off quickly and will give you objective, well-supported advice you can trust. *If I could require one thing of all of my students, it would be to regularly utilize the Writing Center. Beyond college, this is also relevant because people who thrive and are successful know how and when to seek and use support. That is a sign of strength and self-awareness, not weakness.*

"*Any stage is a good stage to seek input...*"

Figure 8.3 Instructor Quote

Student's Final Takeaways on This History Paper Experience

I had a few main takeaways from this experience. Firstly, I never want to write while disliking the writing I'm doing. Writing is such a vulnerable and personal activity in which you're putting your name on something and saying "these are my ideas" for someone else to interpret. So, when you don't feel good about the product, it feels pointless. I can definitely accomplish this goal by holding myself to a higher standard of really believing in my arguments and putting in the work to write things I can be proud of and feel good about turning in. A lot of times, I try to find the argument that's easiest to prove or least controversial, just for the sake of making the assignment as doable as possible, but I've realized that by doing this I'm preventing myself from being truly personal and vulnerable in my work. In the future, I'm going to try to allow myself to really think about how I will use each assignment to express my full and true opinions on something, and explore things I'm interested in.

Secondly, resources are everything! I have learned this over a long period of time because it takes a while to really get in the habit of utilizing the resources available to you. Reaching out for help, whether formal or casual, isn't easy and doesn't come naturally to everyone (certainly not to me). The process of this essay would've been totally different had I utilized my professor earlier on, classmates throughout, and the Writing Center at the end. Each of these would have helped me to develop my ideas and not end up with writing that had only been seen by my eyes. Ultimately, this is because if you are your only editor, you have no idea how your ideas sound and how clear (or not) they are to someone not in your head. Getting input from someone outside your head forces you to really work to hone your ideas so they aren't just communicated in a way that works for you, they are shaped to communicate these ideas to others.

TRY THIS   8.2

Before you even get your next assignment, try writing down all the resources you have available to you so you can better utilize them. Start by writing down the resources you know—for instance, your professor, the Writing Center, the Purdue OWL website, the Public Library, etc. What are the hours that are available to you? Are there online options (for example, does your school's library offer a "chat with a librarian" option on their website or do library inquiries have to take place face-to-face)?

Then, expand into how you might learn about more resources. Perhaps your professor could direct you to an expert in the field you are writing about. Maybe a librarian can direct you to a source you hadn't considered. Keep this list in your writing assignment document so you see it regularly.

Be prepared to share these resources and create a larger list with your classmates.

Thirdly, flexibility is a must in college writing. You get asked to do so many different things, whether it be lengths, topics, citations, or types of writing, and you have to be prepared to take on new ones you haven't done before. Prompts give you a set of directions to follow, and you have to be prepared to follow them while also making your own choices about parts of the process you can control.

TRY THIS _____ 8.3

Sometimes the best resources to use are your peers from class. When a prompt is confusing or ambiguous and you don't feel comfortable asking the professor about it, maybe because you think you should understand it or you are intimidated by them, it can be super-helpful to turn to a classmate and say "Hey, do you get this prompt?" With these peers, you can run ideas by each other, be honest about your confusions or annoyances with the prompt, and even edit each other's essays once you have drafts.

CRITICAL MOMENT

Student—Case Study 2: Biology Research Assignment

This second Case Study comes from a student in an introduction-level biology class; the assignment is a research-based synthesis assignment.

Intro to Biology Assignment:

Employing scientific criticism and literacy; Intro to Biology

Pick a topic in science and find six full articles published within the last 10 years on that topic. These articles could be news articles, non-peer-reviewed journals, and/or peer- reviewed scientific articles.

Determine the following for each article. Be sure to answer each question fully.

1. Article name, journal/website source, date published. (2 points)
2. Provide a weblink, PDF file, or html text. Scans are also acceptable. Must provide the full article; it is not acceptable to provide only the abstract. (2 points)
3. What search engine did you use for the article? How quickly did you find this article? Was it at the top of the list? (2 points)
4. Is the article peer-reviewed? How do you know? (2 points)
5. If not peer-reviewed, do they reference peer-reviewed materials? If peer-reviewed, is it original research or just a summary/recap of findings in the field? (2 points)
6. Are the findings sensationalized? Why or why not? (2 points)
7. What could be done to improve this article (readability, accuracy, relevant pictures/figures)? (2 points)

CRITICAL MOMENT

Student—Case Study 2: Biology Research Assignment (cont.)

Overall Question (Only Answer Once in the Assignment):

Looking at all the articles as a whole, what do they tell you about this topic, and are there conflicting interpretations? Do you think that their agreement/disagreement is related to their "quality" of publication? (16 points) ("Quality" could be determined by peer-reviewed vs. not, sensationalized vs. not, and reputation of publishing journal/site.)

Write up the answers to these questions in your own words. These write-ups, as well as links/copies of the articles reviewed, are due by the date mentioned earlier. Avoid using direct quotes and paraphrase instead. Documents submitted on Moodle must be in .doc, .docx, .pdf, or .rtf format (no Pages files, we cannot open them properly without a Mac; select "Export to PDF"). Send digital copies to the link on the Moodle page where this document was posted.

Total possible points: 100

Notes:

- Use search engines such as Google, Google Scholar, Pubmed, Web of Science, EBSCO, and others.
- Some scholarly articles may ask you to pay for them. Don't pay!
- On a related note, be sure you are accessing the full article. This is particularly relevant for scholarly articles. Some search engines produce only an abstract for scholarly articles, which is a one-paragraph summary of the whole article. This is not the whole article, and you should find the full version if possible. If not, search for a different article that you can access fully.
- Write-up answers should be full sentences, but the answers do not have to be more than a few sentences. The final "overall" question about the group of articles should be answered in a paragraph or two.
- The assignment does not have to be written in paragraph/essay format. It is best to answer the questions in numbered format for each article.

THINK ABOUT IT

What stands out to you in this assignment? What words stick with you or seem important? Does anything confuse you? Is there any key information missing?

Student's Notes About the Context of the Assignment

I took Intro to Biology because I am fascinated by this subject, but I had never studied it before in a class setting. I went in with low confidence because of my lack of experience in STEM classes. This professor was one I really liked; he was funny in class and explained concepts very well while running a well-organized class. The class itself offered little opportunity to discuss with classmates or interact at all, so everyone pretty much showed up at the beginning and sat silently, then left at the end without ever talking to each other. Because of this, there was a distinct lack of class community.

This was our first large assignment for the class, so I was totally unsure of how strict of a grader the professor was, and what type of writing was required in this academic setting. It was early in the semester, so I didn't have many assignments in my other classes and therefore had a lot of free time to devote to this.

The process of doing this assignment was frustrating, because I was constantly thinking about whether I was writing enough, or whether I was writing too much. In theory, the more you write, the more you get out of it, but being realistic, I was annoyed by the idea that I might do twice the amount of work for the same grade that I could've received with less effort. This was during a time when my other classes didn't have many assignments, so I had a lot of time to devote to this and struggled to use it efficiently.

Student: Looking Back on the Context

In order to combat this unproductive usage of my time, I should have set parameters for myself like "only work for two hours at a time" and "if it's taking too long to get an answer, leave a note for yourself and skip to the next one."

Student: My First Reactions

I received this assignment the first week of class. Immediately I was stressed trying to figure out how long it would take me to do, how in-depth I needed to go, and how hard a grader this professor was. Reading the assignment with its enumerated points and simple questions, it immediately reminded me of assignments I've had in the past which felt like a simple checklist of regurgitating information for your professor. The fact that you receive two points for writing down the title, source, and publish date and you also receive two points for expressing your thoughts on how this article could be improved was frustrating to me. Aspects like this made it feel like the professor didn't put a lot of thought into the assignment and made it feel a bit arbitrary.

On the upside, the clear enumeration made it very straightforward and left little room for ambiguity about what questions I was answering. I knew what structure to use and exactly what information I was providing. My main questions going in were related to how I can be sure something is peer-reviewed, what counts as a "full" answer to these types of questions, and how broad a topic I was allowed to choose. These simple and easy-to-answer questions felt too small to go in and talk to the professor about; I felt I should probably already know the answer. So, instead of talking to the professor, I agonized throughout over these aspects and used Google and guessing to determine what the answers to each of them were.

Student: Looking Back at My First Reactions

This assignment is a great example of one where it's helpful to go to the professor right after it's assigned and ask these simple questions. This provides an opportunity to meet the professor face-to-face early on in the class, demonstrate initiative, and get these small questions answered quickly and definitively.

Student: Writing the Paper

My initial feelings of frustration with the structure of this prompt and my confusion on how to execute it did not create a winning process for me. But I tried to begin by implementing some structure. To plot out my first steps, I began with brainstorming and finding sources to see which topics would be more or less challenging in terms of available materials. Realistically, I knew this was the type of assignment that one could probably get done in a matter of days rather than the two weeks we were given. But I know that I tend to spend more time than necessary trying to make sure I do something well. So, I started by setting some goals: Find all of my sources by four days before the due date, and be finished writing the day before the due date so I could edit it some.

These goals ended up not serving me well because I learned that it wasn't simply a matter of finding 10 sources all at once and then writing about them all at once. Each time I found a source, I had to determine whether it had the necessary information and so I naturally began to complete the writing as I was vetting the sources. So, it turned out the pattern was more like: Find a source, answer the questions about it, take notes for the final question, then find the next source and repeat. So, I ended up throwing away those goals and instead following this system. For this reason, I was still finding sources up until the day before the paper was due.

Ultimately, it entailed a lot of searching for articles, a lot of googling about peer review and how it works, and a decent amount of writing time to make sure I felt good about all my wording. Even though the assignment was presented as such, I didn't want my work to feel like a mere checklist of regurgitated information. I wasn't clear on the norms and practices of writing for a STEM assignment, because I'm mostly used to writing in humanities classes. So, the whole time I was also wrestling a little with what wording was most correct, whether using more elaboration would be considered unnecessary, or if certain words would be too vague. Ultimately, I went with my instincts and wrote in the most concise and straightforward way possible, which ended up being sort of liberating. It was very different from the writing I'm used to, so I enjoyed the challenge.

The really challenging part ended up being the process of finding the sources. This is because medical articles are really hard to get access to online. The majority of articles I found via Google asked me to pay to see the whole thing upon opening, which our professor advised us not to do. This was really frustrating and led me to use some sources I knew probably didn't fulfill the prompt the best, just for the sake of having the number of required sources.

Student: Looking Back Now at My Process of Writing This Paper

Looking back, this is an example of where I probably should've asked my classmates, "Hey, are you also having lots of trouble finding sources fully accessible online?" to understand whether it was something I was missing or my struggle was justified. I felt nervous to ask because I assumed no one else was having as much trouble as me and didn't want to have an awkward interaction. But this type of question would've been both an opportunity to connect with my classmates and get clarity on the assignment, which realistically was lower stakes than I was making it out to be.

Unfortunately, I'm the kind of person who will agonize and stress over something no matter how challenging or in-depth, because I want to make sure I am doing it properly. So in the end, I spent much more time on this assignment than I should have because I wasn't sure whether I was "doing it right."

Turn the Tables: From the Professor's Point of View

I literally cringe when I read about your agony with this assignment, because I wonder how many times I've caused that same kind of agony for my students. Frequently, there is a missing piece in what professors want a student to learn and what we actually ask for in the assignment guide. This makes assignments a lot more complicated! This professor is hoping that you learn how to find different types of sources and analyze their credibility using a critical lens, but doesn't spell that out clearly. *This assignment, as written, explains process but not purpose.* Part of the problem for teachers is that we need to always remember that even though we taught this content last semester, it's brand new to the students we're teaching this semester. Identifying the specifics of an assignment that confuse you or that you don't understand (like this student does throughout this case) will help you generate a great list of questions to ask both the professor and classmates. Statements like, "I'm spending a lot of time searching for articles" will prompt your professor to direct you to the resources (like the library) that she uses.

Student: My Takeaways on the Biology Paper Project

Looking back, this assignment wasn't satisfying and didn't feel like my best work, but in a completely different way than my history paper. The main thing that kept me from feeling satisfied was that it felt like a scavenger hunt rather than an assignment to promote learning. I felt that the amount of effort I expended doing it was not proportional to the amount I learned. Easy assignments can be a relief or a nice break, but it's frustrating to me when they still take up enough of my time that they're no longer "easy."

When I got my grade back on this assignment, it was clear this had been graded hastily by the instructor's TA. It basically had no comments and simply checkmarks to make sure everything was answered. Because I filled out every step, I got 100%. Now, I'm definitely not complaining about this grade, but I certainly have really mixed feelings about it. The style of grading confirmed for me that I didn't have to do all the stressing and agonizing about the assignment when it was simply a "yes" or "no" to the points on each question. I definitely could've used easier-to-find resources, answered the questions in a more concise way, and not agonized so much over wording. Definitely a relief to get a good grade! But also frustrating because I put in a lot of extra work that I probably didn't need.

This was an important learning experience because it taught me that you have to know the assignment and know yourself. Take the information you're communicated through the prompt and rubric and do your best to fulfill this without going overboard with overthinking. I was lucky that my other classes weren't busy at this time, but if I had been juggling more serious work alongside this assignment, I would have needed to be more efficient with my work.

From the questions, you can completely tell what my professor was getting at: the importance of identifying differences in sources professing scientific conclusions, and their proper usage in different situations. But in order to really reach this goal, more critical questions would need to be included, which go one step further in the interrogation. The assignment asks explicit questions like "How long did it take you to find this source? Was it at the top of the list?" but doesn't go into the implications of this at all, such as the biases involved with the articles that come up first or the value of digging through sources instead of just choosing the top one.

THINK ABOUT IT

How do you typically start a writing assignment? Once you get an assignment, what's the first thing you do? What is your typical first reaction or feeling?

SECTION **8.3**

Your Turn—Use Simple Strategies to Approach an Assignment

In college, you need to experiment with multiple approaches to the core writing process to figure out what works for you. In the following, we offer several simple strategies you can try when approaching a new writing assignment. We encourage you to try them all to see which works best for you in a given assignment or course.

SIMPLE STRATEGIES

Choose an assignment from any course and mirror the student in Part I.

- Walk through the process steps as this student did in Part I by reading the assignment and annotating it.
- Use these annotations to break it down and plan your approach.

SIMPLE STRATEGIES

Ask a classmate to do an assignment check-in together.

- Walk through the assignment together.
- Check in with each other: Do you have a clear and shared understanding of the expectations for this assignment? What questions do each of you have about the assignment and where will you get the answers you need?
- Discuss your approaches to this assignment. How do they differ and how are they similar?

SIMPLE STRATEGIES

Utilize as many avenues for feedback as possible.

- Look at your school's Writing Center website. What services does the Writing Center offer? What are its hours? Where is it located?
- Make an appointment to meet with a Writing Center consultant.
- Think of two other people (e.g., friend, TA, Writing Center staff, professor) you will have read a draft of your next writing project.

🔑 SIMPLE STRATEGIES

Going to office hours can clear up any confusion about an assignment and the instructor's expectations, and also help lay good groundwork as you approach a project. Office hour visits don't have to involve long conversations. It is fine to ask short, specific questions. Once you read through an assignment and start to process it, try to come up with direct questions that might help you bridge the disconnect. Here are a few:

- Is there a sample assignment that we could review, or an entry/annotation that we could see as a visual guide to the format you're expecting?
- I'm trying to get a sense of how much time this assignment will take. What do you think makes up the bulk of the work for most students: finding the articles, reading them, or writing about them?
- Are there any campus resources you know of that could help me figure out how to identify peer-reviewed articles? (Yes! The library can help. Librarians are amazing and so incredibly helpful with all things research-related.)

These are just a few strategies you can try out as you create your own intentional approach to writing. College will provide plenty of opportunities for you to keep experimenting with different approaches. As we close this section, we want to encourage you to always allow yourself the opportunity to reflect on your process after completing an assignment. It's so tempting to turn the paper in, and then forget about it. "Whew. It's done. What a relief!" But this is a missed opportunity to take a moment to reflect on what worked for you and what didn't. Each assignment is a chance to make your writing even more your own and catapult you into your next assignment better and more capable.

Takeaways

- When given an assignment, pay attention to the parameters and instructions. Don't overthink and make assumptions about what the professor wants or what is "good." If the assignment says "write a few sentences," then writing a few sentences is sufficient.
- Set boundaries for the amount of time to work on something. Setting aside chunks of time to fulfill specific goals will result in a more efficient work process.
- An awareness of one's habits, attitudes, and mindsets around writing will support the writing process and give it a chance to grow and evolve.
- Completing a writing assignment is never a straight line, so an ability to be flexible in approaching each prompt will help the process.
- As soon as a prompt is received, take an action, even if it's the tiniest thing.
- Writing support can be found in many places. Utilize what is available at any point in the process.

Takeaway on Your Terms

- What advice about writing would you give to other students just beginning college?

In Your Own Words: Keep. Quit. Start.

Think about some of the habits you developed in how you approached and planned to complete writing assignments. Think about the next time you are given a writing assignment in class. Having read this chapter, reflect on which of those habits serve you well and how they serve you. Which parts of your habitual approach don't serve your needs and should be discarded or left behind? What new strategies are you most excited to start using? What resources will you try out and why? Write about all this in your journal.

Chapter 8 Assignment

Goals of the Assignment

To practice using all four of the simple strategies outlined in this chapter with a goal of noticing which helps you the most.

Steps of the Assignment

1. Choose an assignment that is due in the next two–four weeks.

   Go through all four simple strategies as you start to unpack and work through the assignment.

   Simple Strategy #1

   Walk through the process steps as the student did in Part I. Read the assignment. Annotate it. Begin to think about how you can use your annotations to break it down and plan your approach.

   Simple Strategy #2

   Ask a classmate to do an assignment check-in together. Walking through the assignment together and checking in about whether you have the key information you need to proceed will be useful for both of you and is an important first step in completing the assignment effectively.

   Simple Strategy #3

   Look at your school's Writing Center website. What does it offer? What are its hours? Make an appointment to meet with a Writing Center consultant. Arrange for two people (e.g., friend, TA, Writing Center staff, professor) to read a draft of your next writing project.

   Simple Strategy #4

   Going to office hours can clear up any confusion about an assignment and the instructor's expectations, and can also help lay good groundwork as you approach a project. Office hour visits don't have to involve long conversations. It is fine to ask short, specific questions. Once you read through an assignment and start to process it, try to come up with direct questions that might help you bridge the disconnect.

What You Need to Hand In

Write one paragraph for each approach, summarizing what you did and what you gained from doing it.

Tools for Managing Your Writing Process and Projects

Amy Lee (one of this book's authors) and Chris Gallagher wrote a book for writing and English teachers called *Teaching Writing That Matters*. The advice they offered teachers in that book also aptly introduces the Process Toolbox:

- Self-assess your writing at different stages: learning to really see your own writing as it is in process is critical to the revision process. Practice doing self-assessments at different stages. Build it into the process.
- Practice project maintenance: break your writing into doable chunks and workable timelines. Set clear goals and expectations for each project.
- Generate *at least two drafts*. This doesn't mean edit a draft; it means revise as in re-see and rewrite and shape your work into a new form. It should be clear by now that none of us "spits out pristine first drafts." Every writer needs to "try out ideas, shape their meaning, develop their purposes," and work to revise for the audience. This is all impossible to do in one sitting or with some polishing (Gallagher & Lee, 2008, p. 120).
- Treat revision as re-seeing. Seeing again. Revision is not about "fixing" your writing, or just proofreading. Impactful revision requires stepping away from your writing—whether literally taking a break, or asking someone else to read it, or (as Joan Didion described previously in Chapter 7) looking at with an editorial eye and questions and not as your own writing.

- Get feedback at various points. Writers need information from others about their writing to create the best draft. You will need different kinds of information at different points in the process. Sometimes you need to bounce ideas around. Other times you need help pulling apart an illogical ordering of ideas or unpacking what your real thesis or core argument is. Getting the wrong kind of feedback at the wrong time in your process can really stifle you. So be mindful about it.

As was discussed in the two chapters about writing, many writers don't have a systematic, consistent process that they deploy each time they write. Instead, you get an assignment or a task, and you just do it in the time you're given. But in the "just doing it" are a multitude of microdecisions and moments of choice that you may not even be aware of, which are based in habits you've developed over time. Slowing down, taking stock of your process, and experimenting with different tools at different phases of your writing process will give you a greater sense of power over your writing. Play around with the different stages and components: prewriting, generating, planning, revising, getting feedback, editing, polishing. It is really important to work the *whole* process and to make the process work *for* you. Don't confuse generating (such as brainstorming) with drafting, or drafting with revision, or revision with editing, or feedback with the word of God.

Key Stages and Tools of the Writing Process

Planning   TB SECTION **2.1**

The next time you get a writing assignment, take a deep breath, then look at the due date. Then, work backward, imagining how much time you want to spend on each step of the process. Be sure to map out taking time off, so you can gain some perspective. Then, put these times into your calendar and use them as a structure for completing this assignment.

To Seek Feedback or Not to Seek Feedback at the Planning Stage:

Yes! Now is a good time to solicit feedback. Check out the prompt—if you have any questions, email your instructor. Or take a moment to visit the Writing Center to get some assistance in laying out a process and timeline you can use to help you navigate the rest of the writing process.

TB SECTION **2.2**   # Generating

The scariest moment is always just before you start.
—Stephen King (King, Hill, & King, 2020)

In the generating stage, it is really important to be able to free up some of your creative brain to explore, express, and produce without thinking about what it means or how to organize it. Every writing project needs some *generating* time in the process. For some people, it works better to plan first—to make an outline, or set some goals, and then to begin generating. For others, generating—in the form of free-writing perhaps—is a great first step.

But all writers know that part of the process is writing without our regular constraints and the harsh critic voice in one's head, which is constantly telling you whether what you are doing is good or not. If you write your work sentence by sentence, editing as you go, it will take you years to write anything. Writers know that sometimes you have to "vomit" onto a page in order to look back and say "that's not what I want to say at all." Sometimes, it takes writing something you *don't* want, in order to know what you *do* want. And for this reason, writers know when to be critical and when to let loose and let themselves just flow through ideas on paper or screen.

Here, Anne Lamott's idea of the "sh&*ty first draft," which we discuss in Chapter 7 applies. As explained in the chapter, the first draft that any writer produces is not publishable, but through a strong writing process, this can be honed and shaped into a wonderful piece of writing that communicates effectively and successfully. Start with an open mind and let your writing run wild for that first draft before you rein it in and begin to revise and edit it into the work you want it to be.

To Seek Feedback or Not to Seek Feedback at the Generating Stage:

This is probably not a great moment to get some feedback about your ideas, because they are raw and fresh. It's best to let them come directly from you. But it might be helpful to have a few conversations with friends or family about the prompt in case their ideas help generate some new thinking for you.

TB SECTION **2.3**   # Brainstorming

Brainstorming is a great way to get your mind around the task. To brainstorm effectively, it's important to remove the usual gates and doors that refine and restrict the thoughts you let emerge from your brain. This is a perfect time to write down all the ideas that come to mind, without restraint, in order to get your brain working in this direction.

TB TRY THIS

The following are some ideas to use in a brainstorming session.

Brainstorm 1

Imagine your task is to write an essay about a person who has had a significant impact on the person you are becoming. Here is how you might move from brainstorm to honing in on an approach to the piece.

1. List at least 10 people in your life who have had a significant impact on your development or education.
2. Choose one of these people and begin generating material.
3. Describe this person's appearance with as much specificity and detail as you can. What characteristics about this person's physical demeanor stand out?
4. Describe the way this person speaks. How do they sound and how do they look when they speak? Are there characteristic gestures this person uses?
5. Describe this person's demeanor. What is their outward manner? How do they "come off" and why? Do they have certain mannerisms? A certain posture or attitude? How can you tell?
6. List various memories or significant moments that you associate with this person.
7. Recreate a conversation (a dialogue) that you had with this person.
8. Explain how this person would feel about you writing about them.
9. Imagine how your life might have been different without this person.
10. Compare this person to something else—another person, place, or thing and elaborate on that metaphor.
11. List the things this person has taught you or brought to your life.
12. Compare yourself with this person.

Brainstorm 2

Observation is really important for writers. Whether you are observing a text closely, such as a poem or a research article, or observing a phenomenon, observation isn't just looking. Observation is about training yourself to notice, and noticing is about paying attention and about really seeing things you might not otherwise see. Like a researcher in a lab, this involves *training* your eyes and attention. The following is an activity to help you practice.

Observation of Student Spaces

Choose a space where students convene and are expected to hang out.

- Where is the space? How do you arrive and what do you immediately notice?
- What sensory adjectives can you use—for sight, sound, smell, touch, taste?
- Who is there? How are they engaged?
- What happens in this space? How do you know?
- What is the atmosphere (inviting, intimidating, sterile, chaotic, etc.)? What physical attributes of the space help create the atmosphere?
- How does the place make you feel? Why? Are you comfortable or uncomfortable?
- Does the place remind you of something or someone? Some association? Why?
- When and to whom would you recommend visiting this spot?

Use your responses to these prompts to construct a paragraph that reports on the student space you observed. Your audience is other first-year students. Your purpose is to introduce them to a student space they might not be familiar with.

To Seek Feedback or Not to Seek Feedback at the Brainstorming Stage:

Again, your writing is still really new and wide open, so it may be difficult for someone to give you meaningful feedback that will support your writing as it develops. Again, this may be a good place to start a conversation with someone about your brainstorming, because they may be able to help you see another perspective that expands or focuses your brainstorming.

TB SECTION 2.4   Getting Stuck and Unstuck

As we have said again and again, writers also struggle. They are not just blessed people from whom great words flow. Writers, just like you, get stuck sometimes, but somehow they keep going, in order to get past those moments of being stuck. This means that when you're stuck, it's not over. You can and will get through it, but only if you're able to find the right strategy. Whether that's pushing through it, taking a break, finding an angle that helps you break into your writing, trying an exercise to express your ideas in a new way, or explaining it to a friend.

To Seek Feedback or Not to Seek Feedback at the Getting Stuck and Unstuck Stage:

This stage can be a good place to get feedback—sometimes someone else's ideas can help push you through when you are stuck. This is not the time to get the most critical person you know to give you ideas. You don't want feedback that will get you more stuck. Think of someone who might be able to help you direct and focus your writing, a motivator.

TB TRY THIS   2.2

Create a "getting unstuck grab bag." Having a grab bag of ways to get unstuck will help you both get unstuck and not get distracted. Some students report that if they walk away from an assignment without a specific task to complete, they go down various rabbit holes of distraction. For this grab bag, write down some getting unstuck strategies on small pieces of paper. Feel free to Google "overcoming writer's block" and add ones that appeal to you to the list that follows. This list is just to get you started. When you feel stuck, grab one and do it. They are generally methods that don't take a lot of time. Eventually, you may develop your favorites and you won't need to use the grab bag, but for some students the randomness of it puts a little fun into the frustration of being stuck.

Write the following on pieces of paper, sticky notes, or note cards that will be put in your grab bag. Keep these around for when you are feeling stuck and realize that staring at the computer will get you nowhere. Pull one out and do it.

- Get physically away from what you're writing. Close the computer, flip over the page, and stop looking at it. Set a timer for 15 minutes with a promise to return to it then.

(continued)

TB TRY THIS — 2.2

- Do something that doesn't require thought, which you instead do by habit, like brush your teeth or fold laundry. What happens when your brain relaxes a bit?
- Try writing your assignment as a letter to a friend. As in, "Hey, what's up? I have to write this writing assignment. It's about...." This can free up your ability to express yourself and give you a new angle with which to view it.
- Pull out a voice recorder and talk to it for three minutes about why your writing isn't working right now.
- What is your favorite part of this writing task? What is your least favorite part? Do a three-minute free-write on these questions.
- Express the ideas of the next paragraph in your writing visually, whether it's a picture drawing or a mind map.
- Go to YouTube and search for "five-minute meditation." Complete the meditation and then return to your writing.
- Do 10 push-ups, or squats, or jumping jacks, or sit-ups.
- Find a piece of writing from your past. Reread it. Take a minute to reflect on the experience of writing that paper. What are you most proud of from that paper?
- Text a friend or family member and ask, "Do you have time for a five-minute phone call? I'm stuck on an assignment and need to talk it out." Then call them.

Revising vs. Editing

TB SECTION **2.5**

For many of you, the word *revision* probably conjures images of writers tweaking and polishing each part of their work until it's just right. Throw that idea of revision out of the window—it's a terrible idea. Let's break down the word "revision" into its two parts: *re* (again) and *vision* (seeing). Writing is revision and revision is, literally, re-seeing. Revision is *not* editing. Revision is about detachment. When we are writing, we often don't even know what we're writing because we are just channeling thoughts and feelings in the form of words onto the page. Once those words are on the page, it's time to step back and see them from the outside.

Think about re-seeing something you've written. For example, if today you looked back at a paper you wrote in the 11th grade, there's no question that you would bring a new perspective to it now. The experiences and time you've had away from it, inside and outside of school, have shaped you in ways that would cause you to see this text differently. This new perspective might illuminate discontinuities in your argument, or places where you missed an opportunity to bring in a great source. We want you to get in the habit of doing this type of "re-seeing" as you write. Giving yourself time to reflect, brainstorm, and analyze during the writing process will help you to see your text in a new way each time you look at it.

You cannot maximize the potential of revision or fully leverage your whole process if you don't leave yourself enough time. Whether stepping away from a project for an hour or a few days, you should build in time *off* from it. If you just sit there staring at it, you really can't see it. It is kind of like when you focus on a point in the near distance with both eyes open, and then close one eye, it looks different, because it is in a different frame. You then close the other eye, and you again re-see the same objects in yet a different frame. You should plan for some time in your process to enable you to shift your frame a bit and re-see what is happening on the page, in your thinking or sequencing or development of ideas. A powerful part of revision comes from a writer's ability to plan. Writers don't just take one hour away from their writing and then suddenly return. They create a schedule where they build in multiple points of "leave and return" in order to re-see multiple times through multiple frames.

TB TRY THIS ————————— 2.3

A. Find an old paper you wrote and pick out what you think is the most important sentence. Put the sentence at the top of a fresh page/doc. Now start writing and write for at least 10 minutes, without stopping, about why this is the most important sentence in the whole paper. What would someone who rushed past this sentence miss? Who might not agree with this sentence or see it the same way? How could you convince them? Who cares anyway? Why should this sentence matter? Where does it show up in the paper and is that the right place for it? (For instance, should it be at the beginning so people know what they're in for, or should it come toward the end because you need evidence and an argument to make the case first?) Once you do this for 10 minutes, reread it. Is it something you could now use to go make that paper better? Did you learn something about your most important idea that you didn't know before?

B. "The one-inch picture frame." Anne Lamott writes about writers and writing, and she encourages herself to focus on the one-inch picture frame. (Lamott, 1995) Most picture frames are a lot bigger and so they put a lot more in the frame. When we write we often stay in that bigger frame, trying to tell the *whole* story, or provide every detail, or make every point in the argument. Because we can see the whole picture, the whole project, in our head, we are overwhelmed trying to get it all down on paper. So she coaxes us to imagine that you are, say, describing your mom or your favorite place in the world or your favorite food. If you had only one inch in which to convey the essence of it, what would go in your one-inch frame? How close can you bring in our focus?

C. And if your fingers are not moving on your keyboard, try using a voice memo app to record you talking about your topic. Talk and talk and talk. Try to get out everything that is in your head around your assignment or topic or even your main idea. And then take a break, at least an hour. Overnight is better. Then listen to your recording and take notes about yourself. What sticks out as important? What can you write down from your speaking? How could you shape this into your paper?

To Seek Feedback or Not to Seek Feedback at the Revising Stage:

Yes! Go for it! This is a great stage to seek outside opinions on your thoughts, the structures you are using, how what you are writing is being read and heard, and a million other things. This can be a perfect place to get momentum and direction from an outside eye, especially if that eye is familiar with giving feedback.

Speaking to Your Audience (Rhetorical Context, Purpose, Form, Norms)

TB SECTION **2.6**

TB THINK ABOUT IT

When you've written in the past, how much have you considered your audience? What audiences have you written for?

At some stage of any writing project, you need to attune your writing to the specific rhetorical context or writing situation. Who is your audience? What is your purpose? What are the conventions or norms for writing to this audience—in terms of the form, formality, voice? For example, from whether or not to use the first-person "I" to whether to use MLA or APA citation style.

We are always writing to some idea of an audience whether we realize it or not. Our sense of audience is often sort of unconscious, mindless, and ill-formed or vague. At a certain point in your writing process, you will be well served by getting a clear sense of your audience because it will influence the type of language you use, the tone of your writing, what you can assume your audience knows, and so on.

Lisa Ede and Andrea Lunsford, scholars in Amy's (one of the authors of this book) field of writing studies, talk about "audience addressed" versus "audience evoked" (Ede & Lunsford, 1984). We tend to evoke or to create an audience with and within our writing. Sometimes, this audience is *not* the same as the audience that is actually going to read our writing or to be addressed by it. An audience evoked is sort of the habitual and often even unconscious way we imagine a sort of default or automatic audience when we write. People internalize vague generalizations, past associations, and what was informally and ad hoc learned about an audience. This impacts every writing session and is the audience we instinctively evoke. For a student, this often looks like, "writing for the teacher." Or for "an academic audience" as though there is something definitive, pinned down, universal, or consistent about such a vague concept. It may look like "writing for reviewers," who may be harsh and oppositional or generative and helpful. (See **TB Figure 2.1.**)

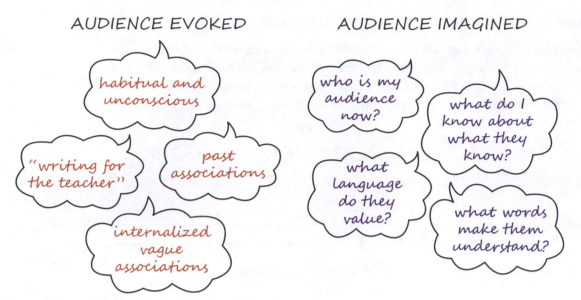

TB Figure 2.1 Audience Evoked vs. Audience Imagined

The proposition here is that the more a writer can become aware of and set aside those internalized associations, they can more consciously reflect on:

- Who is my audience this time?
- What do I know about what they know?
- What rhetorical style do they value? How is authority conveyed to them? Etc.

The more you walk yourself through some of these questions, the better able you are to shape your text (language, tone, examples, style) to communicate effectively to that audience. So, unlearning the unconscious internalized version facilitates more effective and conscious performance. This is the *audience imagined*.

TB TRY THIS _____ 2.4

Write the same letter telling three audiences that you are quitting college (e.g., parent, friend, teacher, stranger, etc.). Try to enter this exercise as realistically as you can and don't think too much. Just give yourself three–five minutes to write or start writing each letter.

Okay. Now look at the three letters. What do you notice? How did you open each one? Did you put your announcement at the start of any or all of them? Which ones and why? Did it come later? If so, why? Did you try to convince or persuade in any of them? How? What does how you wrote each of them tell you about your sense of your audience? Did you assume they already knew you were contemplating this? Did you assume they would be sympathetic? Mad? Argumentative? Did you use different reasons for different audiences?

Chances are your rhetorical analysis reveals you to have an active and attuned sense of rhetorical awareness. The trick is starting to use it intentionally in all of your writing projects, and at the right stage for the project. This toolbox and Chapter 7 and 8 will model rhetorical awareness and prompt you to begin exercising and developing it. Thinking about audience too early, especially when you don't really know your ideas or your audience yet, will often inhibit your generating. So, use this stage of the process carefully, knowing you may need to learn how to tune it out or turn it off at times.

TB TRY THIS _____ 2.5

Read the following two excerpts from drafts of this very book. Each excerpt shows you what a section of our chapter on Engaging Diversity looked like in different stages of drafting. After you read them, we will ask you a couple of questions:

Excerpt I

The word *diversity* is thrown around a lot, often in contexts where it stops meaning anything substantial. If we look to the Supreme Court and their 2003 decisions related to Affirmative Action and race being used as a factor in admission to the University of Michigan, the court agreed that diversity within higher education serves a governmental interest. The government interest rests largely in the fact that we are a country with multiple types of racial, ethnic, religious, and economic differences. It is important to point out here that the Supreme Court decision asserts that there are *important and universal benefits to demographic diversity in higher education.* In other words, the benefits are not simply accruing to historically underrepresented populations. Rather, everyone benefits from interacting with people, ideas, traditions, perspectives, and experiences that differ from their own. Regardless of the topic we are studying in higher education, if students are limited to their own perspective, they've only understood the given topic through one lens: their own.

Excerpt II

Diversity. This important, hot-topic buzzword is used in politics, school, the workplace, peer groups, and maybe even (hopefully) your dinner table. It is mentioned often, in a multitude of contexts, and in ways where all meaning sometimes drains right out of it. However, we have a very specific frame through which we would like to engage your thinking around the term, and practice, of diversity.

(continued)

TB TRY THIS

2.5

It seems as though everyone has an opinion on diversity, including the Supreme Court. If we look to their 2003 decisions related to Affirmative Action and race being used as a factor in admission to the University of Michigan, the court agreed that diversity within higher education serves a governmental interest. The government interest rests largely in the fact that we are a country with multiple points of racial, ethnic, religious, economic difference. It is important to point out here that the Supreme Court decision asserts that there are *important and universal benefits to demographic diversity in higher education.* In other words, historically underrepresented populations are not the only ones benefiting. Rather, everyone benefits from interacting with people and ideas and traditions and perspectives and experiences that differ from their own. Regardless of the topic we are studying in higher education, if students are limited to their own perspective, they've only understood the given topic through one lens, their own.

1. What feels different about these two versions?
2. What literal or actual differences do you notice?
3. What impact do the changes have on the meaning of the writing? On the impact?
4. Do you sense the audience is different for each of them?
5. If you picture the writer/speaker/person behind these, do you picture them differently?

Notice in the first version that we are just getting an idea out, forming and elaborating on that important idea and setting it onto paper. The second version shows us retaining the idea but forming it differently for *this* book and for *you as our audience.* If you look even at just the two different ways we began the writing, you'll see some important things:

Diversity. This important, hot-topic buzzword is used in politics, school, the workplace, peer groups, and maybe even (hopefully) your dinner table. It is mentioned often, in a multitude of contexts, and in ways where all meaning sometimes drains right out of it.

The word *diversity* is thrown around a lot, often in contexts where it stops meaning anything substantial.

The first one is literally plopping down our main idea so we can get going. This word is everywhere to the point it is meaningless. The second version keeps that idea but slows it down a little, and tries to tease it out. It uses more descriptive words, too, and tries to communicate to an audience that isn't already thinking about this all the time. We think the second version is more approachable.

TB TRY THIS

2.6

Audience/Form Exercise

The following is a creative exercise to get you thinking about how the same main idea can be shaped into different forms and how that form shapes the meaning or experience the reader gets from your main idea.

If you could be anywhere right now, where would you be? Explain why, and describe what you would be feeling there. Try describing the space to someone who is totally unfamiliar with this place. Try writing a rhyming poem about this place, or using repetition of a particular word or phrase or sentence structure. Try cataloging sensory details that describe this space (a list of

(continued)

TB TRY THIS _____ 2.6

tastes, sounds, sights, textures, smells.) Describe this place through a dialogue between two people. Or jump right into some action or a scene that is happening in it. Try comparing this place to something else (metaphor.)

Now look at the various writing samples you have created. Which one would be best on a travel brochure? Twitter? In a paper? In a text convincing your friend to join you there?

Questions to Help You Attune Your Revision to the Rhetorical Context

Just as in critical reading, there are helpful questions to begin considering even before you dive into a text for the first time, there are also important questions you should consider before, during, and after drafting a piece of writing. These questions have to do with the rhetorical context in which you are writing. Every piece of writing has a specific rhetorical situation that is comprised of the writer, the audience, the subject, and the purpose. All aspects of the rhetorical context interact with each other to shape the text.

At numerous stages in your drafting (perhaps before you begin, then after a first full draft, and again when you are revising), answering these questions can help you get a better sense of how to shape your text and why, based on various factors that shape the rhetorical situation.

1. What do you, the writer, bring to the topic? How does your history and community shape your perspective and knowledge? *And then*, is it important to communicate this to your readers? How will you do this?

2. Who are you writing to? Who do you wish to reach with your text? What do you know or not know about your target audience? *And then*, how will you address your audience most effectively, how will you engage them, hook them, appeal to them?

3. What is your topic? What kinds of discussion are going on about this topic? *And then*, will you address, acknowledge, or engage in these ongoing conversations about your topic, or differentiate your text from these? How?

4. What is your purpose? Are you writing to inform readers, to change readers' attitudes toward something, to entertain readers, to make them laugh, to get them to take action? Given your intention, what will be the most effective way to construct your text using tone, language, organization, and other writing strategies?

Answering these questions will help you name your text.

To Seek Feedback or Not to Seek Feedback at the "Speaking to Your Audience" Stage

This is a good moment to get someone else's eyes on your work, especially if they are able to explain who they feel you are writing for. A new reader may be able to point out places where the way you speak to your audience works and where it doesn't.

TB SECTION **2.7**   # Getting Feedback and Stepping Back

Whether you ask a friend or two, do an exchange with some classmates, or visit the Writing Center, it is *always* a good idea to get some feedback on your writing. The time to get feedback depends on the project and on your own process, but here are some ways to structure the process. It's also very important to mention that *reading other people's drafts and giving feedback* helps you as a writer. Looking at someone else's piece in process is a lot easier sometimes, and you can get a more detached look at a piece of writing. That experience of thinking about someone else's paper and what is or isn't working and *why* will definitely be of use to you when you go back to your own paper-in-progress or any other writing project.

TB TRY THIS ──────────────────────────── 2.7

Here are three ideas for getting feedback on your writing. You can find more peer review ideas and questions in the bonus activities at the end of this chapter. Adapt and adopt them in whatever way works for you.

1. Mini–Peer Review: Focus on Unified Paragraphs and Digestible Sentences

   Read the following paragraph and decide whether it has effectively used (1) a *controlling idea* that connects everything in the paragraph under a kind of umbrella, so that we as readers can identify the point, purpose, or central idea conveyed by the sentences gathered here; (2) a *signal phrase* that transitions from the writer's voice to the quoted voice; (3) a *parenthetical reference* that gives page numbers in their correct form; and (4) whether the quote has been effectively *sandwiched* between the writer's own words, connecting the outside source back to the writer's controlling idea.

   I'll be the first to admit that, in this, my first semester of college, I have already sat through many hours of long, dull lectures that leave me feeling uninspired about the material presented in the course. I have even nodded off a few times in class, yanking my head back up as it begins to droop toward my chest. It's embarrassing, and I'm not proud of this behavior, but it happens every now and then, even when I come to class well-rested. So, what's my problem? Mark Edmundson, a professor at the University of Virginia, thinks that this lack of enthusiasm among students today is the result of a culture that is "ever more devoted to consumption and entertainment, to the using and using up of goods and services" (807). Edmundson sees the disinterested, disengaged atmosphere pervading his classes and campus as a result of a consumer culture where television, advertising, and "keeping up with the Jones's" has run rampant, and students have been reduced to discerning consumers, not intellectually curious beings. He fears the disappearance of genius. And while there certainly is some truth in this cultural critique, Edmundson glosses over specific classroom and teaching practices that need to be addressed if student engagement is the goal. Poor teaching practices don't serve students well, whether we have been raised on too much television or not.

2. Reader Review Letters

   Exchange copies of your rough draft with two people. Each of you should answer the questions that follow, but *in the form of a letter to the writer*. Remember that the point of responding to these questions is to help the writer get a sense of what is working well and what is not working in their essay. Your task is to help the writer make their essay stronger.

(continued)

TB TRY THIS

When you get to the end of your letter, look back at what you have written and ask yourself: Is this an effective letter? Have I been critical enough? Specific enough? Supportive or encouraging enough? What do you still need to say or explain in order to help the writer?

The following are some questions you could apply:

- What is the controlling idea for the essay? (Remember, this is more than a topic or an issue. It communicates a specific idea, argument, or perspective on an issue.) If you cannot find a controlling idea in the draft, suggest ways the writer can develop a controlling idea.

- Where is this controlling idea best supported? What does the writer do well to make the controlling idea clear, specific, and well-defined? Which places still need more detail, explanation, or support in order to build up, clarify, and support the controlling idea?

- Which places (sentences, examples, ideas, etc.) in the essay don't seem to relate to the controlling idea? Why don't these areas fit? Are there ways to connect these sections or ideas to the controlling idea, or should they be cut out?

- Has the writer used the author's words at least twice in the essay? Do these quotes clearly relate to what the writer is saying? Explain. Are signal phrases, sandwiching, and parenthetical references used correctly?

- Who do you think the writer is trying to reach with this essay? (Who is the audience?) What about the writing itself suggests this? Is there a different audience you think the writer should focus on? Are there appeals, examples, a certain tone, or choice of words that you believe the writer might use to more effectively reach their audience?

- Is each of the paragraphs in the essay unified? Does each have a clear central idea that is developed and supported or explained? Explain which paragraphs are most confusing or unclear and why.

- Does the order of the paragraphs and ideas in the essay make sense? Or do the ideas and thoughts of the writer seem to jump around, making the essay hard to follow? Where do things feel smooth? Where do things feel rough? What's happening in the writing and structure that creates these impressions?

- What has the writer done at the beginning to draw the reader in, to engage you? What could make the opening more effective?

- What has the writer done to close the essay? How do you feel by the time you reach the end? How do you think the writer could make the ending more forceful or effective?

- Would you describe this essay as an argument, a meditation, or a rant? What purpose does the essay serve? What do you think the writer hopes to have happen when a person reads this essay? Explain.

We have included a *rubric* that summarizes these questions, in case you want to organize your thoughts differently in regard to responding to other writers. (See **TB Figure 2.2**.) Using a rubric can be a really great way to organize and make visible where a person's writing currently lies in the process. Often, instructors grade using rubrics, but rubrics also have their weaknesses, too. Try to give feedback and organize your reading in different ways so you are able to see others' writing, and your writing, from multiple perspectives.

(continued)

TB TRY THIS

questions to consider	Answers (yes/somewhat/no + explanation)
What is the controlling idea of the essay? Is it well-supported? Are there parts of the essay which don't relate to it?	
Has the writer used the author's words at least twice in the essay?	
Is the writer's sense of their audience clear?	
Does each paragraph have a clear central idea that is developed? Does the order of ideas & paragraphs make sense?	
Does the beginning draw you into the writing? Does the ending feel like an ending?	
Does the essay have a clear purpose?	
	Notes:

3. Create a Writing Group

    Grab some friends and set up a regular time to read one another's writing. Having a set time/day means you get used to bringing in and reviewing writing at different stages of the process that helps you learn *not* to wait to share your writing until you think it is "done" or "ready." (And if it is done, why would you need peer review or feedback?!)

    It is important in a writing group not to "fix" one another's writing or to focus on polishing and editing. Instead, think about the many dimensions of the writing and how it impacted or communicated with you as a reader and what you hope the writer will attend to or develop or get rid of in the next draft.

Conclusion

This is a full toolbox. We hope it has given you the motivation to try different tools, explore different stages of writing, and experience some creativity and new perspectives in your writing process. It is also a toolbox that you can return to throughout your college career because these tools are very easily adapted and can support your writing in a variety of assignments and projects.

PART III

Beyond College

Investing in Your Well-Being

> **Science and mindfulness complement each other in helping people to eat well and maintain their health and well-being.** —Thich Nhat Hanh
>
> **Knowing that we can be loved exactly as we are gives us all the best opportunity for growing into the healthiest of people.** —Fred Rogers (Mr. Rogers)

In Your Own Words

9.1

In your journal, write down your answers to the following questions. What do you associate with your "well-being"? What factors in your daily life influence your sense of well-being and which of them do you control or can you influence? In what aspects of your life does your personal well-being get compromised?

Introduction to Investing in Your Well-Being

This chapter is about you investing time, energy, and resources into maintaining your health and well-being. There are countless dimensions to this, such as our financial security, the quality of our relationships, our physical health, and our mental state. We control some of these dimensions entirely; others we might inherit or be subject to, in which case we can exert degrees of influence over them but might not be able to fully control. Oftentimes, well-being is about managing rather than eliminating factors that threaten our well-being. For example, during the COVID-19 pandemic and response, many of us are experiencing high levels of stress, anxiety, and financial hardships. This will impact our sleep, nutrition, and mental well-being. We cannot avoid the experience of this pandemic, nor all of its consequences, but we can control how we respond to it by taking care of ourselves during this time and being mindful of what is in our power and what we need right now.

In this chapter, we have chosen to focus on multiple dimensions of well-being: physical, mental, emotional, social, and financial. Attention to each of these elements and a mindful approach to them will support your health and well-being, while inattention to any one of them is likely to impact the others. For example, when you are anxious, it might affect your sleep or eating, so your mental well-being impacts your physical health. If you have a big unexpected expense, and have to take on extra shifts at work, this might impact your stress level and your time for relationships.

Notice that we emphasize three factors in each section: growth mindset, balance, and self-awareness or listening to yourself. These are all fundamental to well-being in any dimension, whether physical, emotional, financial, or something else. In any dimension of your well-being, it is important not to strive for perfection or completion because those are unattainable. It is also important not to approach well-being with a deficit mindset, focused on what you *lack*, because this will lead to self-defeating talk and frustration. Our goal is for you to strive for the habits and practices *that make you feel well* and to know what makes you feel truly well. The goal is not to strive for an image or idea of "perfect," whether it's in your eating habits, relationships, or mental health. This will only lead to strife and stress, and the "all or nothing" attitude of a fixed mindset. Well-being is truly a lifelong process.

SECTION **9.1**

Physical Health (Exercise, Nutrition, Sleep)

Physical health isn't about maintaining a physique or a number on a scale, and it's not about judging your body based on its appearance. It's about accepting the simple but powerful fact that your body is the base of all of your experiences, and should be treated accordingly. Your body takes you where you want to go, does what you want it to do, and keeps you alive. Beware of the fixed mindset trap when it comes to your physical health—for example, labeling yourself as "not athletic" is a fixed mindset that disables your ability to make choices and listen to yourself.

Exercise

We all think of and interact with our bodies in different ways. Some of us think of our bodies as powerful tools, others see them as vehicles for movement, and others rarely even think about their bodies. Regardless of where you fall on this continuum, becoming more in touch with your body and what it needs is very important. Like anything, it's about finding balance: our bodies need movement every day, and we have to find the right amount somewhere between exhausting ourselves with activity and never doing anything.

Moving your body has so many benefits to both your physical and mental health, and it does a lot more than just change your physical appearance. Moving your body gets your blood pumping, strengthens your muscles, increases flexibility, and releases some feel-good hormones, making it a very worthwhile use of time for your body (Colorado Tech, 2017).

Those of you who are working as you make your way through college can also look to the movement you engage in at your workplace. Are you on your feet? Are you lifting heavy items? Are you using your body to get the job done? According to research by Harvard psychologist Ellen Langer, even just being mindful of the fact that any movement you do while engaged in work exercise (whether it's housekeeping, as in their experiment, or another job like delivering packages), actually *increases* the physical benefit of it (Crum & Langer, 2007). If you're moving your body while tending to family or putting in work hours, view it in relation to the benefits it gives you.

THINK ABOUT IT

Write down the top three ways you like to exercise or use and move your body. Do you prefer team sports with a competitive edge, such as basketball or soccer? Or solo activities such as running or biking? Do you like to engage in classes or group fitness apps? Are you someone who likes to take the stairs or grab extra movement wherever and whenever you can? Is there a style of martial arts that you've seen and are eager to try?

How do you find time for exercise when you're always studying, going to class, or managing family obligations, jobs, and various responsibilities as well? Be aware that you can make small choices throughout the day that will increase your physical movement. (See **Figure 9.1**.)

Take the stairs instead of the elevator

Clean your room as fast as you can

Meet a friend for a walk instead of getting coffee

Register for a physical class next semester

Bike instead of driving or taking the bus

Figure 9.1 Make Small Choices to Move Your Body

TRY THIS   9.2

Look into options on your campus or in your community. Many communities have rec centers that offer equipment and classes at discounted prices for students. Perhaps your campus has a rec center or intramural sports leagues. Or are there student groups related to different forms of exercise (e.g., ultimate Frisbee, taekwondo, soccer)? You can also use the internet to find local pickup sports leagues. Outside of these organized forms, try surveying your local area for parks, lakes, or other outdoor areas where you can walk, run, or do a workout. Which two or three of these would be accessible to you and seem fun to try? Think of a friend or family member who might do one of these activities with you.

The more you try new types of exercise, the more you'll figure out which ones you like and the more in tune you'll feel with your body. Like other parts of your well-being, it's about listening to yourself and what makes you feel good, and maintaining balance.

Nutrition

Food serves a multitude of functions in our lives, from giving us energy to connecting us with our cultures to bringing people together. In this section, we will discuss food in its most basic function, which is as fuel for your body. Through this lens, food is incredibly important because it is the thing which is powering your body to help you do fun things, accomplish goals, and stay alive.

THINK ABOUT IT

What foods energize you or just make you feel good, meaning they agree with you and don't result in a moment where you're clenching your stomach saying, "I shouldn't have eaten that"?

The most important principle of nutrition and overall well-being is balance. In college, you'll never be able to eat 100% of the foods you feel good about. Some days, based on money, time, or other limitations, you might eat in a way that leaves you feeling unsatisfied, gross, or regretful. Eating well is not about avoiding these experiences completely. Rather, it's about keeping a mindset in which these days don't derail you. Overeating, and eating things that are not as nutritionally dense, like candy, do not mark you as a "bad" person, but rather as human. It's all about finding balance, so that, on average, in a general sense, you are fueling your body well. There will be ups and downs, and being able to weather them without coming down on yourself or giving up on your commitments to your own health and well-being is key.

Listening to your body is also a key component of your nutrition. If you notice that certain foods make you feel sick or give you low energy, consider minimizing your intake of them. If there are other foods that make you feel energetic and balanced, listen to these feelings and continue to eat them. Although you probably aren't a trained nutritionist, your body can tell you a lot more than you realize about what it needs and what it doesn't like.

In general, college students don't have a great level of control over what they eat. Limitations like money, time, cafeteria options, and available restaurants or grocery stores in the area all affect what foods college students eat. Some college students are also faced with food insecurity. You may rely, in part, on food pantries to meet your dietary and nutritional needs. Increasingly, universities and colleges are recognizing the impact of food insecurity on their campuses and are opening food pantries that serve their students. This lack of control and security related to a need so core to our ability to survive and thrive can take a real toll on college students. Food insecurity carries an emotional toll that is exacerbated by the fact it is not often talked about or acknowledged and yet is increasingly common, especially as COVID-19 shifts our economic well-being and leads many more of us to face food insecurity. Student services offices on campuses are often on the front lines of helping students navigate food insecurity and may be a place to start if you need assistance.

Within the parameters of what is available and accessible to you in terms of your budget, how can you incorporate enough healthy whole foods into your diet? Begin by noticing where fruit or vegetables are available. Does the convenience store in the student union sell fruit? Does the dorm have a salad bar? Can you buy certain foods (fruits, nuts) in bulk to save money? Figure out which ones are most accessible, which you like best, and try adding these to your diet. Finally, consider replacing something more processed with something less processed.

There are creative ways to get around dorm food and eat healthy. Carry around a jar of peanut butter and grab a banana or apple for a nutritious snack on-the-go. Raw vegetables from the salad bar can be steamed with a microwave, a bowl, a plate, and a little water.

THINK ABOUT IT

What is one healthy shift you can make this year for how you fuel your body? How will you accomplish this? Try breaking it down week by week. Focus on outcomes like "have lots of energy" and "feel positive" versus goals around physical appearance, or numbers, or weight.

As a college student, you might not think you have time or need to prioritize whole foods. But it's important to remember that how you eat now is laying the groundwork and creating the pathways for your future habits. You might not feel the effects now, but over time, eating whole foods will help you build a stronger and healthier body. So, how can you start to shape your consciousness around food and diet in ways that your future self will be grateful for?

Sleep

As a society, we are pressured to accomplish more and more in our waking hours, which seems to require we give up some of our sleep. College students are supposed to stay up all night studying, right? The irony, according to research by Matthew Walker, a neuroscientist who studies and writes about sleep, is that all of that information we put into our brain by studying, can't be stored in our brain *unless* we sleep (Walker, 2017). So, if you're staying up late to study and then end up getting less than 5 or 6 hours of sleep that night, your brain won't effectively store the new knowledge you acquired in your classes or in your late-night cram session. Matthew Walker, in his role as professor at University of California–Berkeley, makes sure his students understand that their ability to remember what they learn in his class during the day is dependent on their sleep that night. Lack of sleep also dramatically decreases your immunity, meaning that the less you sleep, the greater your chances of getting a cold or virus.

TRY THIS ————————————————————— 9.3

Watch the TED Talk "Sleep Is Your Superpower" by Matthew Walker (Walker, 2019). Walker discusses a number of ways that sleep benefits a person. On a sheet of paper or in an online document, list them and then rank them according to what you think motivates you the most to prioritize sleep. (Reminder: "Ted.com" is a website where you can search for any of the TED Talks referenced throughout this book.)

Now, identify your current sleep habits by answering these questions with one- or two-sentence responses: How much sleep do you get each night? Is your sleep schedule consistent? What currently makes up your "bedtime routine"? How do you feel when you wake up in the morning? (Awake? Drowsy? Downright sleepy?) Have you ever pulled an all-nighter? How did it make you feel the next day? The day after?

Finally, identify three things you could do today to increase the amount and quality of sleep you get tonight.

Americans are sleeping less, and college students are no exception. Research shows that only 11% of college students sleep well (Division of Sleep Medicine at Harvard Medical School, 2008). Another survey indicates that 19% of college students say that sleep difficulties affect their academic achievement (College Stats, 2017).

Everyone is different, but generally people need 6 to 7 hours of sleep to be fully alert and present. Research shows that most of us do our best with 8+ hours a night. As in all things related to your well-being, balance is important. Sleeping too little can be a problem now and in the future, but sleeping too much can also be an indicator that you might be feeling depressed. You might want to talk to a doctor if you sleep 10+ hours a night.

The challenge during college is to find time for all these hours of sleep, but with some planning and commitment, it is possible to make time for healthy sleep. Experts say that a regular routine before bed is helpful in getting good, regular sleep. Your routine may include showering or bathing, brushing your teeth, reading or journaling for 10 to 15 minutes, and then lights out. Or maybe you prefer a cup of tea and a short meditation. Whatever suits you is best, but the most important thing is that it is consistent from night to night. (See **Figure 9.2**.)

Research has shown that keeping screen time out of your bedtime routine is one of the most important aspects of your sleep hygiene. The blue light from a TV, cellphone, or laptop right before bed will cause your body to delay the process of going to sleep, impacting the amount of hours you're able to sleep each night (National Sleep Foundation, 2020). Think about setting a time after which you won't look at your phone, and try reading or listening to music to help you unwind before you go to sleep.

One of the hardest things about getting to sleep in college, whether you live in a dorm, apartment, or at home, can be people you live with. Moving from social time to sleep can be tough when it's easy to stay up late talking or watching videos. Creating some healthy boundaries around you and your need for sleep might be helpful. Taking the step to inform your friends, family, or roommates that you have certain goals for when you get to sleep can help them support you better.

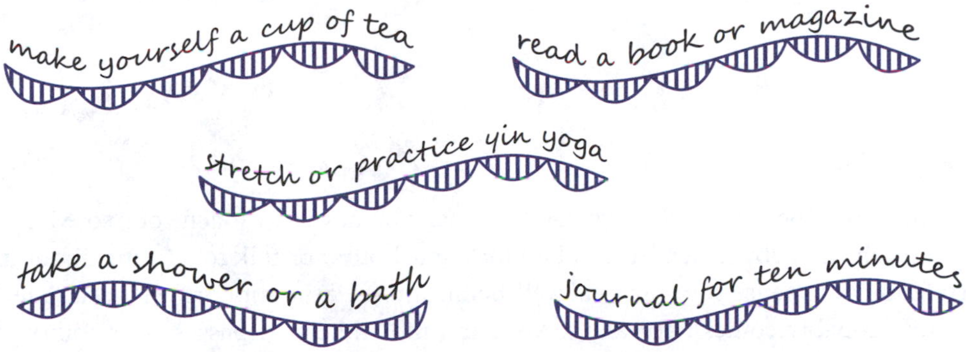

make yourself a cup of tea   read a book or magazine

stretch or practice yin yoga

take a shower or a bath   journal for ten minutes

Figure 9.2 Ideas for a Bedtime Routine

In Your Own Words

9.4

James Clear, author of Atomic Habits, argues that it is much easier to make a 1% change in your daily habits than to do a complete overhaul of them. People are much more likely, he argues, to be successful at making an incremental change than large New Year's resolution-style changes (Clear, 2018).

Using your journal, answer the following questions. Choose an area of your physical health—exercise/movement, nutrition, or sleep habits. What is one change you'd like to make to these? What incremental change could you make today that would point you in the direction of that change?

For example, if you want to start reading a book at bedtime rather than online articles or social media feeds, the first step might be to get a book from the library, or if you already have the book in your possession, the first step might be to pick it up while in bed and read the first paragraph.

List:

1. The change you'd like to make.
2. The small change you can make today to take you in this direction.
3. Tomorrow, return to this document and report back on your success or what got in the way of your success. Add a short, three- to five-sentence reflection summarizing your success or obstacles.

💡 CRITICAL MOMENT

Instructor

In my work with first-year students, I occasionally find myself in my office hours talking to a first-year student about how frustrated or disappointed they are because of their grade in the course or how poorly they did on an assignment. Because of an instructor's vantage point at the front of the classroom, we usually have a pretty good idea about who is short on sleep just based on watching students fighting to keep their eyes open. Many students have busy and complicated lives—jobs, families, lots of homework, and yet the answer is always the same when they can't stay awake in class (or when they are trying to study), they need more sleep. The sleep doesn't have to be during the night. Naps in hallways, student unions, at a desk in a library or another study space help you to refresh. Find a place to store your valuables and embrace the amazing ability that sleep-deprived college students have in catching up on sleep.

SECTION **9.2**

Mental and Emotional Health (Anxiety, Depression, Stress, Substance Use)

Think about the level of concern you feel when you have a headache or a sore back. You might take ibuprofen, rest in bed for a few hours, or talk to a friend about it. Your ability to sense your physical well-being and seek the support you need to feel better probably comes naturally to you, and most likely surpasses your ability to sense when your mental well-being needs support in the form of therapy, kindness toward yourself, medication, or other forms of treatment. A broken leg would stop you from practicing dancing or going for a hike, and unhealthy levels of anxiety or stress can stop you from being able to do the things you want or need to do. And just as physical well-being requires maintenance, such as exercising, eating well, or having a yearly checkup, mental well-being requires maintenance, too. That maintenance can take many forms, such as having good conversations with family and friends, seeing a therapist regularly, or taking mental breaks to do something you enjoy. Despite the importance of mental health, there is still a prevalent stigma that prevents many people from recognizing its validity alongside other aspects of health. It's vitally important for you to understand that mental health is a completely real and very important thing to prioritize.

THINK ABOUT IT

What images or thoughts does the phrase "mental health" conjure up for you? Do you have a lot of experience thinking about your own mental health or that of those around you? Is there anything you're curious about that's related to mental health?

Research shows that the prevalence of undergraduate students who struggle with their mental health is high: *80% of college students report feeling overwhelmed by their college responsibilities, and 50% of college students feel that the quality of their mental health is below average or poor* (College Stats, 2017). (If you are feeling overwhelmed and unsure, even if you don't know what the feeling you're feeling is called, it's important you seek help. Whether it's telling a friend or seeking a professional opinion, it's very important to not go through things like this alone. Many colleges have helpful and life-saving mental health support systems that are free for you to use. This section will introduce you to some of the mental health challenges you may face in college, so you become familiar with the resources available to you.

Dealing with Stress

Stress is something everyone feels at some point in their lives, from giving a speech to playing in an important football game to performing a solo in choir. In these situations, our body elicits the stress hormone cortisol, which is meant to improve your awareness and reflexes in order to perform in the best manner possible. But if your body sits in this stress response for a few days or longer, you begin to move into an unhealthy level of stress, the kind that makes you feel tired and depleted. We all know that college is stressful, so it's important to be aware of how this stress manifests inside you, and how you manage it.

THINK ABOUT IT

How do you typically deal with stress and stressful situations? Do you find a distraction such as Instagram or YouTube? Do you go for a run? Do you talk to a friend or a therapist? Do your coping strategies support your mental health? If not, what might you do to change that?

So many things can cause you stress while in college: budgeting and money, grades, exams, projects, friends, relationships, life after college, and on and on. It affects everyone differently, so this is a really important time to notice when this feeling of stress comes up for you and what it feels like, in order to begin creating healthy habits for dealing with it for the rest of your life. Stress will always exist, but there are healthy strategies you can implement to make coping possible.

We cannot emphasize enough how important it is to seek out help when the stress you are feeling gets to be too much. There are times when you can use your own stress relief techniques to get balance back. This can be found in many different things: talking to family members, exercising, listening to music, baking a treat, sleeping, praying, meditating, watching a movie. Research points to the benefits of deep breathing. Whether you follow an online five-minute meditation or literally just slow your breath down for two minutes, you can make changes in your hormone levels and muscle tension.

THINK ABOUT IT

What activities have you tried in the past to help alleviate stress? Think back to a time in the last few years when you experienced a level of stress that challenged you. Perhaps it was something related to school, like an exam period, or applying to colleges. Or perhaps it was something related to a transition in your relationships or in your family. How did you get through it? How did you and/or the community around you support you? What of these things do you have access to now?

Anxiety and Depression

Anxiety and depression are two of the most common ways to feel unwell mentally. They have a range of different ways of manifesting themselves in our daily lives. There is a difference between having anxious or depressed thoughts and feelings and having clinical depression or anxiety. Every person has these symptoms and feelings at some point in their lifetime. When these symptoms begin to interfere with your daily life, you may need to seek a diagnosis to receive the support you need to feel well. Some symptoms of anxiety are:

- Panic attacks
- Increased sense of worry or dread

- Feeling overly nervous
- Feeling very tense and rigid
- Rapid heart rate and rapid breathing. (See **Figure 9.3**.)

Some symptoms of depression include:

- Lethargy and exhaustion
- Sleeping too much or too little
- Decreased or increased appetite
- Feeling little interest in things
- Pulling away from family and friends, irritability, and thoughts or attempts of suicide

THINK ABOUT IT

Have anxiety and depression affected you, or people in your life?

How did it change you or the person you are thinking about?

Did you or this person take steps to help reduce the anxiety or depression?

On college campuses, students (both traditional and nontraditional) report startlingly high levels of depression (44%) and anxiety (50%). Suicide is the third-leading cause of death in college students (College Stats, 2017). Although stigmas around these issues are declining, they're still a powerful block to seeking help, and the numbers of students who struggle with mental health issues can be a powerful reminder that this happens to classmates and may happen to you. There should be no shame or fear associated with asking for help when you feel you may be experiencing problems with your mental health.

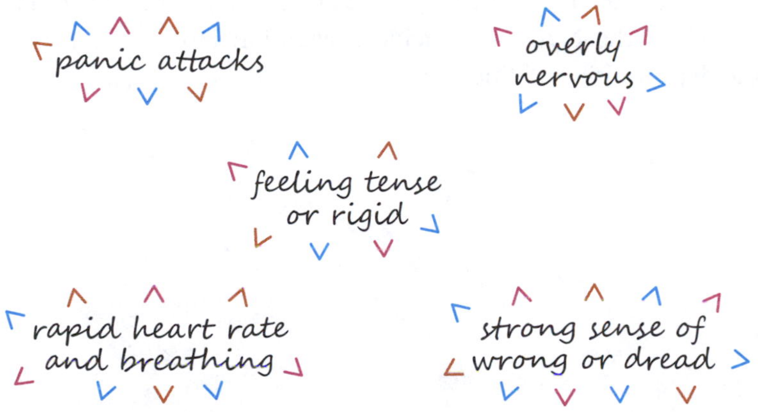

panic attacks

overly nervous

feeling tense or rigid

rapid heart rate and breathing

strong sense of wrong or dread

Figure 9.3 Symptoms of Anxiety

In order to effectively deal with anxiety and depression, it's important to listen to yourself. Ask yourself the following questions: What makes you anxious? What do you need to feel calm and focused? What may trigger depression in you? Are there things you can do to address these feelings before they become pronounced? Above all, it is important to know that your mental health is something that can be nurtured every day and addressed as your needs arise. During this time of great transition, remember to be kind to yourself, and forgiving. You will make mistakes. You will experience failures. These things have no bearing on your worth as a human.

Resources for Yourself or a Friend

Statistically, you or a friend will most likely have some of these symptoms during your college careers. Keep in mind that schools have mental health services for just this reason. If the mental health services at your school aren't a good fit, there are a broad range of services and hotlines available nationally.

It's important to care for yourself every day, not just at the most stressful or anxiety-inducing times. The more you attend to the way you're feeling every day, the more likely you will be able to help yourself cope with the ups and downs you experience in your life. If you are ever feeling overwhelmed to the point that it interferes with your life, your studies, your eating habits, or your sleeping, please take the time to reach out for support. There are many ways to do this, whether it's talking with a friend or academic advisor, making an appointment with your school's counseling services, or calling a hotline. Whatever you choose, it's important you choose something to support your well-being during stressful times in college. In addition, now is an important time to speak with your friends to offer them support if you feel they are not coping well with the demands of their lives, whether it be from school, family, work, or other pressures they're feeling (Bruce-Sanford & Soares, 2019). Reaching out can be awkward and challenging, but know that the value of your safety and the safety of those around you totally outweighs the need to make sure people are comfortable. If you find yourself or a friend talking about or attempting self-harm, it is important to act. You can always call 911 or the National Suicide Prevention Hotline at *1-800-273-8255* (https://suicidepreventionlifeline.org).

COMMUNICATION SITUATION

One unfortunate result of the stigma around mental illness is that it often prevents people from reaching out for help. Because it's not talked about often, you probably don't have a lot of experience in how to have this conversation. For this communication situation, imagine a scenario where a college student is talking to a friend, a family member, an instructor, a residence hall adviser, or an academic adviser trying to find support and resources.

• How would you approach this conversation? How does it feel?
• How do you best communicate this message?
• What is at stake in this communication?

Now imagine you are the audience.

• How would you feel, and how would you respond to this conversation?

Write a dialogue where the student communicated to someone, whether it's a friend or family member or an instructor, and the person responds. Aim for 8 to 10 turns for each speaker so you flesh out the dialogue and the scene.

Substance Use and Substance Use Disorders in College

Addictive substances will most likely be available to you during college and it is important to consider this in the context of your health. Regardless of whether or not you use them in college, this is a serious issue which affects people at many different times during their lives, so it is important for you to absorb this information, not only for yourself but for those around you.

Not everyone in college drinks or does drugs. This stereotype does a disservice to those who think they have to drink in order to belong. The reality is that there are a multitude of other options you have at college for having fun and making friends. Don't feel pressured to fit into a certain lifestyle at college, because there are way more than you can imagine, and it's worth it to try to find the one that's right for you. And if you do choose to partake in these substances, keep your health in mind and seek help if you need it.

Rather than focusing on the dangers of using drugs and alcohol, we want to help you understand the neuroscience of it. The dangers are well-publicized and widely known, whereas the actual effects on our brains are less widely understood. Ruth Potee, MD, is a family doctor and addiction medicine specialist. She also gives talks to a variety of audiences (e.g., parents of teens, EMTs, opiate task forces, public health officials, etc.) on the physiology of addiction. (Note: Her website at www.ruthpotee.com has a number of these videos available for viewing.)

We will present here the core of Potee's explanation about substances and the brain. Basically, our brains release dopamine as a way to reward us for doing something that is good for us, such as having a good meal (we won't starve) or having sex (our species will continue to exist) or even getting a good grade (success in the future). (ActonTV, 2019) The dopamine, a neurotransmitter, is released in our brain and feels good. The brain works this way so that we continue to seek out those things that will help us to survive.

Our baseline dopamine level goes up when we do something pleasurable (again, like eating good food or hearing a favorite song), and then goes back to its baseline level. Substances, like drugs, also impact our dopamine levels. But rather than the moderate-sized spike in dopamine levels that we get from a piece of pizza, the spike in dopamine from a drug like cocaine is huge. The brain, in reaction to so much dopamine, experiences significant pleasure and starts to adjust its reaction to dopamine in order to cope with this excessive amount. So, on the one hand the brain is saying, "Yes! I want to do that again!", on the other it's saying, "Wow, that's too much dopamine! In order to protect myself, I'll find ways to reduce the impact of that dopamine." The dopamine that is released with the intake of different drugs varies from drug to drug and many of the intricacies of what goes on in the brain differ (you've likely learned about depressants versus stimulants at some point), but Potee argues that all drugs, including alcohol, impact the amount of dopamine released.

When the brain has this overload of dopamine and starts to protect itself by reducing the impact of the dopamine, two important things start to happen. First, the user needs more of the substance to get to the same level of pleasure. You might know or understand this as building up a tolerance. So, if one beer used to give a person a tipsy feeling and now three beers are required to get to that same feeling, the dopamine produced by the brain is likely not having as big of an impact as before. The second impact is that the way your brain feels when you're not exposing it to the substance is different. Your baseline dopamine level is lower, meaning your general sense of pleasure is lower. Mondays feel worse. The work ahead feels worse. The joy that you usually get from a walk or dinner with a good friend isn't quite the same. Potee, specifically talking about dopamine in the brains of addicts, states, "People who struggle with addiction use [the substance] to feel normal." (See **Figure 9.4**.)

Some of you reading this might be asking, "Why the science lecture?" Others might be saying, "I'm not an addict!" Why are we including this in the text? Like so many things we've addressed in this text, the world tends to think of addiction as either/or, in which you either have a substance problem or you don't. Substance use disorder is actually a continuum of sorts. To diagnose this, doctors follow the guidelines from the most recent edition of the *Diagnostic and Statistical Manual*, (DSM-5) , which lists 11 criteria for substance use disorder

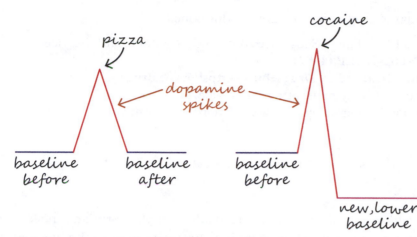

Figure 9.4 Dopamine Spikes: Pizza versus Cocaine

(American Psychiatric Association, 2013). A person can be diagnosed as having a mild substance use disorder if they have just two or three of the criteria. So, it's important to not see this as a binary of people who have problems and people who don't. Rather, people are on a scale, and certain behaviors can move us into more severe or concerning territory. The most important thing is to be aware of your relationship with any substance, and know how it fits into your life.

We also hope that explaining this in terms of neuroscience will help you to understand that addiction is not a character flaw, or a failure of sorts. It is a complex issue which can be very hard to control, and due to certain genetics or other factors, can affect each person differently. Therefore, you should never feel shame about reaching out for help, or approaching a friend to discuss it.

Due to the prevalence of substance use in college, it's also important to be aware of the bystander or Good Samaritan laws in your state. This is legislation that can protect you from getting in trouble for your own consumption of alcohol or other substances if you need to call 911 or your campus security to help a friend who is experiencing alcohol poisoning or a drug overdose. These are very important and save the lives of students every year by removing the fear of getting in trouble and allowing people to seek help for their friends when they need it.

College campuses typically have a number of resources you can reach out to if you're struggling with anything related to substance abuse, such as:

- Health center
- Counseling services
- Recovery groups on campus
- Sober-living facilities

Additional sources of information on this issue:

- National Helpline of Substance Abuse and Mental Health Services: 1-800-662-HELP (4357)
- National Institute on Drug Abuse: https://www.drugabuse.gov
- Alcoholics Anonymous: https://www.aa.org
- Addiction Center: https://www.addictioncenter.com

Social Health (Support Systems, Sexuality, and Consent)

Social health centers on how you relate to other people. Forming connections and bonds with people is very important in maintaining your health, no matter how much you believe you can do it on your own. In this section, we will help you understand what a support system is, and how you can build the one which will work best for you. Most of all, we want to convey the importance of connections with others in tough as well as happy times. Being surrounded by people who validate and support you in all situations in your life is key to your overall well-being. As with the other facets of well-being, college brings new opportunities to meet people, grow your community, and make lasting connections. As you branch out and become more independent by owning your college experience, one of the most powerful things you can do is find people who support you.

Support Systems and Connections

College is a time when you come into contact with many new people, from instructors and faculty to roommates and classmates. For some people, it's exciting to meet new people and develop friendships, but for others it can feel overwhelming to be placed in so many new social situations. It is helpful to spend a little time noticing how you react to new social situations.

THINK ABOUT IT

What is your favorite community you belong to or have been a part of? What relationships in your life are the most healthy and supportive? How do these relationships change the way you see your life?

Being mindful about creating a community starts with knowing yourself and being able to identify what you need, whether it's a small group of close friends, or a large network of people who can fulfill different needs for you. The people you spend time with are integral to shaping you, and so it's important to spend this time wisely, with people and groups that make you feel good about yourself, allow you to do things you love, and make you a better person. Finding people you connect with feels grounding and is an important way of discovering a sense of belonging in your college community. Within groups, it is normal to fall into a pattern of replicating the actions of other people in the group, good or bad, such as being very active, or drinking alcohol. It's important to be honest with yourself so you can recognize whether these actions are in line with how you want to be spending your time. Friendship and social connection are important, but ultimately you know what is best for you and your well-being. It's important to listen to your gut. Making choices that meet your needs and maintain your priorities is a valuable skill and you never need to apologize for doing this.

Being conscious of your social health doesn't mean you must have a certain number of friends, or that you can't be an introvert. It's not about forcing yourself to interact with other people. Instead, it's about having meaningful relationships and interactions that help you feel supported and healthy. If this means having two people in your life who you really trust and open up to, that's a support system. If this means having lots of people around you who you go to for all different types of issues, that's also a support system. In order to build positive and meaningful relationships, you must learn to communicate your needs to others. Whether you need advice, space, or a hug, it is important you let the people around you know how to support you by communicating with them.

Making friends is really hard and it's not usually an easy and automatic thing. Putting yourself out there is the first step, and while not easy, allowing yourself to be vulnerable and brave creates a lot of strength. For many of you, the last time you had to make new friends was when you were in kindergarten. Know that you are not alone; the vast majority of your classmates at college will also be looking for new friends, and probably feeling nervous in doing it.

Sexuality and Consent

The authors of this book made a deliberate choice to include a section on sexuality and consent in this chapter on well-being. This is a component of your well-being that is interconnected with your physical, mental, and social health. But sexuality may seem like a strange topic to include in this text. Study skills in one chapter and then sexuality in the next? For some, it may seem an inappropriate or taboo topic, while others may be quite comfortable with the subject matter. All of this is okay. Like most of the big themes we cover in this book, the topics of sex and sexuality are discussed in terms of how the habits you develop now in college will impact your thoughts, feelings, and actions in the future. So, now is the time to spend some time and energy in thinking about how you have seen your sexuality in the past, how you want to be right now, and what you might consider for the future.

There are many pervasive stereotypes about college students and sex. Specifically, there are many myths around the idea that everyone participates in a "hook-up culture," in which people are frequently engaging in sex, often with people they don't know. While these ideas are persistent, it's important to know that this experience is absolutely not how everyone experiences sex in college. There are a wide variety of ways that people engage with sexuality in college, and it's important you stay true to what you want, whatever that looks like. Don't fall for the idea that "everyone is doing it" and then risk doing things you don't feel ready for or comfortable with. Regardless of the approach you take, we want you to be informed so you can stay healthy and safe, and seek help if necessary.

The ability to choose comes up over and over in this text. You can choose how you want to collaborate with classmates, how you communicate in different situations, and how you want to see yourself as a writer. We also think it is up to you to choose how you want to express your sexuality. But your ability to choose does not override someone else's ability to choose. This is called *consent*: everyone involved must actively say "yes" to everything that is happening. If at any point anyone strays away from "yes," even just one degree, consent is no longer present. That means it's time to stop. Consent is a very important part of your sexual health, and we suggest you err on the side of overcommunicating to ensure everyone is comfortable with what is happening. This is an important opportunity for you to advocate for yourself and communicate your needs to other people.

Your college likely has multiple resources available for you as you're navigating your sexuality. This is a part of your life that can have many effects on your mental, physical, and social health, so we encourage you to take advantage of any of the following resources:

- Campus clinics can screen for STDs and STIs, as well as offer many different contraception options.
- Planned Parenthood has clinics in many towns and cities. They offer inexpensive or sliding scale services, including screening for STDs and STIs, pregnancy tests, etc.
- Many campuses have a confidential office or center to support students who are victims of sexual assault, relationship violence, stalking, or sexual harassment.
- Advisors, counselors, and therapists are all available to help you connect with resources you may need. Sometimes it feels best to start with someone you know.
- The National Sexual Assault Hotline can be reached at 1-800-656-4673, 24 hours a day.
- The Trans Lifeline 24-hour hotline is 1-877-565-8860.
- The LGBT National Youth Talkline is 1-800-246-7743.

You may or may not spend a lot of time focused on your sexuality in the next few years. Either way, know that there are places to go and people to consult when you have questions, feel worried or unsafe, experience feelings that are overwhelming, or simply want to know more information.

Financial Health

Financial health has a big impact on your overall well-being because it can profoundly impact your opportunities, stress levels, and other parts of your health. Therefore, it is important we include it in a chapter on well-being. We discuss financial health in terms of your mindset, the role of balance, and the importance of developing good habits that serve your goals. As with the other kinds of health we have covered in this chapter, financial health is a matter of understanding your past experiences, naming your habits, thinking about whether these habits contribute to your overall well-being, and shifting your mindset to support new habits.

THINK ABOUT IT

What do you know about money? Debt? Loans? Budgeting? Saving? Investing? Credit cards? Can you name when and how you developed this knowledge?

Everyone has a different relationship to personal finances, including different associations and experiences, resources, levels of comfort, and levels of literacy with their finances. Statistics show that seven out of 10 college students claim that their finances are a source of stress, so the chances are good that you will feel some stress about your money during your college years, and so will your peers and friends (Tran, Lam, & Legg, 2018). Financial knowledge is power, and in this chapter we begin providing some of the basic knowledge to help you claim that power. But this chapter doesn't cover everything it is helpful to know, so view this as a starting point for you to take action and learn more. The internet is full of resources for college students seeking financial literacy, and your school also probably has resources as well. Check out the Financial Aid Office to see if they have any free materials, so you can be purposeful and mindful in managing your money.

Personal Finances

You are starting college with one or more different ways to pay for school. You could be taking out loans, be on a scholarship, or using the GI bill. Perhaps you are working to pay tuition and living expenses, or relying on support from parents or other family members. Most likely, you are using some sort of combination of all of these.

When you break down your finances for college, you should know the difference between your tuition and your living expenses. Tuition is the cost of taking classes. Living expenses are the costs associated with living: food, housing, transportation, parking, insurance, books and other school supplies, social and fun things, to name a few. You get a tuition bill from your school that tells you how much tuition you owe based on how many credits you are taking. Your living expenses can vary from month to month, and it is best to create a budget to try to estimate how much you think you will spend.

TRY THIS ─────────────────────────────── 9.5

Guess how much your total cost will be for attending college this semester, considering all the relevant expenses. Write that number down. Now, gather the actual data for all of your expenses This includes: tuition, fees, transportation, housing, and food. Is the number about what you expected? Way off? What accounts for the difference?

Income

Your income is the money you earn, typically from working at a job. As tuition rates go up, more and more college students are working more and more hours. There is an inherent conflict here: You are spending a lot of money on tuition, so if you aren't able to get to class, do your homework, and study because you have to be at work, what's the point? There is usually a sweet spot, say 10 to 20 hours a week, where you can earn some income, but are not so busy that school-work takes a hit. Try to be realistic about how many hours you can work while still having time for your studies and taking care of yourself.

Some of you are working full-time or near full-time as you start to take your first-year courses. While not easy, it's a reality that many students face. Some students cope by taking multiple courses online so that their schedule has maximum flexibility. Others don't schedule face-to-face courses on one or two days a week so they can work long shifts on those days. Make sure your instructors are aware of your schedule and time constraints if there are class expectations that require you to be available outside of class time periods (to attend a speaker or event, or to do service learning, for example) and plan ahead.

Some students come into their first year of college already having a part-time job. If this works with your schedule and commute, great. Another option to consider is finding a job on campus, which has a few advantages. These jobs are close to where your classes are and so travel time is short, and they follow the same calendar that your school does, so when it's exam time, there may be some flexibility in terms of the shifts you work. Many campus jobs have supervisors and other adults whose life work is working with undergraduate students. They can become excellent resources, both as you are navigating classes and majors, and as you are thinking about the road ahead and graduation. Not only do you learn real work skills in these positions, you also build your network.

Work-Study

Work-study is a part of some financial aid packages. It is a federally funded program that pays part of the wages you earn while working in work-study jobs. Many on-campus jobs hire work-study students, and some *only* hire work-study students. While you don't make more money because of it, your employer only has to pay a part of your wage. The rest comes from the federal government. This means that you cost less to the employer and therefore are a more desirable hire. When jobs on campus are scarce, having access to work-study funding is a benefit. The mechanisms for hiring vary from campus to campus, so consider contacting your financial aid office for help finding work-study jobs. (See **Figure 9.5**.)

Expenses

Expenses include everything you have to pay for in order to live and go to school. There are big expenses like tuition and housing, and then there are the daily things that you tend to have more control over. Tuition is fairly out of your control, but there are choices to be made when it comes to housing. On-campus housing and off-campus housing come with their own costs and benefits. Students and their families have a variety of different approaches for figuring out what works best for them and their financial situation and provides the desired college experience. There is no one-size-fits-all or better choice, rather it is a matter of figuring out what is possible and optimal for you. You can talk to your Financial Aid Office to understand how your financial aid will be affected by your housing choice.

At college, there is a growing expectation that every student has a laptop and cellphone. These are not inexpensive items to buy or maintain. While there is pressure to have the newest and greatest, there is no shame in making do with what you have. If buying a new computer is going to use so much of your budget that it will cause you stress, ask yourself if you really need it or if you are just being convinced that you need it because of advertising or because someone sitting next to you has it. Look into whether your library has public computers or laptop rentals you can take advantage of if buying a device is out of the question.

Do I need to pay back my...

	YES	NO
work-study		X
scholarship		X
loans	X	
grants		X

Figure 9.5 What Do I Need to Pay Back?

Your daily and weekly budget is where you can most control the money you spend. Your daily and weekly expenses are usually the least expensive items (like food), but they still make a large impact on how much money you spend each semester. As you start to develop some independence with your finances, pay attention to where you spend your money and begin to decide if it's worth it. For example, is a fancy coffee at a coffee shop on the way to class *that* much better than what you can make in your kitchen? Are you spending money because you didn't think ahead and make yourself a sandwich before leaving home? These are choices you can make by paying attention to how you spend your money.

Daily expenses when peer groups are involved are a bit more complicated. Do you find yourself going out with friends and having little control over the restaurant where you go, the things that others order and then, when the bill comes, just splitting it? You can feel a lot of pressure and high expectations around getting together and spending money—and often the pressure and expectation is real. It takes courage to say, "I'd love to join you but I only have $5, so I'm just going to get a soda." While it's hard to say these things, likely there are others who will appreciate it. Saying something like that starts to normalize the idea that saving money benefits everyone. You can also respond to an invitation to go out with another invitation, such as "There's a free movie/concert/event. Do you want to join me at that?"

TRY THIS ———————————————————— 9.6

Track everything that you spend for one week. You can use an app or just use a notebook and pencil. At the end of the week, assess your expenses with the question, "Was it worth it?" You get to decide what makes something "worth" it? Whether it's enjoyment or some equation related to how long it would take you to earn that money, you decide.

At the end of the week, in 100–250 words explain what you would like to do differently in the week ahead, or if you wouldn't do anything differently, explain why you think your spending worked so well for you.

Loan/Interest Rate/Debt

If you have taken out a student loan, you likely know that you are borrowing money either from the federal government or from a private lender and that you will have to pay it back. You will pay back the amount you borrowed, as well as any interest accrued while you had the loan. The interest rate on federal student loans tend to be lower than from private lenders.

There are multiple resources, both online and at your institution, to help you understand the repayment plans for student loans and how and when repayment will start. Learn as much as you can as soon as you can, because college debt can greatly impact your life for the first 10 years after you graduate (the standard length of time for paying your loans back).

Student loans are good because they allow you to get your education, but it's still money you have to pay back. This impacts your choices after you graduate from college. It impacts how much money you need to earn, if you have money for travel, how much money you are able to save for a home or for retirement. Keep this in mind when you're ordering pizza or planning a spring break trip or buying the newest phone. One college campus had a public service campaign a few years back that had a pretty good tagline, "Live like a college student now so that you won't have to later." (See Figure 9.5.)

CRITICAL MOMENT

Student

I didn't really understand what a loan was until I graduated from college. I understood that I had to pay the money back, but I think I had thought more about the fact that there's interest on it and less about the fact that every month, for 10 years, that I would make a payment for the education I had received in college. I didn't realize that this impacted my opportunities after college— the types of jobs I could take (ones that pay more rather than ones I was more interested in), the types of adventures I could have now that I didn't have school (that payment was due every month, no matter what I was doing or where I was), and how soon I could start to save for the things that I really wanted. I'm grateful for my education and I know that the loans let me get it, but I wish loans were the types of things that you could understand BEFORE you take them out. I might have made different choices about how I spent some of my money.

Scholarships

Apply for scholarships. Even if it's only for $500, apply for it. Use the formula "how much money is the scholarship for" divided by "how many hours will it take you to apply for it." If a scholarship is $500 and it takes you five hours to complete the application, you earned $100.00 per hour. Many scholarship applications require you to write an essay and get a recommendation. Writing essays builds your essay-writing muscles. Asking for recommendations helps you to have a conversation with an instructor, *and* when you need another recommendation, you can ask them if they are willing to revise it to fit the new scholarship. (See Figure 9.5.)

Grants

Grants are need-based or merit-based and do not have to be paid back. They are free money to help pay for education. (Note: Collegescholarships.org is a good resource for learning about different grants and scholarships.) (See Figure 9.5.)

Overall, college finances include some things that you can control and some things you can't. Here are a few things you can control:

- You can pay attention to how much tuition costs and how you are paying for it.
- You can carefully budget your money. A budget is a reflection of your values. Do a personal spending diary for two weeks to see where your money is going.
- You can use your budget to keep your debt as small as possible.
- You can start building credit now.
- You can be frugal. Focus on what you have, not what you don't have.
- No matter what, you can keep track of what you are spending.
- Consider using an app such as "Mint" or "You Need a Budget."

Takeaways

▶ Investing in your well-being is about giving attention, care, and time to yourself and your well-being, and finding a balance that works for you that doesn't involve going to extremes.

▶ Your well-being is a complex thing made up of many factors, and maintaining it is about paying attention to each of these factors, keeping them at healthy levels, and ultimately being forgiving of yourself when things don't go as planned.

▶ Physical health is about maintaining the health of your body so it's able to help you do the things you love.

▶ Mental health is a critical aspect of well-being that requires maintenance, just as do other parts of well-being.

▶ Being aware of the effects of addictive substances on your brain gives you the power to make an educated choice about your usage of them.

▶ College students report that they have symptoms of depression and anxiety at a statistically high rate.

▶ Campuses often have mental health support services for students, and the National Suicide Prevention Hotline number is 1-800-273-8255.

▶ Regarding your sexual health, consent and communication are key parts of staying healthy and safe.

▶ Working to develop relationships with people and groups that make you feel good about yourself, allow you to do things you love, and make you a better person will contribute to your overall well-being.

▶ Financial health is all about awareness and knowledge. The more you know about and pay attention to your finances, the more you will be able to be in control of your finances now and into the future.

Takeaways on Your Terms

▶ Which area of your well-being feels like a strength for you? Why?

▶ Which area of your well-being feels like something you would like to improve? Why? What will you do to bring more awareness to this area?

In Your Own Words: Keep. Quit. Start.

Think through the various components of your well-being discussed in this chapter: physical exercise, nutrition, sleep, mental health, stress, and social and financial health. For now, just choose one and identify things you do within that component that you want to keep, things you want to quit, and things you want to start. Later, return and think through another component. How can you incorporate your goals of keep, quit, start into your daily habits? Log all this in your journal.

Chapter 9 Assignment

Goals of the Assignment

To actively engage in something available on your campus that will support some aspect of your health.

Steps of the Assignment

Challenge yourself and choose one of the following actions. Complete it. If it is easier for you, you can do your activity with a friend, but be sure to engage with others as well. You should choose an activity that is new for you, not something you already do on a regular basis.

- Ask a classmate or two if they are interested in studying for an upcoming exam together.
- Seek out a student group on campus that you're interested in learning more about and attend a meeting.
- If your school has a recreation center, go to a fitness class or a pick-up game.
- Seek out a book talk or an academic talk on campus (instructors often post these events on class websites or mention them in class). See if someone from your classes or dorm would like to go with you.
- Find out what kinds of on-campus events are held on the weekend—cheap movies for example—and make plans to go with someone.
- Do research to find out if your school has "culture" houses/groups where different cultures are showcased, supported, and celebrated. Are there events you can attend?
- Other activities: Find something outside your normal circle that lets you engage with people.

What You Need to Hand In

After you attend the event, write up a short report on it. Your first paragraph should state the date, time, and location of the event, as well as a description of the event. Subsequent paragraphs should cover the following:

- The Who, What, Where, When, How, and Why of the event
- A few sentences explaining your feelings about doing something new with new people
- Your analysis of what aspects of your well-being this activity supported
- If you would recommend that others on your campus engage in this way

Investing in Your Future

> " *Now I think it's one of the most useless questions an adult can ask a child—What do you want to be when you grow up? As if growing up is finite. As if at some point you become something and that's the end.* —Michelle Obama
>
> *...if you know how to attack the job market, your opportunities will be vast.* —George Anders
>
> *As young people, we are surrounded by expectations that may have little to do with who we really are, expectations held by people who are not trying to discern our selfhood but to fit us into slots.* —Parker J. Palmer "

In Your Own Words

10.1

1. At the beginning of Chapters 1–9, you were prompted to complete an "In Your Own Words" journal entry. Those opening prompts set a stage for the work and focus of each chapter, while also inviting you to reflect on your starting point in relation to the concepts and competencies of that particular chapter.
2. Reread the introductory "In Your Own Words" journal reflections you wrote for Chapters 1–9.
3. Spend 15 minutes free-writing in your journal about what you observed. What did you notice about your growth and development? The level of enthusiasm or engagement you invested? What did you notice about how your conceptual understanding has changed over time? For example, if you look back at how you approached terms such as diversity, or collaboration, what do you feel has evolved or changed?

Approaching or "Attacking" the Job Market

According to the Economic Policy Institute's *Class of 2019: College Edition* report, fewer than 20% of adults aged 21–24 are college graduates. (Gould, Mokhiber, & Wolfe, 2019) The U.S. Census Bureau reported in 2017 that fewer than 33% of Americans, aged 25 or older, are college graduates. These statistics suggest that you will already have a competitive edge when you enter the job market, by virtue of having a college degree. However, a college degree in and of itself is not a golden ticket to a dream job. As George Anders, Pulitzer Prize–winning journalist, author of *You Can Do Anything*, and Senior Editor at LinkedIn, wrote in one of the opening quotes of this chapter, *how* you approach or attack the job market matters. This is in keeping with our message throughout this book: How you approach a project (whether it is engaging diversity, collaboration, well-being, or a writing assignment) matters as much as what you bring to the project.

Being career ready means knowing what employers seek and value, being self-aware and comfortable enough to articulate how the skills and talents you bring align with what they value, and having confidence and dexterity as you approach your job search. (See **Figure 10.1**.) So, the good news is that being career ready is an extension of the growth mindset, process approach, and reflective practice you have been cultivating throughout this book. The goal in this chapter is to help you make connections between what you are doing today and what you will do in your future career. It also gives you the opportunity to practice and gain confidence in representing your skills and talents in a career context.

Figure 10.1 Being Career Ready

What Skills Are Employers Looking for from College Graduates?

In 2014, the *National Association of Colleges and Employers (NACE®)* surveyed 606 representatives from over 20 different types of organizations (for-profit; non-profit; large, small, government/public) who hire college graduates through direct recruiting and relations with universities across the country. (NACE, 2014) Respondents were asked to indicate the importance of seven core competencies when they review new college graduate candidates for their workplaces. (See **Table 10.1**.)

As NACE reported, it is noteworthy that four of these were identified as absolutely essential or essential by 90% or more employers.

THINK ABOUT IT

What stands out to you about this list? What surprises you? What is unsurprising? How confident are you in these competencies?

Professionalism/Work Ethic	97.5%
Critical Thinking/Problem Solving	96.3%
Oral/Written Communications	91.6%
Teamwork/Collaboration	90%
Information Technology Application	72%
Leadership	55.9%
Career Management	45%

Source: NACE 2014 Employer Survey

Table 10.1 Career Readiness Competencies Identified as Essential or Absolutely Essential (by Percent of Respondents)

Cognitive complexity, or the ability to translate knowledge and skills across different contexts, is also a competency that employers value. According to the Strada Institute's 2016 Report on Long-Term Labor Outcomes for Liberal Arts Graduates, "'LinkedIn data estimates: Between 2010 and 2013, the growth of liberal arts majors entering the technology industry from undergrad outpaced that of computer science and engineering majors by 10%...' *Companies are looking for intellectual dexterity just as much as they need technical expertise.*" (Strada Institute, 2016, p. 7).

As described by the concept of *intellectual dexterity*, employers are less interested in what classes you took and more interested in your ability to articulate and apply the skills and knowledge you learned in settings outside of a class or college. They want to feel confident that once you move from the classroom to the workplace, you will be able to—with some degree of independence—translate and attune your skills to the new setting.

We have brought your attention to the following consistently: As you enter new situations, you will encounter unique demands and specific factors that will require you to attune and refine your skills to be effective in that context. When you write a memo at work, for example, your supervisor will not hand you an assignment sheet or a rubric or a schedule for your drafts. Another way to think about this is: You might have perfected a complex piano solo at home playing alone, but this will feel and sound different if you perform in a crowded concert hall or if you add a full orchestra. So, you will need to prepare yourself to translate the performance alone at home to these new arenas. You will also need to prepare mentally, by imagining and thinking through the differences, and do so practically, too, by visiting and practicing in the setting to get a feel for it in your body, not just in your mind. Acknowledging and preparing to translate your competency from one situation to another is part of what strengthens your skill and makes it more durable and resilient. (See **Figure 10.2**.)

Figure 10.2 Translation, Attunement, Revision

TRY THIS ——————————————— 10.2

To practice attuning your skills to different contexts, we will guide you through a short writing exercise that helps demonstrate how different audiences affect how we communicate the same ideas. To start, imagine one of your friends just taught you how to do something that you find very cool: It could be a card trick, a way of playing an instrument, a new soccer move, or anything that makes you excited.

1. Imagine how you would tell another friend about this new skill you gained. What words would you use to describe it? How animated would you be in telling them? Would you let them ask questions, or just talk through it all at once?
2. Replace the friend with a parent, guardian, or another important adult in your life. How do the words you use differ? Are you still as animated and descriptive? How does your telling of the story differ?
3. Lastly, think about telling this same story to someone interviewing you for a job. Think about how your description of this skill differs, in your word choice, hand gestures, level of detail, and any other factors.

Look at these three different ways of talking about the same topic and reflect on how they differ. Did this happen naturally, or did you think about it intentionally as you wrote? How much do your accounts differ, and what does that tell you about your skill of attuning to the audience?

Beyond specific measurable and demonstrable competencies, respondents to the NACE survey also reported that candidates who demonstrate a competitive edge have strong self-awareness. Self-awareness is not measurable, but it is demonstrated by candidates' ability to comfortably and directly state the skills they bring, and to articulate their goals. Respondents reported that "candidates who had a clear sense of their career aspirations, direction, and goals have a distinct advantage over other candidates" and tended to "move up in the organization more quickly than those who don't have the same level of competency." In other words, employers value candidates *who know what they bring and can clearly articulate how it fits* with the role at hand. Employers value applicants who have reflected on their aspirations and can express them.

Entering the Arena   SECTION **10.2**

> It is not the critic who counts; not the man who points out how the
> strong man stumbles, or where the doer of deeds could have done
> them better. The credit belongs to the man who is actually in the
> arena, whose face is marred by dust and sweat and blood; who strives
> valiantly; who errs, who comes short again and again, because there
> is no effort without error and shortcoming; but who does actually strive
> to do the deeds; who knows great enthusiasms, the great devotions;
> who spends himself in a worthy cause; who at the best knows in the
> end the triumph of high achievement, and who at the worst, if he fails,
> at least fails while daring greatly... —**Theodore Roosevelt** (Roosevelt, 1910)

TRY THIS

1. Write down three job titles that interest you. They could be "dream jobs," careers you could picture yourself doing, or even jobs you've heard of but know very little about.
2. Go to https://www.onetonline.org/find/ and use their "Find Occupations" section, where they provide detailed information about the qualifications required, the day-to-day abilities that are most valued, and the experience of the work itself.
3. Search the three job titles you listed, and read through each of the pages devoted to them.
4. Pay particular attention to the "Skills" section. Do these surprise you? Are they what you expected? Do you have experience practicing them? Do they affect whether you believe you could do this job, or whether you would enjoy it?
5. Find three new jobs you've never heard of and explore their qualifications and job descriptions. Reflect on the same questions posed earlier in this list, thinking about what parts of these jobs make you more interested in them and which ones make you think they may not be a good fit

As we've discussed throughout this text, your mindset, your habits, and your ability to *approach with purpose* will prepare you for whatever path you choose. We've also emphasized that there is no growth without risk; no growth without some failure. An individual who is trying new things and stepping outside of their comfort zone regularly is going to experience failure. This is part of the process, and reframing failure as a growth opportunity is essential.

As we move from information about what employers value and expect to readying yourself mentally and practically to enter the arena, it is by no means an easy or comfortable journey. It requires a lot from you in terms of effort, reflection, resilience, and grit. The resources and tools offered in this section can serve to guide you through this process of cultivating self-awareness of your skills and goals, and confidently and comfortably communicating that to others.

Representing and Communicating Your Skills

According to the 2018 Strada/Gallup report, only about a third of current college students express confidence that they will graduate with the skills and knowledge they need to be successful in the job market (34%) and in the workplace (36%). (Strada-Gallup, 2018)

To start, it is absolutely essential to be aware of and comfortable expressing your skills and competencies, and to do so in ways that communicate effectively to prospective employers. As you make your way through your undergraduate experience, you will take a variety of courses and experience diverse opportunities in and out of school, from jobs to internships or research opportunities, to community service activities and cultural events. Be mindful that each of these opportunities has the potential to support your development of some core skills and competencies you are in college to cultivate. As we have discussed throughout the book, skill development takes time, practice, and the opportunity to reflect.

The College of Liberal Arts (CLA) at the University of Minnesota has dedicated significant resources to supporting their undergraduates' career readiness. (Amy Lee, one of the authors of this book, directs the faculty engagement component of CLA's Career Readiness initiative. Maggie Bergeron, another author, has served on the faculty advisory team for the initiative.) We highly recommend you take a look at the rich and robust resources CLA has developed and provided, many of which are public and available. (Note: The CLA can be found at http://get-ready.cla.umn.edu/.)

One of those resources is a tool that provides structure for students to document and practice communicating about the competencies they are developing as they make their way through their undergraduate career. The tool is called RATE which stands for the stages in the metacognitive process the tool walks students through: Reflect, Articulate, Translate, and Evaluate. The RATE tool is a way to habituate yourself to the practice of observing, charting, and articulating your growth and invites students to truly engage with their education as an experience instead of a transaction.

While RATE is only available to UMN students right now, it is possible to move through the steps of a RATE on your own in order to be able to take a step back from and really investigate an experience that develops a skill or competency. It is also a helpful habit to regularly engage in as a metacognitive practice, because it can help you develop an understanding of the way you speak and write about yourself, something that is deeply important in the job search process from writing a cover letter to developing your résumé to interviewing.

As part of their Career Readiness framework, the College of Liberal Arts at the University of Minnesota has identified and defined 10 Core Career Competencies that students will cultivate over the course of their undergraduate experience in their coursework and in co-curricular and extracurricular experiences. These core competencies were developed through consultation with employers, alumni, faculty, and professional organizations such as NACE. (Note: You can learn more about all 10 Core Career Competencies at http://get-ready.cla.umn.edu/core-career-competency-videos.html#problem.) For our purposes in this chapter, we will highlight four of the Core Career Competencies, because those four have been at the center of this book and are core components of your first-year experience.

1. *Analytical and Critical Thinking* comprehensively explores issues, ideas, knowledge, evidence, and values before accepting or formulating an opinion or conclusion. Those competent in Analytical and Critical Thinking.

2. *Engaging Diversity* cultivates awareness of one's own identity and cultural background and that of others through an exploration of domains of diversity, which may include race, ethnicity, country of origin, sexual orientation, ability, class, gender, age, spirituality, etc. This requires an understanding of historical and social contexts and a willingness to confront perspectives of dominant cultural narratives and ideologies, locally, nationally, or globally.

3. *Teamwork and Leadership* builds and maintains collaborative relationships based on the needs, abilities, and goals of each member of a group.

4. *Oral and Written Communication* intentionally engages with an audience to inform, persuade, or entertain.

TRY THIS   10.4

You can choose to write or type your RATE, or you can make short videos, or even speak into a voice recorder app. All of these modes of capturing your thinking are valid and important. Try to vary the form you use to complete RATES so you are exercising all of these different communication muscles.

Steps to complete a RATE:

1. *Choose an experience* to focus on for this RATE. It could be an assignment or project you did for a class. Or you could choose a community service activity or extracurricular event you attended. Once you have an experience in mind, think about the core competencies employers said they valued: from as small as a paragraph in a paper or an interaction with a group to as large as an entire class or internship. Then, choose one of the competencies shown in the previous list (Analytical and Critical Thinking, Engaging Diversity, Teamwork and Leadership, Oral and Written Communication) that you feel connects to your experience.

2. *Reflect* on your experience. Take some time to document what this experience entailed. What did you do? How did you do it?

3. *Articulate* how this experience connects to the competency you chose. What did you do that grew your capacity for this competency? What choices did you make that made them feel purposeful? What choices did you make that made them feel not as purposeful?

4. *Translate* how your experience with this competency might connect to a job or workplace. What part of this experience feels like it applies to the "real world"? What part of this experience might be valuable in a workplace?

5. *Evaluate* how competent you feel in this competency. If you had to give yourself a 1–3 score, with 1 being very inexperienced and 3 being an expert, where would you land? Why?

Consultation and Network-Building

According to the Strada/Gallup 2017 College Student Survey of 32,585 currently enrolled college students, "Students who receive career-specific support feel most prepared for the workforce." (Strada-Gallup, 2017)

The report notes that this support might take a variety of forms from frequent conversations with faculty or staff about career options, to having at least one conversation with them about their career options, but that students who believe someone in their school is committed to helping them will "express significantly more confidence in their preparation for the workforce than students who have not experienced the same support." Stop and think about this; students report that informal conversations have a significant impact on their sense of being career ready.

THINK ABOUT IT

Set a timer for three minutes and free-write on the following: How do you feel when you hear the term "networking"? Why do you think you feel that way? What are your associations with this term? Direct experiences?

It may feel uncomfortable to seek out these conversations, but the reality is that it is essential. Contacting people for guidance, insight, and information requires effort, planning, initiative, and courage. All of those are also essential practices when you enter the job market, so this is a good, low-stakes way to exercise those qualities. Second, the expertise, contacts, information, and mentoring you might find will be helpful as well. According to statistics, more than 70% of professionals get hired at companies where they have a personal connection, and job candidates who are referred by an employee are eight times more likely to get hired. (Fisher, 2017)

College is a prime time to expand your social network. Your access to a variety of people previous to college was often limited to your community and who your family and friends were connected to. While this can be a rich resource, the more people you know, the more this network expands. Your instructors at college are now part of your network, as are guest speakers in your classes and alumni of your institution. Just as your classmates are textbooks that go unread if you don't engage with them in your class, the professionals you are exposed to throughout your college journey are contacts into the world of work that become part of your network once you engage with them. Engaging can look like many things, whether it is sending someone an email letting them know you're interested in their work, or scheduling an informational interview to find out more about what a person's job entails. When you make genuine connections with people, keeping in touch with them won't feel like a chore.

SIMPLE STRATEGIES

Be consistent about keeping your contacts up to date. When you meet someone, reach out to them and friend them on LinkedIn or another such social media platform. Your future self will thank you.

While it can be uncomfortable to put yourself out there, pushing through this vulnerability is critical to growth and to deepening your understanding and your network. Regardless of how extroverted you are, this may be uncomfortable at first. You won't always get the response you want—in fact, you may not get a response at all—and this isn't easy for anyone. This is an important time to practice resilience by not letting this stop you from reaching out next time. Every time you put yourself on the line, you are opening yourself up to the possibility of failure, but also the possibility of making a positive connection with someone that shifts your outlook and career prospects in a meaningful way.

TRY THIS   10.5

Choose five people you would like to meet for an informational interview. Why did you choose them? What about them is interesting or aspirational? How could you connect with them?

Next, carry out your plan with three people. How does it feel to reach out in this way? Did anything come of your inquiries?

In addition to leveraging individual connections, find out what career resources your school offers. The Strada/Gallup 2017 College Student Survey reports that 4 in 10 students have never visited their school's career services office or used online career resources, including more than one-third of seniors. Overall, 39% of current students have never visited their school's career services office or used their online resources. Though juniors and seniors are more likely than first- and second-year students to have used their career services office, still, 35% of seniors say they have never used this resource. This report goes on to note that, "black and Hispanic students, as well as first-generation college students and nontraditional students, are more likely than other students to rate the guidance they received from their career services office as very helpful."

TRY THIS _____ 10.6

1. Find out if your school has a career center or career services office. Make an appointment or drop by and explore what they offer. Many campuses provide you with the opportunity to actually sit down with a qualified professional counselor who will help you with formal and informal self-assessments and work with you through all stages of the career decision-making process. This is a specialty area just like the Writing Center, and it is one that is often underused, overlooked, or misunderstood. If you were to pay a career consultant, it would be over $100/hour, so take advantage of this resource while you are in college! Here are some of the things you might find available to you:

> Career counseling
> Résumé writing workshops or consultations
> Mock interviews
> Career fairs
> Internship connections and placement help

2. Figure out how you can access the resources available to you. You may need to:

> Make an individual appointment
> Register for a workshop
> Show up for a drop-in appointment
> Access online tutorials and materials

In Your Own Words
10.7

At the end of Chapter 5, you completed an assignment where you interviewed someone about collaboration in their workplace. At the end of Chapter 7, you interviewed someone about writing in either a specific discipline or in a particular workplace. Now, return to those assignments and reread your notes from the interviews and what you actually turned in.

In your dedicated journal space, spend some time thinking and writing about the following questions.

1. What struck you or surprised you about how the people you interviewed applied skills such as collaboration or writing in the workplace? Where did you see connections to what you're doing in college? Where did you see disconnections?
2. What was your impression of this person's environment when at work or engaged in their discipline? What did you perceive to be their excitement or motivation related to their job?
3. Overall, what did those interviews show you about the world of work?

Be prepared to discuss in a small group:

▶ One connection or disconnection to what you've been doing in college

▶ One detail about the environment that your interviewees work in

▶ Your overall impression of the world of work

Résumés

Ultimately, résumés are the tool by which you communicate the skills and qualities you bring, demonstrating self-awareness and your alignment with the opportunity. It is important to be aware of the rhetorical constraints and challenges of résumés as a form or mode of writing, and it is also important to talk about the fact that résumés are a representation of you and your skills, attributes, and talents, and so it might make you feel vulnerable and awkward. Just as you learned in Chapter 8, you need to prepare yourself for this project and be mindful of what you know, don't know, and need to know, and what aspects of it will be especially challenging for you.

We begin with the form of the résumé. Strategically presenting your experiences and skills in a résumé is hard. The space limits are typically intense. So you can't communicate or simply list all of your attributes and achievements. You have to select, curate, and strategize. There also isn't a universal résumé genre, either. The conventions and expectations can differ in trivial and substantive ways across types of jobs and employment sectors. So you need to be informed about, and attuned to, what your audience wants, in terms of form and conventions, as well as key words and phrases that will be effective. Your résumé is the "first look" employers will have, not only at the relevant skills and qualifications you hold, but also at you—what kind of colleague you will be, what kind of producer, and what kind of contributor.

The style and substance of résumés vary greatly, depending on the field, type of work, and the country and culture of the organization or corporation. So, begin with research related to the different forms that are out there, and focus on the ones you're most likely to use.

COMMUNICATION SITUATION

A résumé is, in short, a form of communication with a potential employer. You can develop a deeper understanding of the moves that applicants make when putting together a résumé by seeking out example résumés and analyzing them. For this Communication Situation, you will need two or three résumés. These can be found online, picked up from your school's career center or shared by a friend or family member. For each résumé, answer the following questions.

When looking at each résumé, consider:

- The layout
- The tone
- The visual presentation
- The sequence of the information
- The length
- The type of language used

When you are comparing your sample résumés, what stands out to you as different? Do those differences reflect the individuality of the applicant? Differences in the audience? Differences in the field? Or something else?

Now seek out sample résumés in your potential career field. Answer the preceding questions for those résumés. If possible, discuss your samples with people in the field in order to assess how typical, relevant, and current they actually are.

Some companies that receive résumés still have humans scanning the documents for whether or not a candidate is a good fit for a first-round interview. However, more and more companies and institutions are using technology to scan résumés for specific words and phrases. Writing a résumé that will scan well is a very specific kind of writing. If your institution has a career center, this is a good place to learn more. Online resources like Purdue Owl's résumé resources are also a good resource for learning more about how résumés should be put together in terms of spacing and punctuation, so that your keywords are seen. (Purdue University Online Writing Lab)

TRY THIS _____ 10.8

Search online on at least five different websites for job listings that appeal to you, using keywords that reflect your interests and aspirations. Read through 10 different job listings that fulfill your criteria for a job that you would want. Look through the required and preferred skills for patterns or commonly used phrases, such as "strong communication," "proficient in Office," or "skilled in collaboration." What do you notice? What skills show up in all of them?

Your résumé will represent a collection of your concrete, tangible competencies (e.g., proficiency in different computer programs), as well as speak to your less tangible competencies such as the four identified in Section 10.2 of this chapter. The art of writing a résumé that captures this and is attuned to the appropriate audience is one, like all of writing, that benefits from starting early, doing multiple revisions, and getting adequate feedback. Rather than being overwhelmed by the task when you start seeking a position, start now. Create a document that can be a place to record your growing and developing competencies. When it comes time to put yourself out there professionally, you will be grateful for having started this beforehand.

Beyond the challenge of making rhetorical choices about how you represent yourself to future employers, résumés are also difficult because they ask you to promote yourself. To some, this comes naturally, but to many, it is uncomfortable because it is an act that renders us vulnerable. There is no advantage here to being humble and trying to avoid sounding self-promotional. By nature, a résumé forces you to promote yourself, and this is an important opportunity to not shy away from your accomplishments, but celebrate and communicate them. This is a good time to reflect on other parts of the text, such as the writing chapters, in which we asked you to really *own* your work and your experience. You have put in the work to cultivate relevant skills and gain experience in certain areas, so be proud of it, and put in the time to communicate it well in order to give yourself the best possible chance of being hired.

Takeaways

▸ Becoming informed about the job market and what employers are looking for will help you "attack" the job market in the most intentional and informed way possible.

▸ You have already cultivated skills and qualities that are desirable to future employers, and the key is becoming aware of them and learning to communicate them.

▸ Employers are looking for particular skills, such as professionalism/work ethic, critical thinking/problem solving, oral/written communications, and teamwork/collaboration.

▸ Practicing intellectual dexterity and self-awareness is key to having a competitive edge in the job market.

▸ The RATE (Reflect, Articulate, Translate, and Evaluate) tool is a valuable way of reflecting on and charting your growth in particular skills and competencies.

▸ Utilizing the available resources is key to having the most informed approach to your career process possible.

▸ Résumés are a difficult but necessary part of the process, and you will benefit from starting early and continuing to adapt and change as you learn more about yourself.

Takeaways on Your Terms

▸ Which part of this chapter made the most sense to you? Why?

▸ Which part of this chapter seemed the most far away to you? Why?

In Your Own Words: Keep. Quit. Start.

In your journal, reflect on the way you have viewed your future career in the past. Has it felt distant? Exciting? Daunting? Something you have complete control over, something out of your hands? What about this approach and view is productive, and that you want to keep? What about it will you quit doing? And what will you start doing to integrate yourself into this view and approach?

Chapter 10 Assignment

Goals of the Assignment

To dive into a person's career journey in order to learn about the various steps different individuals might take on their path to a career.

For this assignment, you will need access to a person's journey. Depending on the type of career you are wanting to research and whether or not you know someone with that career, there are multiple ways to approach this assignment. Here are a few.

A. Think of a person you could talk to who has a job that sounds cool or appealing to you. Either friend that person on LinkedIn or ask them if they'd share their résumé with you. From a résumé or LinkedIn profile, you can likely gather information on their educational journey and where they've worked and in what positions. Having a connection to the person also gives you some potential to later interview them.

B. Think of a person who you don't know personally but who has a job you want to know more about or that you aspire to have. This could be someone moderately in the public view, like the superintendent of a school district or a public health official at the state level, or the person who wrote a screenplay for your favorite TV show, or someone whose YouTube channel you subscribe to. Search the internet for information on this person. Read interviews. Listen to podcasts. What can you piece together about their background? Search websites connected to their current employer. See if there is a résumé or a curriculum vitae (cv) for that person.

C. Choose a job title you are interested in learning about. An internet search for that job title + the word "résumé" will bring you to a number of résumé-building sites that show sample résumés for that career and that also compile the type of job qualifications for job postings seeking candidates in that field. Alternatively, you can search LinkedIn or similar networking sites (your institution may have its own networking site) to see actual résumés for individuals on those sites who have that job title.

Once you've gathered your information, complete the following steps. These steps will vary some, depending on how you've gathered your information.

Steps of the Assignment

1. In chronological order, start to list the steps of their journey. Consider the following:

A. Where did they go to school?
B. What was their major?
C. What jobs have they had since completing their education?
D. What other activities are included on their résumé? Other types of certifications? Awards? Publications?

If this is a person you have access to, once you've looked at their LinkedIn Profile or their résumé, ask if you can interview them. Questions to potentially ask include:

A. How did you decide on your major?
B. How did your vision of what you wanted to do evolve?
C. What excites you about your job?
D. What do you see as the most helpful things you did to prepare for the work you do now?

2. Annotate the chronological list, so the list represents the facts of their journey, and the annotations are your reflections, questions, and ideas on their journey. If you're in a Google doc, highlight small sections of it (one or two key words) and then add a comment. In those comments identify:

▸ What surprises you and why (e.g., How connected does their major seem to their current job?)

▸ Things they have done that you had not thought of before as part of this journey.

▸ What seems to be essential. (For example, what credentials are necessary for certain job titles?)

3. Look back over the "journey" that you've mapped out and your annotations. How would you describe their journey? How does this change or reinforce your own ideas about your journey through college and the postcollege job market? If you were able to either interview a person OR listen to interviews with them, do you see evidence of them engaging in the practice of reflecting, articulating, translating, or evaluating?

What You Need to Hand In

Your final product will be an annotated list of steps that either a specific person made, or an amalgamation of the people that you researched have made, along with a 200-word reflection summarizing what you learned.

CRITICAL MOMENT
Your Turn

Throughout this book, we have offered you "Critical Moments" to read and consider. Each of those critical moments was provided by instructors and first-year students we have worked with in our courses or research projects. Many of these reflections came from a long-term research project conducted by Amy Lee (one of the book's authors) and her collaborators who collected journals from approximately 375–400 first-year students every semester for three years, with each student writing at multiple points in time in the semester.

In the final entry each semester, students were asked to reflect on a Critical Moment: to choose a significant moment, event, or incident within the course or the semester; describe it thoroughly; and reflect on its meaning or value to them. The idea is to cultivate reflective practice, which many educational and cognitive theorists believe is a critical component in moving from implicit to explicit knowledge. In other words, reflection helps you become aware of what you might know implicitly and thereby deepens the knowing. That is why, throughout this book, we have asked you to compose journal entries "In Your Own Words."

Now, it is your turn to offer a Critical Moment. Brainstorm a list of moments that stand out to you from your first year of college. Choose any one of those moments and describe it in detail for someone who wasn't there. Set the scene a bit. Where were you? What was the context of the moment? What was going on? Then spend some time analyzing and reflecting on the significance of that moment. Why does it stand out to you as a Critical Moment? What did you take from it, and what impact did it have? Why do you remember it?

Conclusion to Approaching College with Purpose

In times of change, learners inherit the earth, while the learned find themselves beautifully equipped to deal with a world that no longer exists. —Eric Hoffer

In Your Own Words: Conclusion

Take some time to read through your *In Your Own Words* journal entries. As you read, make a note by (or star or underline) things that stand out to you. Pay attention to the ideas and themes that recur in your entries. What are the big questions you keep returning to? What do you notice and learn about yourself as you read through all of these? Once you are finished, spend 10–15 minutes free-writing your final journal entry. Think about your mindset, level of self-awareness, and approach to college. What do you remember about the way you approached your journal that first day? How is that different from how you approach writing this final one? What areas of growth and change feel particularly meaningful to you? How does this make you think about future growth?

Attending college is a huge accomplishment. You are taking classes and having other experiences that expand your body of knowledge, worldview, and understanding of yourself and how you fit into your community and the world. Congratulations on taking this step, and try to not lose sight of this accomplishment.

As you continue your studies, you will make small and large decisions each day, both in and out of class, that will impact your college experience. Engagement is a tool and a choice that is in your hands. Throughout this book, we've tried to emphasize the importance of *you* as the center of your college experience. Rather than seeing yourself as being along for the ride on this journey, we hope you can see yourself as an agent of your own destiny. Work hard to stay attuned to yourself and listen to your inner voice through this time of growth and change. Keep journaling to stay reflective and mindful. Don't lose sight of the importance of your voice and your perspective in shaping your experience.

The work you have done in this book will serve you well during your time in college and beyond. Please consider this book a resource for your future—come back to your journals and assignments to see where you were at this time, and do some of the features and assignments again next year or the year after. Let them serve as a barometer for who you are, how you've grown, and where you want to go.

Onward.

GLOSSARY

A

Ability to tolerate ambiguity: Ability to function even in an environment of uncertainty; this means being able to produce and interact when there is uncertainty or conflicting directions or views.

Active listening: Taking in, processing, and focusing on what is being said.

Anne Lamott's "sh*#ty first drafts": The countless previous drafts full of errors, poor wording, and total chaos required to get to a final draft. The compelling, life-changing, beautiful texts that people love are the product of a sh*#ty first draft, plus a lot of revision, and new ideas, and outside input, and more and more revisions.

Anxiety: The state of being when your feelings of worry and dread affect your ability to function. Some symptoms of anxiety are panic attacks, feeling overly nervous, feeling very tense and rigid, rapid heart rate, and rapid breathing.

Attunement to Audience and Context: Steering your communication into the style best suited for the audience and the material.

Audience evoked: The habitual and often even unconscious way we imagine a sort of default or automatic audience when we write. People internalize vague generalizations, past associations, and what was informally an ad hoc learned about an audience.

Audience imagined: Unlearning the unconscious internalized version of the audience to facilitate a more effective and conscious performance.

B

Being purposeful: When you stay open to your growth and change, are honest about habits and practices that haven't served you well in the past and you want to leave behind, and you are intentional about the new habits and attitudes you adopt.

Bravery: A feeling of courage to act in the way you feel is right. Bravery does not exist without vulnerability. The vulnerability, through the susceptibility to harm, is what makes actions we see as brave in the light we do. If there were no possibility of harm or failure, these actions would not require courage. Bravery can be discovered through vulnerability.

Bulleting: A form of notetaking where you list ideas from the text, reactions you have, and connections to class material in bulleted form.

C

Career ready: Knowing what employers seek and value, being self-aware and comfortable enough to articulate how the skills and talents you bring align with what they value, and having confidence and dexterity as you approach your job search.

Change State: A place between comfortable and uncomfortable where a perspective shift can take place. Change state is absolutely necessary for intercultural development.

Charge: In many business settings, when a group is formed, employees are given a charge, in the form of a clear outcome, or set of outcomes, that they are asked to achieve.

Cognitive complexity: The ability to recognize and acknowledge differences, and to synthesize; the ability to engage seemingly oppositional views or facts.

Collaboration: Where a group works together to achieve something.

Confirmation bias: When we see a person we've prejudged behave in a way that supports the stereotype, our idea is confirmed. When we see that person behave in a way that conflicts with our judgment, we tend not to notice it or we see it only as an exception. Social scientists call this confirmation bias.

Consent: When everyone involved actively says "yes" to everything that is happening. If at any point anyone strays away from "yes," even just one degree, consent is no longer present. That means it's time to stop. Consent is a very important part of your sexual health.

Controlling idea: The controlling idea connects everything in the paragraph under a kind of umbrella, so that readers can identify the point, purpose, or central idea conveyed by the sentences gathered here.

D

Deep learning: Deep learning is interacting with new content or ideas in ways you can incorporate into how you see the world and the choices you make inside that world.

Deficit mindset: To be focused on what you *lack*, which will lead to self-defeating talk and frustration.

Depression: The state of being when you lose interest, focus, and energy in a way that affects your daily life. Some symptoms of depression include lethargy and exhaustion; sleeping too much or too little; decreased or increased appetite; feeling little interest in things; pulling away from family and friends, irritability, and thoughts or attempts of suicide.

Direct plagiarism: The writer copies words of another author and does not cite the source or use quotation marks. It's also considered plagiarism if you *do* cite the source but *don't* use the quotes, or vice versa.

Diversity: Diversity refers to all the forms of human difference—social group and individual, visible or invisible—that define cultural identity as perceived, imposed, or self-defined. Diversity includes individual differences (personal history, life experience, educational background, learning preferences), as well as group or social differences (race, ethnicity, religion, language spoken, socioeconomic class, sexual orientation, country of origin).

E

Effective groups: An effective group has members who feel like they belong, have a shared, stated goal (short-term and long-term), have norms/rules that are agreed upon, recognize the value in having multiple perspectives, listen to each other, support each other, and foster risk-taking.

Engaging diversity: Engaging diversity is much more than just exposure to different perspectives. It is about being able to communicate and form relationships with one another. Engaging diversity is a process requiring practice, coaching, and mentoring to develop the skills and confidence needed for a globally interconnected world of work and life.

Equal social status: Equal participation from all group members.

Extrovert: A person who displays a willingness to participate in a group and do the work by behaving in an outgoing and gregarious manner.

F

Financial well-being: Financial health has a big impact on your overall well-being because it can profoundly impact your opportunities, stress levels, and other parts of your health. This includes how you manage your personal finances, income, and expenses.

Fixed mindset: A person inclined toward a fixed mindset tends to see their ability to learn as set, or *fixed*, at a certain level. They see challenges that they can't solve as being due to the limits of their intellect or abilities.

Food insecurity: Lack of control and security in regard to food access.

Free-writing: Free-writing is the act of writing nonstop and turning off that inner judgmental voice so you don't think about what you're writing.

G

Glossing the text: One of the least time-consuming methods of note-taking that consists of writing annotations, or notes, in the margins.

Grants: Grants are need-based or merit-based and do not have to be paid back. They are free money to help pay for education.

Grit: Grit is passion and perseverance for very long-term goals.

Group identity: It is usually a low-stakes task that requires a newly formed group to brainstorm and then come to a consensus. It allows the group to get to know each other on a human level before the work of the team begins. This is the beginning of building psychological safety within the team.

Group norms: Establishing clear expectations about how things are going to happen. While group norms are important for all groups, no matter how small or short-lived they are, they are essential for groups that are going to work together on larger-scale projects over a longer period of time. If the group members don't actively establish norms that the group discusses and agrees upon, those norms will be formed anyway, but likely not in a purposeful, or useful, way.

Growth mindset: A growth mindset is oriented to chalk up failures to not investing enough effort or not being ready yet. This type of mindset makes a person more likely to be willing to take on a future challenge and thrive, seeing any failures as a reflection of their effort rather than a determination of their worth.

H

Higher-level learning: Higher-level learning is when you're able to apply new knowledge to a variety of situations and go beyond understanding and into application and analysis.

I

Identifying multiple perspectives: Actively seeking different interpretations or ways of seeing an issue or idea, or approaching a problem from different directions.

Income: The money you earn, typically from working at a job.

Informational interviews: Interviews to find out more about what a person's job entails.

In-group bias: Typically, we tend to be able to acknowledge, see, and understand many kinds of differences among the members of a group when we are a part of that group. Social scientists call this *in-group bias*. Because we are a part of the group—a religious organization, for example—we know there are all sorts of different types of people with different attitudes toward their faith within the organization.

Intellectual dexterity: Your ability to articulate and apply the skills and knowledge you learned in settings outside of a class or college. With some degree of independence, being able to translate and attune your skills to new settings.

Intercultural development: Examining preconceived notions or accepting, integrating, and finding space for other perspectives within your own frames of reference.

Introvert: A person who prefers and generates energy from being alone.

Ivy Lee Method: Before you go to bed, you list out the six most important tasks you need to accomplish the next day and then prioritize them 1 to 6. The next day you start with number 1, do it until it's complete, and then move on to number 2.

L

Loan: Money you borrow either from the federal government or from a private lender that you will have to pay back, as well as any interest accrued while you had the loan. The interest rate on federal student loans tend to be lower than from private lenders.

Long-term groups: The strategy behind forming long-term groups is that it mirrors how professionals work—in teams, over longer periods of time. It provides a manageable way to complete a large or complex assignment when there is more work to be done than one person can do on their own. Long-term groups provide consistency.

Looking-glass self: A sociological concept coined by Charles Horton Cooley that argues that we form our self-concept, in large part, based on how we believe others see us. This means that rather than form a sense of our self from our own experiences and our own interpretation of those experiences, we look to others, observe their reactions, and let our understanding of their response inform our sense of self.

M

Mental well-being: Maintenance of anxiety, depression, stress, and substance use. That maintenance can take many forms, such as having good conversations with family and friends, seeing a therapist regularly, or taking mental breaks to do something you enjoy.

Metacognition: To develop an awareness of what you know, how you know it, and how it connects to other information. It means the ability to step back, assess, and plan.

Microdecision: A microdecision is a small decision that you make in the course of your day that, under normal circumstances, you might not think has any impact.

Mindfulness: A state of being open to new perspectives and adapting to change.

Mindlessness: Characterized by entrapment in old categories, by automatic behavior that precludes attending to new signals. Being mindless is like being on automatic pilot.

Mindset: Mindset describes habits of our mind that are shaped by previous experience. Although it only constitutes a pattern of thought in your brain, it shapes your actions, interactions, habits, and way of life.

Monolithic: We tend to view groups we don't belong to as monolithic. We attribute sameness or generalized shared qualities to all members of the group. This can lead to the formation of stereotypes about a certain group of people.

N

Networking: Contacting people for guidance, insight, and information.

O

Openness/humility: The capacity to remain open to and influenced by new information, even if it contradicts ideas that may be deeply held or believed to be true.

P

Parenthetical reference: A parenthetical reference gives page numbers in their correct form.

Passive listening: Instances where we are hearing noise but not distinguishing words on a conscious level, and yet we can still repeat some of it back if we had to.

Patchwork plagiarism: In this case, the writer might use some direct words, phrases, or ideas from another author but doesn't cite the source they came from. Sometimes, we see writers who take someone else's text and try to move things around, paraphrase here and there, and then present the work as their own. This is plagiarism. In general, everything that is not an original idea to you and is not common knowledge (e.g., Minnesota became a state in 1858) needs to be cited.

Peer-to-peer instruction: The process of working with classmates to understand and articulate content from your classes. The act of having to express your ideas to someone outside your perspective who won't automatically know what you mean forces you to refine and more deeply understand your own thoughts.

Physical well-being: Maintenance of exercise, nutrition, and sleep.

Plagiarism: When you take the words and/or ideas of another person and use them without giving credit to the source. There are three general categories of incidents of plagiarism: 1. Intentional—A student copies and pastes from sources and turns it in as their own work when they understand the concept of plagiarism. 2. Unintentional (doesn't know the rules)—A student doesn't understand the rules of attribution (giving credit to the original author) and does it incorrectly. For example, often students will paraphrase an author and not realize that this still requires a citation. 3. Unintentional (doesn't have the right habits)—A student has poor note-taking habits, and does their research without following a clear system. This student then writes a paper unsure of where the information came from and doesn't use proper citations.

Productive discomfort: In the classroom context, this means actively and intentionally supporting students as they process a disruption in their thinking about difference—and sometimes this involves crafting and introducing the disruption itself to start the process.

Project maintenance: When you break your writing into doable chunks and workable timelines by setting clear goals and expectations for each project.

S

Sandwiched: When quoting from an outside text in writing, you need to introduce the quote, quote the quote, and then analyze the quote. Some call this a "quote sandwich" with the person adding the "bread" around the meat of the outside text's words. The top bread introduces the quote (the context, the author, sometimes the title of the work). The bottom bread connects the outside source back to the writer's controlling idea.

Scholarships: Money offered by schools or organizations that you are able to put toward your tuition and/or living expenses while in college. Many scholarships require an application. Scholarships do not need to be paid back.

Self-awareness: Ability to listen to yourself.

Self-concept: Self-concept refers to how you come to view yourself, and what you think about your abilities, worth, tastes, and talents. Your self-concept impacts your sense of self-worth, and your belief in your potential, and these impact whether or not, and how, you pursue opportunities and interactions.

Self-plagiarism: Here a student uses previous work that they created for another course and either hands it in again or modifies it a bit and hands it in for a different course. Self-plagiarism also occurs when a student hands in one paper for two separate courses without permission of both instructors.

Sense of belonging: A person's sense of belonging changes depending on any number of factors, including whether a person feels like an outsider or an insider. It's the tip of the iceberg when it comes to discomfort, but in the context of learning and your college education, it is valuable to push through this discomfort to engage diversity.

Signal phrase: A signal phrase transitions from the writer's voice to the quoted voice.

Single story: A single story—whether transmitted by social media or news agencies or family lore—limits and distorts truth and complexity and creates stereotypes. They make one story become the only story.

Social construction: This is a phrase used to explain things that have meaning because our collective society gives them meaning.

Social well-being: Social well-being centers on how you relate to other people. It's the maintenance of support systems, sexuality, and consent.

Stereotypes: Seeing a group as having sameness or generalized shared qualities and projecting this onto all members of the group.

T

Think-pair-share framework: Sometimes instructors will use the "think-pair-share" framework, where you have a moment to reflect on a question, then turn to a neighbor and exchange your ideas and eventually join another pair (or in some cases come back to the full class) to share your ideas further.

Time management: Time management is part using your time wisely by pairing the time that you have to an appropriate task, and part project management because of the need to identify the individual pieces of any given project so you can prioritize and complete them as needed.

Transformational Learning Theory: Sociologist Jack Mezirow argues that people operate from deeply engrained habits in thinking and point of view. These are formed and reinforced over time, and they eventually constitute one's "frame of reference." Mezirow argues that productive discomfort is necessary to disrupt one's own preconceived notions and "to encounter different perspectives and to accept, integrate, and find space for those perspectives in our own frames of reference."

V

Vulnerability: Professor Brené Brown defines vulnerability as "uncertainty, risk, and emotional exposure…. Vulnerability is the core of all emotions and feelings." Ultimately, it's the experience of being open to possibilities and being willing to risk some degree of exposure.

W

Well-being: Well-being is complex and made up of physical, mental, social, and financial factors. Maintaining well-being is about paying attention to each of these factors, keeping them at healthy levels, and ultimately being forgiving of yourself when things don't go as planned.

Work-study: Work-study is part of some financial aid packages. It is a federally funded program that pays part of the wages you earn while working in work-study jobs. Many on-campus jobs hire work-study students, and some *only* hire work-study students.

Writing process: Writing is a process that requires time and effort and involves writing what Anne Lamott calls a "sh*#ty first draft," seeking feedback, and revising in order to make it the best it can be. The different stages and components consist of prewriting, generating, planning, revising, getting feedback, editing, and polishing.

CHAPTER REFERENCES

Chapter 1

Ambrose, S., Bridges, M. W., DiPietro, M., Lovett, M. C., Norman, M. K., & Mayer, R. E. (2010). How learning works: Seven research-based principles for smart teaching. Jossey-Bass.

Dewey, J. (1897). My pedagogic creed. E. L. Kellogg & Co.

Duckworth, A. (2016). Grit: The power of passion and perseverance. Scribner.

Duckworth, A. (2020). Grit scale. https://angeladuckworth.com/grit-scale/

Duckworth, A. L. (2013) Grit: The power of passion and perseverance [Video]. https://www.ted.com/talks/angela_lee_duckworth_grit_the_power_of_passion_and_perseverance

Halberstam, D. (2008). Everything they had: Sports writing. Hyperion.

King, S. (2016). Awaken. CreateSpace Independent Publishing Platform.

Langer, E. (1997). The power of mindful learning. Addison-Wesley.

Rose, R. (2018). Raphael Rose: How failure cultivates resilience [Video]. https://www.ted.com/talks/raphael_rose_from_stress_to_resilience

Chapter 2

Adichie, C. (2009). Chimamanda Ngozi Adichie: The danger of a single story [Video]. https://www.ted.com/talks/chimamanda_ngozi_adichie_the_danger_of_a_single_story

Brown, B. (2010). Brené Brown: The power of vulnerability [Video]. https://www.ted.com/talks/brene_brown_the_power_of_vulnerability

Cooley, C. H. (1902). Looking-glass self. The production of reality: Essays and readings on social interaction.

Dweck, C. S. (2008). Mindset: The new psychology of success. Random House Digital.

Lorde, A. (1984). Sister outsider: Essays and speeches (Crossing Press feminist series). Crossing Press.

Schnall, M. (2017). Madeleine Albright: An exclusive interview. https://www.huffpost.com/entry/madeleine-albright-an-exc_b_604418

Seuss, T. (2011). Oh, the places you'll go! HarperCollins Children's Books.

Chapter 3

Allport, W. (1954). The nature of prejudice. Addison-Wesley.

Antonio, A. L. (2000). Developing leadership skills for diversity: The role of interracial interaction. Paper presented at the Annual American Educational Research Association in New Orleans, LA.

Antonio, A. L. (2004). The influence of friendship groups on intellectual self-confidence and educational aspirations in college. Journal of Higher Education, 75(4), 446–472.

Bennett, J. M. (2009). Cultivating intercultural competence. In D. Deardorff (Ed.), The Sage handbook of intercultural competence (pp. 121–140). Sage Publications.

Bowman, N. (2010b). College diversity experiences and cognitive development: A meta-analysis. Review of Educational Research, 80(1), 4–33. doi:10.3102/0034654309352495

Clayton-Pedersen, O'Neill, & McTighe-Musil. (2009). Making excellence inclusive: A framework for embedding diversity and inclusion into college and universities' academic excellence mission. Association of American Colleges and Universities.

Commission on the Future of Undergraduate Education (2017). The future of undergraduate education: The future of America. A report from The American Academy of Arts & Sciences. https://www.amacad.org/publication/future-undergraduate-education

Deardorff, D. K. (2004). The identification and assessment of intercultural competence as a student outcome of internationalization at institutions of higher education in the United States. [Unpublished doctoral dissertation]. North Carolina State University.

Deardorff, D. K. (2006). Identification and assessment of intercultural competence as a student outcome of internationalization. Journal of Studies in International Education, 10(3), 241.

Gottfredson, N., Panter, A., Daye, C., Allen, W., Wightman, L., & Deo, M. (2008). Does diversity at undergraduate institutions influence student outcomes? Journal of Diversity in Higher Education, 1. 10.1037/1938-8926.1.2.80.

Gudykunst, W. B. (1993). Toward a theory of effective interpersonal and intergroup communication: An anxiety/uncertainty management (AUM) perspective. In R. L. Wiseman, & J. Koester (Eds.), Intercultural communication theory (pp. 33–71). Sage Publishing.

Gudykunst, W. B. (1998). Applying the anxiety/uncertainty management (AUM) theory to intercultural adjustment training. International Journal of Intercultural Relations, 22(2): 227–250.

Gurin, P., Dey, E. L., Hurtado, S., & Gurin, G. (2002). Diversity and higher education: Theory and impact on educational outcomes. Harvard Educational Review, 72(3), 330–367.

Hu, S., & Kuh, G. D. (2003). Diversity experiences and college student learning and personal development. Journal of College Student Development, 44(3), 320–334.

Hurtado, S. (2001). Linking diversity and educational purpose: How diversity affects the classroom environment and student development. In G. Orfield (Ed.), Diversity challenged: Evidence on the impact of affirmative action (pp. 187–203), Harvard Education Publishing Group.

Lee, A., Poch, R., O'Brien, M., & Solheim, C. (2017). Teaching interculturally: A framework for integrating disciplinary knowledge and intercultural development. Stylus Publishing.

Lee, A., Poch, R., Shaw, M., & Williams, R. (2012). Engaging diversity in undergraduate classrooms: A pedagogy for developing intercultural competence: ASHE higher education report, Volume 38, Number 2. John Wiley & Sons.

Lorde, A. (1984). Sister outsider: Essays and speeches (Crossing Press feminist series). Crossing Press.

Milem, J. F. (2003). The educational benefits of diversity: Evidence from multiple sectors. In M. J. Chang (Ed.), Compelling interest: Examining the evidence on racial dynamics in colleges and universities (pp. 126–169). Stanford Education.

Milem, J. F., Chang, M. J., & Antonio, A. L. (2005). Making diversity work on campus: A research-based perspective. Association of American Colleges and Universities.

Pettigrew, T. F., & Tropp, L. R. (2008). How does intergroup contact reduce prejudice? Meta-analytic tests of three mediators. European Journal of Social Psychology, 38(6), 922–934.

Saenz, V. B., Ngai, H. N., & Hurtado, S. (2007). Factors influencing positive interactions across race for African American, Asian American, Latino, and White college students Research in Higher Education, 48(1), 1–38.

Tatum, B. D. (1997). Why are all the black kids sitting together in the cafeteria? Basic Books.

Chapter 4

Liebowitz, R. (2014). The value of discomfort. http://www.middlebury.edu/about/president/addresses_archive_copy/archive/baccalaureate2007/node/470112

Lorde, A. (1984). Sister outsider: Essays and speeches (Crossing Press feminist series). Crossing Press.

Montoya, M. (2000). Silence and silencing: Their centripetal and centrifugal forces in legal communication, pedagogy and discourse. 33 U. MICH. J. L. REFORM 263. https://repository.law.umich.edu/mjlr/vol33/iss3/4

Tools for Managing Assignments, Workload, and Projects

Clear, J. (n.d.). The Ivy Lee method: The daily routine for peak productivity. https://jamesclear.com/ivy-lee

Flippo, R. & Caverly, D. (2008). Handbook of college reading and study strategy research. Routledge.

Mueller, P. A., & Oppenheimer, D. M. (2014). The pen is mightier than the keyboard: Advantages of longhand over laptop note taking. Psychological Science, 25(6), 1159–1168. https://journals.sagepub.com/doi/10.1177/0956797614524581

Rhoder, C. (2002). Mindful reading: Strategy training that facilitates transfer. Journal of Adolescent & Adult Literacy, 45(6), 498–512. http://www.jstor.org/stable/40014738

Silberberg, M. & Amateis, P. (2015). Chemistry: The molecular nature of matter and change. McGraw-Hill Education.

Chapter 5

Allport, W. (1954). The nature of prejudice. Addison-Wesley.

Brown, B. (2018). Design is a function of empathy. https://brenebrown.com/blog/2018/04/19/design-is-a-function-of-empathy/

Cain, S. (2012). Quiet: The power of introverts in a world that can't stop talking. Crown.

Cain, S. (2012). Susan Cain: The power of introverts [Video]. https://www.ted.com/talks/susan_cain_the_power_of_introverts

Duhigg, C. (2016). What Google learned from its quest to build the perfect team. The New York Times Magazine, 26, 2016.

Kirch, C. (2014). BEA 2014: Jacqueline Woodson: Remembering a brown girl's childhood. Publishers Weekly.

Kuh, G. D., Schneider, C. G., & Association of American Colleges and Universities (2008). High-impact educational practices: What they are, who has access to them, and why they matter. Association of American Colleges and Universities.

Chapter 6

Lee, A., Poch, R., O'Brien, M., & Solheim, C. (2017). Teaching interculturally: A framework for integrating disciplinary knowledge and intercultural development. Stylus Publishing.

Mezirow, J. (1997). Transformative learning: Theory to practice. New Directions for Adult and Continuing Education, 74, 5–12. http://dx.doi.org/10.1002/ace.7401

Parker, Clifton B. (2014). Stanford research shows that working together boosts motivation. Stanford News Service. https://news.stanford.edu/pr/2014/pr-motivation-walton-carr-091514.html

Silko, L. (1977). Ceremony. Viking Press.

Chapter 7

Atkins, A. (2016). George RR Martin and Stephen King [Video]. https://www.youtube.com/watch?v=v_PBqSPNTfg&feature=emb_err_woyt

Dahl, R., & Blake, Q. (2019). Billy and the minpins. Puffin Books.

Lamott, A. (1995). Bird by bird: Some instructions on writing and life. Anchor.

Lee, A. (2000). Composing critical pedagogies. NCTE.

NAEP Exams. https://www.nationsreportcard.gov/testyourself.aspx

Parker, S. F. (Ed.). (2018). Conversations with Joan Didion. Univ. Press of Mississippi.

Plimpton, G. (1989). The Writer's chapbook: A compendium of fact, opinion, wit, and advice from the 20th century's preeminent writers. Viking.

Chapter 8

Butler, O. (2000). Persistence. Locus Magazine. https://www.locusmag.com/2000/Issues/06/Butler.html

Dead Poets Society (1989). Touchstone Pictures [Film].

Saroyan, W. (2000). WRITERS ON WRITING; Starting with a tree and finally getting to the death of a brother. The New York Times. https://www.nytimes.com/2000/10/09/arts/writers-on-writing-starting-with-a-tree-and-finally-getting-to-the.html

Tools for Managing Your Writing Process and Projects

Ede, L., & Lunsford, A. (1984). Audience addressed/audience invoked: The role of audience in composition theory and pedagogy. College Composition and Communication 35: 155–171.

Gallagher, C., & Lee, A. (2008). Teaching writing that matters. Scholastic.

King, S., Hill, J., & King, O. (2020). On writing: A memoir of the craft. Scribner.

Lamott, A. (1995). Bird by bird: Some instructions on writing and life. Anchor.

Chapter 9

ActonTV [Ruth Potee] (2019). Physiology of addiction with Dr. Ruth Potee [Video]. https://www.youtube.com/watch?v=twdeTt-XD_8

American Psychiatric Association (2013). Diagnostic and statistical manual of mental disorders (DSM-5). APA.

Bruce-Sanford, G., & Soares, L. (2019). Mental health and post-traditional learners. https://www.higheredtoday.org/2019/04/22/mental-health-post-traditional-learners/

Clear, J. (2018). Atomic habits: An easy & proven way to build good habits & break bad ones. Avery.

College Scholarships (n.d.). Scholarship search engine. http://www.collegescholarships.org/financial-aid

College Stats. (2017). Mental health guide for college students. https://collegestats.org/resources/mental-health-guide/

Colorado Tech. (2017). 4 reasons college students should make time for exercise. https://www.coloradotech.edu/blog/2018/march/4-reasons-college-students-should-make-time-for-exercise

Crum, A. J., & Langer, E. J. (2007). Mind-set matters: Exercise and the placebo effect. Psychological Science, 18(2), 165–171.

Division of Sleep Medicine at Harvard Medical School (2008). Sleep and memory. http://healthysleep.med.harvard.edu/need-sleep/whats-in-it-for-you/memory

National Sleep Foundation (2020). Sleep hygiene. https://www.sleepfoundation.org/articles/sleep-hygiene

Oprah: A conversation with Thich Nhat Hanh about savor. (2010). http://www.oprah.com/spirit/a-conversation-with-thich-nhat-hanh-about-savor/all

Potee, R., MD. (n.d.). Ruth A. Potee, MD. https://ruthpotee.com/

Tran, A. G. T. T., Lam, C. T., & Legg, E. (2018). Financial stress, social supports, gender, and anxiety during college: A stress-buffering perspective. The Counseling Psychologist, 46(7), 846–869. https://www.apa.org/education/ce/financial-stress-college-students.pdf

Walker, M. (2017). Why we sleep: Unlocking the power of sleep and dreams. Simon and Schuster.

Walker, M. (2019, April). Matthew Walker: Sleep is your superpower [Video]. https://www.ted.com/talks/matt_walker_sleep_is_your_superpower

Chapter 10

Anders, G. (2017). You can do anything: The surprising power of a "useless" liberal arts education. Little, Brown and Company.

Fisher, C. (2017). Let your connections help you get the job. https://blog.linkedin.com/2017/september/12/let-your-connections-help-you-get-the-job

Gould, E., Mokhiber, Z., & Wolfe, J. (2019). Economic Policy Institute: Class of 2019: College edition report. https://www.epi.org/publication/class-of-2019-college-edition/

National Association of Colleges and Employers (2014). Career readiness competencies: Employers survey results. https://www.naceweb.org/career-readiness/competencies/career-readiness-competencies-employer-survey-results/

Obama, M. (2018). Becoming. Crown.

Palmer, P. (2000). Let your life speak: Listening for the voice of vocation. Jossey-Bass.

Purdue University Online Writing Lab. (n.d.). Welcome to the Purdue OWL. https://owl.purdue.edu/owl/purdue_owl.html

Roosevelt, T. (1910). Citizenship in a republic. [Speech given at the Sorbonne in Paris, France]

Strada Education Network & Gallup (2017). Strada-Gallup 2017 college student survey. https://news.gallup.com/reports/225161/2017-strada-gallup-college-student-survey.aspx

Strada Education Network & Gallup (2018). 2018 Strada-Gallup alumni survey: Mentoring college students to success. https://go.stradaeducation.org/strada-gallup-alumni-survey

Strada Institute (2016). The real, long-term, labor market outcomes for liberal arts graduates. https://www.economicmodeling.com/wp-content/uploads/2019/01/Robot-Ready_Outcomes-DIGITAL.pdf

INDEX

Note: Page numbers followed by *f* or *t* indicate figures and tables, respectively.

G

Gallagher, Chris, 196
gender, 63
goals
    college degree as, 101
    crazy, 103
    future self, idealizing, 104
    mapping, 100
    measuring progress, 102–103
    misalignment, 104
    modifying, 104
    reflections on, 102
    setting, 8, 103
    shared by groups, 125–126
    size, 101*f*
    structure, providing, 103
Good Samaritan laws, 229
Google Calendar, 99
Google Drive, 98
grants, 238
grit, 13
group differences, 47
group identity, 124
group presentations. *See* presentations
groups
    access, 124
    belonging, 123–125, 147–148
    business settings, 125
    communication, 123, 130
    dynamics, 119
    dysfunctional, 145
    effectiveness, 121
    individual differences within, 123, 133
    listening to each other, 122–123
    member status, 128
    multiple perspectives, 128–129
    names, knowing, 124
    norms, 122, 123, 126–128
    shared goals, 125–126
    supportive environments, 130, 131*f*
groupwork
    active engagement, 123
    case studies, 148–151
    conflict management, 133
    fairness issue, 120
    groundwork, 121–122
    in-class, 138, 141–142
    long-term projects, 142–143
    paired discussions, 138–139

reflecting on past experiences, 117–121, 132
research-proven benefits, 152
skills, 145
stumbling blocks, 145–148
growth mindset, 26–31, 27*f*, 215

H

habits, 6, 23, 106
health. *See* physical health
help seeking, 9, 223, 226
hotlines, 226
housing, 235
How Learning Works (Ambrose), 16
humility, 46, 56

I

identity, 6, 13, 28, 33, 37
immune system, 220
income, 234
individual differences, 47
information seeking, 36
in-group bias, 49*f*
insiders, 72
integrity, 104
intellectual dexterity, 244
intelligence, 13, 26
intention, 6, 8
interest rates, 236
internal states, 13
interpersonal skills, 46
Ivy Lee Method, 81

J

job market
    approaching, 242, 246
    career readiness, 242*f*, 243*t*, 247, 249
    entering, 245–246
    network-building, 249–250
    skills needed, 243–245
jobs. *See* employment
journaling, 158

K

Kelly, Margaret Delahanty, 89
King, Stephen, 16, 156, 157
knowledge, 16

L

labels, 32
Lamott, Anne, 167, 170, 198
Langer, Ellen, 8, 217
leadership, 248
learning, 14
   opportunities, 11, 16, 52, 152
   process, 16–17
   self-directed, 16, 18
Lee, Amy, 167, 196
limitations, 26, 32
listening. *See* active listening
living expenses, 233, 234, 235
loans, 236–237
looking-glass self, 32–34
Lorde, Audre, 49
love, 39
Lunsford, Andrea, 203

M

Martin, George R.R., 156, 157
mental health, 215, 222–223
mental health services, 226
metacognition, 17*f*
Mezirow, Jack, 140
micro-decisions, 6
mindfulness, 7, 8
mindlessness, 7, 8
mindset
   description, 23–24
   facets, 24–26
   fixed versus growth, 26–31, 27*f*
   looking-glass self and, 32–34
   power over, 5, 23
   reframing for online learning, 112–113
   single stories and, 34–38
   well-being and, 215
mistakes, 16
Montoya, Margaret, 67
multitasking, 84, 147

N

National Association of Colleges and Employers
   (NACE®), 243
navigation, 6
network-building, 249–250
news consumption, 53
nontraditional students, 6

nonverbal communication, 130
norms, 126–127
notetaking
   bulleting, 95
   glossing text and, 89–90, 90*f*
   in-class, 95–96
   mindful reading, 91
   outlining, 92–94
   outside-of-class, 89, 95
   paper versus computer, 98
   personal methods, 89
   shorthand, 97–98
   during small group discussions, 96–97
   teacher language and, 97
nutrition, 218–220

O

occupations, 104
online learning, 7, 110
   connection and, 113
   in-person classes versus, 112*t*
   mindset for, 112–113
   structure, 110–112
open-mindedness, 29, 37, 38, 39
openness, 8, 46, 56, 73
opportunities
   engaging diversity, 62
   growth, 26, 28
   learning, 11, 16, 52, 152
   openness to, 29
organization, 98–100
outsiders, 73

P

participation, 67
partner work, 138–140
passion, 13
peer reviews, 143–144
peer-to-peer instruction, 140
perceptions, 33, 34
perfectionism, 170
perseverance, 13
persistence, 14
personal beliefs, 23, 24
personal discovery, 29
personal finances, 233–234
personal growth, 11, 45. *See also* growth mindset
perspectives, 52, 53*f*, 56, 128–129, 133
physical activity, 216–218, 217*f*